Good Housekeeping

STEP-BY-STEP

low-fat
cooking

Good Housekeeping

STEP-BY-STEP
low-fat
cooking

OVER 150 QUICK & EASY RECIPES

EBURY PRESS
LONDON

First published in Great Britain in 1999

1 3 5 7 9 10 8 6 4 2

First published by Ebury Press,
Random House, 20 Vauxhall Bridge Road, London SW1V 2SA

Random House Australia (Pty) Limited
20 Alfred Street, Milsons Point, Sydney, New South Wales 2061, Australia

Random House New Zealand Limited
18 Poland Road, Glenfield, Auckland 10, New Zealand

Random House South Africa (Pty) Limited
Endulini, 5A Jubilee Road, Parktown 2193, South Africa

The Random House Group Limited Reg. No. 954009

www.randomhouse.co.uk

A CIP catalogue record for this book is available from the British Library.

Design: Ruth Prentice
Editorial: Jo Younger, Fiona Hunter, Hilary Bird

ISBN 0 09 187259 6

Papers used by Ebury Press are natural, recyclable products made from wood grown in sustainable forests.

Printed and bound in Spain by Printer Industria Grafica S.A.

COOKERY NOTES

Follow these general guidelines to get the best results from the recipes.
- Both metric and imperial measures are given for the recipes. Follow either metric or imperial throughout as they are not interchangeable.
- All spoon measures are level unless otherwise stated. Sets of measuring spoons are available in both metric and imperial sizes for accurate measurement of small quantities.
- Ovens should be preheated to the specified temperatures. Grills should also be preheated. The cooking times in recipes assume that this has been done.
- Large eggs should be used except where otherwise stated. Free-range eggs are recommended.
- Use freshly ground black pepper and sea salt unless otherwise stated.
- Use fresh rather than dried herbs unless dried herbs are suggested in the recipe.

CONTENTS

INTRODUCTION

The aim of this book is to provide delicious low-fat recipes that will satisfy every taste, and that are easy to prepare using the step-by-step instructions. First, however, you will find on the following pages the basic guidelines for healthy eating – in which low-fat cooking plays a vital role – and discover how choosing the low-fat option is an important part of enjoying a healthy diet and lifestyle. Experts are agreed that low-fat cooking benefits our health but it is not always easy to start to follow a new regime.

Each recipe in the main part of the book gives the calories and the amount of fat and saturated fat contained in a portion. If you decide to cook a dish which has one of the slightly higher fat contents, choose lower-fat meals and snacks during the rest of the day. You don't have to go hungry when you are eating low-fat foods but if you have a sweet tooth remember that it's much healthier to snack on a piece of fresh fruit or perhaps a selection of vegetable crudités, like carrots, celery and broccoli, rather than fill yourself up with a piece of cake, a biscuit or a chocolate bar. At the top of each recipe, preparation and cooking times are given, together with any additional time required, perhaps for marinating or soaking, so you can choose dishes that fit in with the amount of time you have to spend on producing a meal.

Whenever you pick up a newspaper or magazine these days you are more than likely to find at least one article on food and health-related matters. There is no doubt that what we eat greatly affects our health. However, eating well is only one ingredient in the recipe for helping you to live longer and enjoy a better quality of life. The other 'essentials' for a healthy lifestyle are being more physically active, not smoking and taking 'time out' for relaxation.

In fact, scientists and nutrition experts recommend the following five key guidelines for a healthy lifestyle:
● Be active in your daily life.
● Take pleasure in active leisure.
● Aim for five or more servings of fruit and vegetables every day.
● Base meals on starchy foods.
● Check out more lower-fat choices.

The theme of this book is low-fat cooking, showing you step-by-step how simple it is to produce tasty, nutritious lower-fat meals. In this section, we explain how to incorporate these guidelines into your diet as a whole.

FOOD AND HEALTH: THE FACTS

● A diet high in saturated fat is known to be one of the risk factors for cardiovascular disease (heart disease and strokes), which accounts for nearly half of all deaths in the UK. Some foods might protect us against heart disease, such as oil-rich fish, and fruit and vegetables.
● Diet is estimated to be linked to between 10–70% of all cancers (cancer accounts for approximately 25% of all deaths in the UK), particularly some of the common cancers such as large bowel and stomach cancer.
● Diet is a contributory factor in the development of obesity (nearly half the British population is overweight). Being overweight can increase your health risk, and can affect other risk factors for heart disease like high blood pressure. Being overweight can also aggravate other existing health problems you may have, such as osteoarthritis.

The good news is that even small changes in your daily lifestyle can make a real difference to your health. Choosing to follow a lower-fat diet might seem like a lot of effort at first, but soon healthy eating will become your normal routine, and you'll begin to see and feel the range of benefits.

BY TAKING POSITIVE STEPS TO IMPROVE YOUR LIFESTYLE, YOU GAIN:
● More confidence in how you look and feel about yourself.
● A lowered risk of developing heart disease, high blood pressure, diabetes, obesity and some cancers.
● A positive outlook and feeling of well-being.
● Better control of your weight.

READY FOR ACTION? FOLLOW THIS ACTION PLAN TO GET STARTED:
● Adopt a positive frame of mind. Think of the benefits to you and your family (see above) and think positively e.g. 'From today, I choose to eat more healthily, and look forward to enjoying my food.' Find your own words, but make sure you use the present tense, and not some time in the future, or it might never happen!
● Elicit the support of a family member or close friend – you'll need it if things get tough. It's good to have someone to share success with.
● Check your store cupboards and refrigerator/freezer for any foods which may not fit into your new healthy eating plan. Use them up quickly (invite some friends over), or give them away.
● Browse through the recipes in this book, and plan ahead for a few days, choosing some easy, tasty, low-fat recipes to try out.
● Write a shopping list for ingredients of the recipes above, and other everyday lower-fat foods, such as skimmed/semi-skimmed milk; low-fat yogurts; reduced-fat spread; extra fruit and vegetables; healthy cereals, bread and pasta.
● Think about those times in the day when you might be tempted to snack on a high-fat food – e.g. between meals, children's tea time, early evening, late evening – and think of alternatives. This might be finding an activity to take your mind off eating, such as reading, ironing, having a bath, going for a walk, gardening (whatever suits you and your mood at the time), or, if you're genuinely hungry, a healthy snack (see page 16). Remember to add some of these snacks to your shopping list so that you're well prepared for tempting times.

THE KEY TO HEALTHY EATING: BALANCE AND VARIETY

Keeping an eye on the fat content of your diet is just one of a number of important aspects of your healthy eating plan. Choosing a variety of different foods every day is an easy way of making up a healthy, well-balanced diet, to ensure you get all the essential vitamins and minerals your body needs. No single food contains all the nutrients, which is why you need to vary your diet.

Foods can be grouped together by the nutrients they contain. The chart opposite lists the main food groups; summarises the essential nutrients provided by each group; suggests healthier options and indicates how much you need from each on a daily basis. Use the quantities as a rough guide only, as we all have slightly different needs. The quantities in the chart are aimed at adults, but the principles of balance and variety from each food group apply to everyone.

Children under five have different needs. They often have small appetites, so they need the fat in foods for energy, as well as foods which are rich in essential nutrients. Bulky, high-fibre diets are not appropriate for young children as these foods can fill them up too quickly so that they may not get enough calories, vitamins and minerals which they need to grow and develop. A young child should be given full-fat milk unless your doctor or health visitor advises otherwise.

FOOD GROUP/MAIN NUTRIENTS	TYPES OF FOOD TO CHOOSE WHENEVER YOU CAN	HOW MUCH TO CHOOSE
BREAD, CEREALS, RICE, PASTA AND POTATOES These foods provide energy, some protein, calcium, iron and B vitamins. Wholegrain varieties are high in 'dietary fibre'	Wholemeal varieties of bread, pasta, rice, pitta bread; boiled, baked or mashed potato; wholegrain breakfast cereals	Include some with every meal
FRUIT AND VEGETABLES These provide vitamins e.g. vitamin C, carotenes, folates, some minerals and fibre	All types. Eat a wide variety of fresh, frozen and canned fruit and vegetables, dried fruit and fresh fruit juice	Aim for five or more servings every day
MILK AND DAIRY FOODS Foods in this group include milk, cheese, yogurt and fromage frais. They provide calcium, protein, vitamins A and D and vitamin B12	Lower-fat varieties e.g. skimmed/semi-skimmed milk; low-fat yogurt and fromage frais; lower-fat cheeses e.g. Edam, Camembert, cottage cheese	Eat or drink moderate amounts, approximately 2–3 servings daily to meet calcium needs. One serving = 1 carton yogurt, 200ml (7fl oz) milk, or 25–40g (1–1½oz) hard cheese
MEAT, FISH AND ALTERNATIVES These include meat, fish, poultry, eggs, nuts, beans and pulses. Foods in this group provide iron, protein, B vitamins (especially B12), zinc, magnesium	Lean cuts of meat; all types of fish; beans, peas and lentils are low in fat and high in fibre – use in stews, casseroles and curries	Moderate amounts. As a guide, aim for 2–3 servings a day of these foods e.g. 50–75g (1½–3oz) meat, 100–150g (3½–5oz) fish, 200g (7oz) beans/pulses, 40g (1½oz) hard cheese, 2 eggs
FATS AND OILS These include margarine, butter, other spreading fats, and cooking oils. They provide some vitamins (A,D and E) and essential fatty acids, but are also high in fat and energy (calories)	Low-fat spreads, or use smaller amounts of margarine/butter. Unsaturated pure vegetable oils for cooking such as olive, rapeseed or sunflower oils	Small amounts of spreading and cooking fats
OTHER FATTY/SUGARY FOODS Foods in this group include cakes, biscuits, savoury snacks; confectionery; and other 'snack' foods. They are often high in fat and sugar and therefore calories	Plain biscuits, fruit cake, bread muffins, scones, currant buns, tea cakes, savoury crackers, crispbreads	Small amounts. Keep high-fat/sugary foods as occasional foods

DRINKS

Drinking plenty of fluid is essential for good health, but it is not always easy to know exactly how much you need. As a guide, aim for a minimum of 6–8 large cups, mugs or glasses a day. Try to include a variety, including water, low-sugar/calorie drinks, fruit juices, and hot drinks, including tea and coffee. Most health experts agree that it is best to avoid or reduce our intake of caffeine (found in coffee, tea and colas), so try decaffeinated drinks or substitute them with one of the many herbal and fruit teas available.

ALCOHOLIC DRINKS
Scientific evidence suggests that a small amount of alcohol might protect us against heart disease, but remember that too much alcohol can result in long-term health problems, especially liver damage. If you do drink alcohol, it's a good idea to stick to the guidelines issued by the Department of Health and the Health Education Authority, and to have at least one or two alcohol-free days a week.

Sensible limits for women are 2–3 units a day, although pregnant women should try to abstain from alcohol altogether, and 3–4 units a day for men. One unit is a small glass of wine, a small measure of spirits, or half a pint of ordinary lager or beer.

EAT MORE FRUIT AND VEGETABLES

One of the key messages about healthy eating is to eat more fruit and vegetables. In Britain we lag far behind many other European countries in terms of our fruit and vegetable consumption. The World Health Organisation, UK Government and Cancer Research agencies all recommend that we eat more fruit and vegetables. Research has shown that they contain compounds which can help to protect us against disease. In countries where the people consume large amounts of fruit and vegetables, the incidence of heart disease is low, and this is thought to be due, in part, to the high consumption of fruit and vegetables.

FIVE GOOD REASONS TO EAT FIVE OR MORE PORTIONS EVERY DAY:
● They're low in fat and calories, so you can eat plenty without worrying about your waistline.
● They're packed full of essential vitamins and minerals.
● Brightly coloured fruit and vegetables, and dark green vegetables are our main source of antioxidants – compounds which help to protect us from heart disease and some cancers.
● They're a great source of dietary fibre – essential for a healthy digestive system.
● Fruit and vegetables of all varieties add flavour, texture, colour and taste to almost any meal or snack.

If you're wondering how you can reach five or more servings of fruit and vegetables every day, try some of the following suggestions. Add in an extra portion and gradually build up to a target of five or more.

BREAKFAST TIPS
● Add fresh or dried fruit to cereal e.g. sliced banana, raisins or apricots.
● Have half a grapefruit or canned grapefruit segments in fruit juice.
● Include a glass of fruit juice.
● Try to include at least two different lightly cooked vegetables with main meals.

MAIN MEALS TIPS
● Add frozen vegetables such as peas, sweetcorn or mixed vegetables to rice or pasta as it's cooking.
● Add vegetables or fruit (dried apricots, apple or prunes work well) to stews or casseroles.
● Always add salad or other vegetables to sandwiches.

SNACK MEALS TIPS
● Fresh fruit is the ideal convenient snack – enjoy it on its own, or add to other foods, such as low-fat plain or fruit yogurt.
● If you're out and about, or going to work, take two or three pieces of fruit to enjoy throughout the day. Put it out on your desk so that you remember to eat it!
● Fingers of raw vegetables, such as peppers, celery and carrots, make a tasty low-fat snack when served with a salsa or yogurt-based dip.

NOTE
● *Remember to wash raw fruit and vegetables before eating them.*

FAT MATTERS

Both the quantity and quality of the fats you eat is important for good health. We all know that eating too much fat is not good, but how much fat should you be eating, and with so many to choose from, how do you decide which are the best types of spreading and cooking fats to use?

A small amount of fat is an essential part of a healthy, well-balanced diet to provide us with the fat-soluble vitamins A, D and E, and some essential fats which our bodies cannot make. In Britain, however, we tend to eat more fat than we really need. How much fat you require depends on your age and how active you are. Use the following as a rough guide to a healthy fat intake.

PER DAY	WOMEN	MEN
calories	2000	2500
fat	70g	95g

These figures for fat equate to approximately 35% of dietary energy, the guidelines for fat recommended by the Department of Health, and the target we considered when selecting the recipes in this book. But how does this relate to the actual food you eat?

GUIDE TO DIETARY FATS

There are two main types of dietary fat: saturated and unsaturated fats.

SATURATED FATS
Saturated fats are not essential in the diet, and eating too much saturated fat is linked to an increased risk of developing heart disease. Saturates can raise the level of cholesterol in the blood, one of the main risk factors for heart disease.

DIETARY SOURCES
Saturated fats are found mainly in:

● Full-fat dairy products such as full-cream milk; hard cheese; cream; full-fat yogurt.
● Butter, margarine, fat spreads and other animal fats such as lard, dripping and suet.
● Fatty cuts of meat e.g. lamb, pork and beef; meat products such as sausages, burgers and ready-made pies, cooked meats, luncheon meats.
● 'Hidden' sources such as biscuits, cakes, confectionery, savoury snacks and nuts.

RECOMMENDATIONS
● Limit your intake of foods high in saturated fats. These should make up no more than 10% of the total calories (energy) that you eat and drink per day.

UNSATURATED FATS
There are two types: polyunsaturates and monounsaturates, both of which play an important role in the diet.

POLYUNSATURATES
Small amounts of polyunsaturates are needed in the diet to provide essential fatty acids. The term 'polyunsaturate' covers a range of essential fatty acids; some of these fatty acids are found in vegetable oils, and others in oil-rich fish. The fatty acids in vegetable oils help to lower blood cholesterol but, at high intakes, these fats may be linked to an increased risk of developing heart disease.

DIETARY SOURCES
Polyunsaturated fats are found mainly in:

● Vegetable oils such as sunflower, safflower, corn and soya oils; fat spreads made from these; meat, nuts and seeds.
● Research has shown that the essential fatty acids in oily fish help reduce the tendency of blood to clot, thereby offering protection against the final stages of heart disease. Fish oils may also have other beneficial health effects.
● Oil-rich fish include: salmon, mackerel, sardines, pilchards and herring trout (these may be fresh, smoked or canned).

RECOMMENDATIONS
● Eat small amounts of vegetable oils and/or fat spreads which are high in polyunsaturated fats.
● Eat oily fish once a week.

MONOUNSATURATES
Although not essential in the diet, monounsaturates are a good replacement for saturates in the diet. Evidence suggests that they also help to lower blood cholesterol, and can, therefore, protect us from heart disease.

DIETARY SOURCES
These fats are found mainly in olive and rapeseed oils and fat spreads made from these; meat, nuts and seeds.

RECOMMENDATIONS
● Eat foods containing monounsaturated fats to replace those foods high in saturates.

TRANS FATS
These fats are found naturally in small amounts in butter, beef and lamb fat. Most, however, are produced during hydrogenation – the industrial process of hardening oils used in the manufacture of margarines, spreads, biscuits, cakes and other products.

There is some research evidence to suggest that trans fats raise blood cholesterol, and are therefore linked to a higher risk of developing heart disease. In the UK, trans fats only contribute approximately 2% of dietary energy, so our intake of these fats is relatively low compared to saturated fats. It's a good idea, however, to limit your intake of foods containing trans fats.

DIETARY CHOLESTEROL

Eating foods rich in cholesterol does not, in general, seem to affect blood cholesterol levels, because the amount eaten is much lower than that of total fat or saturates.

SOURCES OF DIETARY CHOLESTEROL

Egg yolks, offal, shellfish, and other foods which tend to be high in saturates e.g. meat products, full-fat dairy products, butter.

HEALTHY COOKING METHODS

The way in which you prepare foods greatly affects both the fat content in your diet and the nutritional values of the food. Some cooking methods are much healthier than others. For instance, frying foods in generous quantities of fat will obviously increase your intake of saturated fats. The following cooking methods are all beneficial for healthy eating.

STEAMING

Steaming is one of the best methods for cooking vegetables, but it is also suitable for fish, shellfish and grains. It helps to retain the flavour and colour of vegetables and, most importantly, the water-soluble vitamins which are easily lost during other cooking methods.

You can buy special steamers in which the water is boiled in the bottom of the steamer and the food is cooked in the compartment above. Alternatively, you can use a metal basket-type steamer which will fit into a saucepan, or a bamboo steamer that is used in conjunction with a wok. Both are available from most cookware shops, are easy to use and inexpensive to buy.

STIR-FRYING

You need much less fat to stir-fry food than if you shallow-fry so this is a very healthy cooking method. Use a wok or deep-sided frying pan and make sure that the oil you use is really hot before you add any ingredients. When you prepare vegetables or meat for stir-frying, cut them into similar-sized pieces to ensure that they cook evenly and in the same amount of time. Cooking Chinese and Thai food at home has become increasingly popular, and you will find oils and sauces suitable for stir-frying readily available in supermarkets as well as specialist stores.

MICROWAVE COOKING

Microwaves are a valuable additional piece of kitchen equipment and are fast, clean and efficient to use. They are especially useful for cooking fresh vegetables and fish because there is no need to add extra fat or large amounts of water so all the nutrients, textures and colours are retained during the cooking. This method helps to retain vitamins, particularly the water-soluble B vitamins and vitamin C, that are often destroyed or diminished by other cooking methods.

To keep food moist while it is being microwaved, cover it with a plate, lid or piece of microwave film (not clingfilm). Pierce the film or leave a gap at the side so that any steam can escape. Wrap 'baked' potatoes in absorbent kitchen paper, which can also be placed on foods like bacon that might splatter inside the microwave.

As a general guide, most foods can be cooked in a microwave in about one third to one quarter of the time it takes to cook them in a conventional way (depending on the density of the food, whether it is frozen and the amount involved). The more food you cook, the longer it takes. If a microwave recipe specifies standing time, always allow for this as the food continues to cook during this period.

Microwaves are especially useful for thawing and reheating food. If you plan to cook straight from freezer to microwave, freeze the food in a container that can be put straight in the microwave (plastic is ideal – avoid metal or any item that is gilded with metallic paint).

BOILING
Water-soluble vitamins found in vegetables can be very easily lost during this method of cooking. And if you boil vegetables in large amounts of water up to 70% of their vitamin C content can be destroyed. To retain as much of their vitamins as possible, add freshly prepared vegetables to only a small amount of boiling water. Cook for as short a time as possible, until they are just tender but retain their crunchiness and 'bite'. Make the most of any water-soluble vitamins by using the water that the vegetables have been cooked in to make gravy, stock or soup.

GRILLING
This is an excellent cooking method for many cuts of meat, poultry, fish and some vegetables. It is a much healthier alternative to shallow-frying

as it requires little or no fat to be added during cooking.

Grilling is ideal for cooking even-sized, tender cuts of meat that are not too thick (like pork chops). But it is unsuitable for tough cuts as the intense heat of the grill will simply toughen the meat even more. Marinating meat before it is grilled helps to tenderise it and will also improve the flavour. Ideally, leave the meat to marinate overnight but for at least 1 hour if this isn't possible.

Grilling is a good method to use with oily fish such as herrings or mackerel. Take care, though, when grilling more delicate, white-fleshed fish because it tends to dry out quickly.

To grill vegetables like mushrooms, courgettes, peppers, aubergines and tomatoes, brush them first with just a little oil and grill them under a moderate heat.

ROASTING

This is a healthy way to cook meat and poultry. Place the joint or bird on a rack in the roasting tin so that the fat drips underneath. Before you use the juices to make gravy, remove any fat by skimming the surface, drawing it off with a cooking syringe/baster or pouring it into a separating jug.

As with grilling, roasting is a good way to cook certain vegetables including aubergines, courgettes, onions, garlic and peppers. Cut the vegetables into large, even-sized chunks, blanch in boiling water and thoroughly drain in a colander. Place in a large roasting tin, drizzle with a very little olive oil, season well with salt and pepper and cook in a moderate oven until tender.

STEWING

For tougher cuts of meat, stewing is an excellent option as the meat will be tenderised during the long, slow cooking. Cook the meat with vegetables and just enough liquid to cover them. If stews and casseroles are cooked the day before you need them, cool them quickly, and refrigerate. Before you reheat a stew, remove any excess fat that has come to the surface.

SPREADING AND COOKING FATS

With such a choice of fat spreads and cooking oils on the market, it can be difficult to decide which one is best for you and your family. Below are some points which you might like to think about when choosing a fat spread:

● Choose one which is low in saturates; hard margarines, lard and butter are high in saturates.
● When using fat in cooking, always use an oil, soft margarine or reduced-fat spread which is high in either polyunsaturates or mono-unsaturates.
● If you are overweight or want to maintain a healthy weight, it might help to choose a spread which is low in total fat, and so cut the calories as well as the fat.
● If you like to do a lot of baking, choose a fat spread which contains more than 60% fat to use in your cooking to make sure you get the best results.
● A wide range of low-fat spreads (with less than 40% total fat) are now available, and these can be used in cooking as well as for spreading. Very low-fat spreads (with a fat content of around 20% are only suitable for spreading because of their high water content.
● Low-fat spreads can be used successfully for all-in-one cake and biscuit recipes, all-in-one sauces, choux pastry and for gently cooking or sautéeing vegetables.
● As well as the nutritional and cooking properties, the other important aspect is taste. So choose a spread which you know you and your family will enjoy.
● When choosing an oil for cooking, opt for a pure vegetable oil high in mono or polyunsaturates and low in saturates, such as olive, rapeseed, sunflower, safflower, corn or soya oil.
● Some nut oils, such as palm oil, coconut oil and peanut oil are higher in saturated fat than the pure vegetable oils, so try not to use them too often.

IDEAS FOR HEALTHY BREAKFASTS

Breakfast is an ideal opportunity to get your day off to a healthy start. Even if time is limited in the morning, it's important to have something to eat or drink. Breakfast, as the name suggests, is 'breaking a fast', and it's often a long time since your last meal the night before. It's an opportunity to start the day with a healthy meal, which should see you through until lunchtime, without wanting to snack on a high-fat/high-sugar food mid-morning.

INCLUDE A MIXTURE OF THE FOLLOWING FOODS FOR A HEALTHY START TO ANY DAY:

● Breakfast cereal (preferably high fibre) with semi-skimmed or skimmed milk, topped with fresh or dried fruit.

● Homemade muesli with rolled oats, wheat flakes, sunflower seeds and dried fruit.
● Fresh or canned grapefruit in fruit juice.
● Dried fruit compote with low-fat yogurt.
● Low-fat fruit yogurt.
● Fresh fruit with low-fat natural yogurt.
● Wholemeal toast, low-fat or reduced-fat spread and yeast extract or marmalade.
● Boiled, poached or scrambled egg on toast.
● Grilled bacon and tomatoes on toast.

CUTTING THE FAT IN SNACKS

Food eaten between meals can often be high in fat and/or sugar, especially if you are 'eating on the go'. With a bit of planning, however, it's possible to enjoy between-meals snacks which are lower in fat and calories. Use the chart below as a guide to healthy snacks, and look at the fat and calories you can save just by making some changes to the type of snacks you eat.

Key: lower-fat alternatives

	Fat (g)	Calories (kcal)
Chocolate coated biscuits (2)	11	210
Plain digestive biscuit (2)	6	141
Banana (1)	0.3	95
Danish pastry (110g)	19	411
Plain fruit cake (80g slice)	10	283
Doughnut (130g)	19	437
Toasted crumpet (40g)	3	133
with low-fat spread and jam		
Potato crisps (30g bag)	11	164
Bread sticks (4)	1	80
Greek-style yogurt (125g)	11	144
Thick and creamy yogurt (125g pot)	4	131
Low-fat yogurt (125g pot)	1	70
Very low-fat yogurt (125g pot)	0.2	51

EXCELLENT SNACKS AT ANY TIME OF DAY
Some foods are naturally low in fat and are therefore sensible snacks:
● Bananas are one of the healthiest convenience foods – they are low in fat, high in fibre and an excellent source of a range of vitamins and minerals. Unlike other fruit, bananas are also filling.
● All fruit, of course, is low fat and nutritious, but dried fruit, due to its concentrated sweetness, is not a 'tooth-friendly' between-meals snack, so it is best to keep dried fruit for mealtimes (this is especially important for young children whose teeth are just developing).

● Breakfast cereal and low-fat milk makes a nutritious snack and is a popular evening 'filler'.
● Low-fat yogurt and fruit, savoury crackers and cottage cheese, bread muffins, plain biscuits, scones, fruit cake and toasted tea cakes are all low-fat but quite filling snacks. Remember to spread any fat spread you might use thinly, otherwise these bread-based snacks can easily become high-fat snacks.

TIPS FOR LOWER-FAT EATING

● Choose 'low-fat' foods and lower-fat alternatives whenever possible.
● Buy smaller amounts of meat; replace meat with more vegetables, beans or lentils.
● Use low-fat yogurt, reduced-fat mayonnaise or low-fat fromage frais as the basis for salad dressings.
● Check food labels for more low-fat options (with 3g fat or less per portion).
● Limit your intake of cakes, biscuits, savoury snacks and confectionery. Try lower-fat alternatives such as fresh fruit, plain biscuits, scones and tea cakes.
● Limit the amount of spreading fat you use; try spreading it thinner, or opt for a low-fat spread.

CUTTING THE FAT IN COOKING
Switching from traditionally high-fat cooking ingredients to lower-fat alternatives can cut both the fat and calories of a dish, without compromising on taste. Compare the figures below to see the huge difference in products.

	FAT (G)
Double cream	14.0
Crème fraîche	18.0
Soured cream	3.0
Single cream	3.0
Greek-style yogurt	4.0
Creamy fromage frais	4.0
Wholemilk yogurt	1.0
Low-fat fromage frais	0.5
Low-fat yogurt	0.4

● Greek yogurt, creamy fromage frais or wholemilk yogurt are excellent substitutes for cream or crème fraîche: they still produce a creamy tasting sauce but with less than half the fat and calories. When using low-fat yogurt or fromage frais for an even lower-fat option, always add at the end of cooking, gradually mixing it in, to prevent curdling.
● Trim the visible fat off meat before cooking, and buy the leanest cuts you can afford.
● Cook meat without adding fat e.g. in stews and casseroles.

● Dry-fry mince and other meats, drain off excess fat before adding vegetables and other ingredients for casseroles etc. Steam, boil or microwave food whenever possible.
● Grill, bake or microwave food rather than frying.
● Use mashed potato or a mixture of cooked, mashed root vegetables, such as potato, carrot and swede, to top savoury dishes instead of using pastry.

● When using oil in a recipe, measure it out accurately using a measuring spoon rather than pouring the oil straight from the bottle.
● 'Sweat' or cook vegetables in a covered pan in their own juices, rather than shallow-frying or sautéeing them. Alternatively, soften vegetables in a little stock or wine.
● For a week, keep a record of everything you eat and drink so that you can see your true fat intake and take steps to reduce it further.

HOW TO HAVE A LOWER-FAT DAY

By making small changes to your everyday diet, you can cut the fat and still enjoy what you eat. The example below shows a high-fat day and the changes needed to meet the lower-fat target of 70g per day for women.

HIGH-FAT DAY

BREAKFAST	HIGH FAT
Bran flakes & full-fat milk	4.1g
2 slices wholemeal toast, butter & marmalade	18.1g
Tea/coffee & full-fat milk	1.2g

MID-MORNING	HIGH FAT
Chocolate digestive	4.3g
Tea/coffee & full-fat milk	1.2g

LUNCH	HIGH FAT
Chicken salad sandwich on wholemeal bread with butter & mayonnaise	21.2g
Greek-style yogurt	9.4g

MID-AFTERNOON	HIGH FAT
25g bag dry-roasted peanuts	12.5g

EVENING MEAL	HIGH FAT
Spaghetti bolognese, salad & garlic bread	32.0g
Apple crumble & double cream	27.8g

LOWER-FAT DAY

BREAKFAST	LOW FAT
Bran flakes & semi-skimmed milk	1.8g
2 slices wholemeal toast, low-fat spread & marmalade	9.8g
Tea/coffee & semi-skimmed milk	0.6g

MID-MORNING	LOW FAT
Plain digestive	3.1g
Tea/coffee & semi-skimmed milk	0.6

LUNCH	LOW FAT
Chicken salad sandwich on wholemeal bread with low-fat spread & reduced-calorie mayonnaise	15.6g
Low-fat fruit yogurt & a banana	1.2g

MID-AFTERNOON	LOW FAT
Toasted crumpet, low-fat spread & jam	3.0g
Tea/coffee & semi-skimmed milk	0.6g

EVENING MEAL	LOW FAT
Spaghetti bolognese, salad & French bread	21.8g
Apple crumble & custard	11.9g

TOTALS 131.8G   70.0G

COLOUR INDEX

Your starting point for choosing low-fat recipes and planning a menu is the Colour Index on the following pages. This shows a photograph of every recipe in the book (so you can see at a glance whether the overall appearance and colour of the dish suit your purposes), and also gives:

- a brief description of the dish
- the number of people it serves
- the page on which the recipe appears in the book

You will find the information for the recipes for Soups on page 20, Starters on page 24, Fish and shellfish on page 26, Meat dishes on page 31, Pasta and rice on page 36, Vegetables and salads on page 39, Vegetarian dishes on page 44, and Desserts on page 47.

SOUPS

CHILLED MELON AND GINGER SOUP

A summery soup, pretty and with an exotic flavour, to serve for a special occasion.

● SERVES 4 ● *page 56*

LEEK AND POTATO SOUP

A rich and hearty soup that is simple to make – it requires no stock – and is based on a Portuguese recipe.

● SERVES 4 ● *page 60*

CHILLED ASPARAGUS SOUP

A light, creamy soup that brings out the distinctive flavour of asparagus.

● SERVES 6 ● *page 57*

CHILLED TOMATO SOUP WITH AVOCADO CREAM

This soup needs no cooking and the Italian plum tomatoes provide lots of colour.

● SERVES 6 ● *page 58*

CARROT AND CORIANDER SOUP

This is a traditional combination of flavours that never fails to please.

● SERVES 6 ● *page 59*

SOUPS

RED PEPPER AND SWEET POTATO SOUP
The roasted red pepper blends beautifully with Caribbean sweet potato in this flavourful soup, which makes a colourful starter.
● SERVES 4 ● *page 62*

MUSHROOM AND ARTICHOKE SOUP WITH WALNUTS
Jerusalem artichokes give their distinct flavour to this delicious soup.
● SERVES 4 ● *page 64*

CHICKEN CONSOMMÉ
A classic recipe, this concentrated clarified stock is flavoured here with tender pieces of chicken.
● SERVES 4 ● *page 61*

CURRIED CARROT AND SPLIT PEA SOUP
This is the perfect remedy during the cold winter months – a warming, thick and wholesome soup.
● SERVES 4 ● *page 63*

BUTTERNUT SQUASH SOUP WITH PARMESAN CROSTINI
The sweet, buttery flesh of the squash combines well with the crostini.
● SERVES 4 ● *page 65*

SOUPS

MINESTRONE

This is a typically Italian, delicious and filling soup packed with interesting textures.

● SERVES 6-8 ● *page 66*

VEGETABLE, NOODLE AND TOFU BROTH

The flavours of this Thai soup, especially the lemongrass, root ginger and coriander, are subtle, refreshing and surprisingly delicate.

● SERVES 4 ● *page 68*

SPICED BEEF AND NOODLE SOUP

A filling soup with fragrant Asian flavours that can be served as a meal in itself.

● SERVES 4 ● *page 67*

PRAWN BROTH WITH ORIENTAL MUSHROOMS

A chunky soup with a delicate flavour.

● SERVES 6 ● *page 70*

MUSHROOM AND OMELETTE SOUP

Eggs are often used in Thai cooking; here omelette pieces are stirred in before serving.

● SERVES 4 ● *page 71*

SOUPS

MUSHROOM TOM YAM
A Thai soup that makes an unusual starter or light lunch for those who like hot, spicy food.
● SERVES 4 ● *page 74*

HOT AND SOUR PRAWN SOUP
The flavours of this soup are light, refreshing and quite delicate.
● SERVES 4 ● *page 72*

**HOT AND SOUR SOUP
WITH CRAB-STUFFED WONTONS**
Wontons make this Thai dish satisfying and filling.
● SERVES 4 ● *page 73*

**TURKEY, HAM AND SPINACH BROTH
WITH SPLIT PEAS**
A hearty, nourishing main-course soup.
● SERVES 6 ● *page 75*

STARTERS

FATTOUSH
An Arabic salad that can be served as a starter or as an easy lunch or supper dish.
● SERVES 4 ● *page 78*

MINTED CITRUS SALAD
Exotic fruits are combined with fresh mint in this refreshing summer salad.
● SERVES 4 ● *page 79*

ZESTY ORANGE AND ASPARAGUS SALAD
A delicious tangy salad that makes a perfect light lunch as well as a starter.
● SERVES 4 ● *page 80*

ROASTED GARLIC AND TOMATO TAPAS
Ideal finger food, these Spanish appetisers are bursting with Mediterranean flavour.
● SERVES 6 ● *page 81*

LIME AND GIN MARINATED SALMON
Japanese sushi of rice and marinated salmon are ideal nibbles before a substantial meal.
● MAKES 15 ● *page 82*

SMOKED SALMON AND SCALLOP PARCELS
Chilli, lime and coriander flavour the salmon and scallops in this punchy starter.
● SERVES 6 ● *page 83*

STARTERS

LEEK TERRINE WITH WARM LEMON AND CAPER DRESSING
A light and low-fat terrine that brings out the subtle flavour of tender young leeks. It is much easier to assemble than it looks and the time it takes is well worth the effort.
● SERVES 8 ● *page 88*

MUSHROOM PÂTÉ WITH MADEIRA
A delicious, rich vegetarian starter using a variety of fresh and dried mushrooms.
● SERVES 6 ● *page 87*

MARINATED SALMON
A dill and lime juice marinade makes wafer-thin slices of fish melt in the mouth.
● SERVES 8 ● *page 84*

MUSSELS WITH GINGER, CHILLI AND CORIANDER
A spicy alternative to moules marinières.
● SERVES 4 ● *page 85*

GRILLED KING PRAWNS WITH CHILLI SOY SAUCE
Succulent prawns served with a hot sauce.
● SERVES 4 ● *page 86*

FISH AND SHELLFISH

SPICED FRIED FISH

A tasty spiced fish dish with chillies, cumin seeds and coriander.

● SERVES 4 ● *page 92*

GREMOLATA SWORDFISH WITH LEMON AND MINT BULGHAR WHEAT

Grilled fish steaks served with a colourful salad – bright red cherry tomatoes contrasting with chopped fresh mint and black olives – and garnished with lemon rind, garlic and parsley.

● SERVES 4 ● *page 93*

SEAFOOD WITH GARLIC, PARSLEY AND LEMON

A simple starter to prepare – you need only prawns, squid, lemon juice, garlic and whichever fresh herbs are available.

● SERVES 6 ● *page 94*

GRILLED COD WITH SWEET CHILLI GLAZE

A wonderfully quick dish of moist fish in a crispy coat. The recipe works with mackerel and other fish, too.

● SERVES 4 ● *page 95*

GRILLED TURBOT WITH CHERVIL AND TOMATO SAUCE

Grilled turbot steaks served with a creamy tomato and chervil sauce.

● SERVES 4 ● *page 96*

FISH AND SHELLFISH

SEAFOOD KEBABS
Seafood interspersed with lime and cucumber served on a bed of salad leaves makes a delicious summer supper or dish for a barbecue.
● SERVES 4 ● *page 100*

GRILLED SCALLOPS IN BASIL LEAVES
Fresh scallops wrapped in colourful coats of basil leaves and grilled peppers.
● SERVES 4 ● *page 102*

PARCHMENT BAKED FISH
This method of cooking ensures maximum flavour as the fish cooks in its juices, flavoured with fennel and cucumber.
● SERVES 4 ● *page 97*

ROLLED PLAICE WITH PESTO
A nutritious dish – plaice rolls flavoured with pesto, served on a bed of colourful and crunchy steamed vegetables.
● SERVES 4 ● *page 98*

SWEET AND SOUR MONKFISH KEBABS
Monkfish wrapped in bacon so it retains its succulence, then marinated in a sweet sauce and grilled until tender.
● SERVES 4 ● *page 99*

FISH AND SHELLFISH

PRAWNS FRIED WITH GREENS
A delicious stir-fry dish of large prawns, Chinese greens and spices.
● SERVES 4–6 ● *page 104*

MUSSELS WITH GARLIC AND PARSLEY
Mussels stuffed with garlic, herbs and Parmesan and baked in the oven to bring out their distinct flavour.
● SERVES 4–6 ● *page 103*

FISH BAKED WITH HOT SPICES
Firm white fish fillets, such as cod, monkfish or sea bass, marinated in a delicious mixture of spices.
● SERVES 4 ● *page 106*

FISH STEW WITH ARTICHOKES AND OYSTER MUSHROOMS
A special occasion fish stew with tender pieces of haddock cooked in white wine sauce.
● SERVES 4–6 ● *page 110*

SQUID AND VEGETABLES IN A BLACK BEAN SAUCE

A particularly authentic Thai dish with squid, spices and colourful vegetables in a delicious bean sauce. It takes a while to prepare but very little time to cook.

● SERVES 4 ● page 108

ROASTED MONKFISH WITH MEDITERRANEAN VEGETABLES

A strongly flavoured monkfish dish.

● SERVES 4 ● page 107

DILL-GLAZED SALMON

Dill and salmon are perfect partners, and this recipe is no exception to the rule. The resulting moist fish is perfect for a cold buffet.

● SERVES 8 ● page 111

THAI SEAFOOD SALAD

A combination of seafood tossed in a generous sweet and sour dressing, with crunchy vegetables.

● SERVES 4 ● page 112

CRAB SALAD

One of the best ways to serve freshly cooked crabs, with a hint of spice and lime juice and a selection of bitter salad leaves.

● SERVES 6 ● page 113

FISH AND SHELLFISH

SEAFOOD AND MELON SALAD WITH GINGER LIME DRESSING
Prawns, mussels and squid with fragrant melon.
● SERVES 4 ● *page 114*

MARINATED SALMON WITH LIME AND CORIANDER DRESSING
Wafer-thin salmon slices in a lime-based marinade make a delicate starter or even a light lunch or supper dish.
● SERVES 4 ● *page 117*

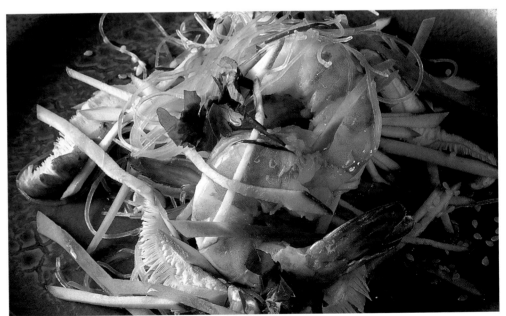

LIME MARINATED HALIBUT WITH AVOCADO AND RED ONION SALSA
A salad based on the Mexican dish ceviche.
● SERVES 4 ● *page 116*

PRAWN AND GLASS NOODLES SALAD
Prawns, mushrooms and vegetables served with transparent noodles make an impressive starter or light lunch.
● SERVES 4 ● *page 115*

MEAT DISHES

CHICKEN, BEAN AND SPINACH CURRY
Strips of chicken breast in a curry sauce to your taste make a substantial supper dish that can be prepared in just 30 minutes.
● SERVES 4 ● page 123

AROMATIC CHICKEN PARCELS
A headily aromatic dish with flavours of North Africa.
● SERVES 8 ● page 120

CHICKEN CASSEROLE WITH HERB DUMPLINGS
A warming, filling stew that also includes prunes and leeks.
● SERVES 6 ● page 122

TANDOORI-STYLE CHICKEN
Chicken cooked with a spicy yogurt crust under an intense heat.
● SERVES 4 ● page 124

CHICKEN FAJITAS
Mexican-style chicken served with tortillas, guacamole and soured cream.
● SERVES 6 ● page 125

MEAT DISHES

GREEN CHICKEN CURRY
A Thai green curry paste forms the basis of this hot dish.
● SERVES 4 ● *page 126*

BARBECUE CHICKEN
Baby onions, small potatoes and chicken thighs or drumsticks are coated in a rich barbecue sauce and baked in the oven until tender.
● SERVES 4 ● *page 127*

GRILLED CHICKEN WITH A SPICED YOGURT CRUST
Yogurt forms a delicious soft crust and retains the moistness of the meat.
● SERVES 4 ● *page 128*

CHICKEN BAKED WITH SPICES
A tasty and easy-to-prepare supper to serve with a crisp green salad and rice. Best made in advance so the chicken is well marinated.
● SERVES 6 ● *page 129*

VENISON WITH POMEGRANATE
Lean and tender venison sautéed very quickly and served with an extravagant mushroom and pomegranate sauce.
● SERVES 4 ● *page 130*

LAMB AND BAMBOO SHOOT RED CURRY
Thai red curry paste is used to flavour this exotic lamb curry – a mouthwatering dish that is easy to make and best accompanied by rice or noodles.
● SERVES 4 ● page 132

LAMB CUTLETS WITH MINTED CUCUMBER SALSA
Juicy, spring lamb with orange and mint sauce.
● SERVES 6 ● page 133

DUCK BREASTS WITH PICKLED PLUMS
Thai-spiced duck cooked with pickled plums which provide a sharp contrast to the richness of the meat and its sauce.
● SERVES 6 ● page 131

GRILLED LAMB WITH COURGETTES AND ROSEMARY
Tender lamb infused with rosemary and flavoured with creamy roasted garlic.
● SERVES 4 ● page 134

SPICED LAMB MEATBALLS
Lightly spiced minced lamb meatballs make an ideal family or informal supper – delicious served with a feta cheese salad.
● SERVES 4 ● page 135

MEAT DISHES

LAMB FILLET AND PEPPER STIR-FRY

Lean pieces of lamb quickly stir-fried and served with a tangy sauce.

● SERVES 4 ● *page 136*

LEMON-ROASTED PORK WITH GARLIC AND BASIL

Pork fillets wrapped around a filling of herbs and garlic and roasted, for a meal packed with flavour. The meat needs to marinate overnight but the results are well worth it.

● SERVES 6 ● *page 140*

SPICED LAMB ESCALOPES

Herbs, garlic, ginger and chilli marinate these escalopes that simply melt in the mouth.

● SERVES 4 ● *page 138*

PAN-FRIED LIVER WITH TOMATOES

A warming dish of wafer-thin liver cooked in a rich Marsala sauce.

● SERVES 4 ● *page 139*

STIR-FRIED PORK WITH BABY CORN

Morsels of pork stir-fried with vegetables and a light soy sauce.

● SERVES 4 ● *page 142*

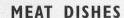

LAMB AND ROSEMARY RAGU
Minced lamb cooked in a traditional, rich tomato sauce flavoured with heady scent of rosemary. The ragu sauce also works well with beef, if you prefer.
● SERVES 4-6 ● page 146

STIR-FRIED PORK WITH CHINESE GREENS
A cheat's stir-fry using ready-repared vegetables – quick and easy to prepare.
● SERVES 6 ● page 147

GLAZED BAKED GAMMON
This is a perfect joint for large gatherings, studded with cloves and glazed with honey.
● SERVES 8 ● page 143

BEEF SALAD WITH ROASTED VEGETABLE PASTE
Based on a Thai dish, seared beef is served with a paste of roasted vegetables.
● SERVES 4 ● page 144

SWEET AND SOUR SPICED PORK
Chinese-style pork cooked with a chilli, ginger, garlic and plum sauce.
● SERVES 4 ● page 148

PASTA AND RICE

WARM SEAFOOD AND PASTA SALAD
Pasta with a selection of mixed seafood to serve warm or cold.
● SERVES 4 ● *page 152*

TAGLIATELLE WITH CHICKEN LIVERS AND SPINACH
An iron-rich and highly nutritious pasta dish, packed with lots of flavour and with a pleasing colour contrast supplied by the tomatoes and spinach.
● SERVES 6 ● *page 153*

ORECCHIETTE WITH PEPPERS, CAPERS AND ANCHOVIES
Smoky, sweet roasted peppers and anchovies lend a distinct flavour to this wonderful dish.
● SERVES 4 ● *page 154*

PASTA AND RICE

SPAGHETTI WITH CHILLI AND GARLIC

A classic recipe known as *aglio olio* in Italy, this is simple to make, delicious to eat, and makes a substantial dish for hungry pasta-lovers.

● SERVES 4 ● *page 155*

BROAD BEAN AND LEMON RISOTTO

Buttery broad beans and tangy lemon contrast well in this creamy risotto.

● SERVES 4 ● *page 157*

MEE GORENG

A Malaysian dish of seafood, steak and spices.

● SERVES 4–6 ● *page 156*

PRAWN AND LEMON RISOTTO

Saffron and lemon are added to this risotto for an attractive and tasty one-pot supper.

● SERVES 4 ● *page 158*

PASTA AND RICE

AUBERGINE AND CHICKPEA PILAF

A fragrant, elegant dish of chickpeas and delicate spices.

● SERVES 6 ● *page 161*

GARLIC AND PARMESAN RISOTTO

This is a good starter recipe for those new to risotto; simple and delicious, it is a useful one-pot dish when only basic ingredient are to hand.

● SERVES 4 ● *page 160*

RICE AND DAL PILAF

Chana dal cooked with rice, nuts and sesame seeds for a nutritious dish.

● SERVES 4–6 ● *page 162*

RICE WITH ASPARAGUS, CRAB AND PINEAPPLE

Vegetables, crab and spices with Thai fragrant rice – an exciting combination of flavours for those who like sweet and sour food.

● SERVES 4 ● *page 163*

VEGETABLES AND SALADS

GRILLED PEPPERS WITH PINENUTS
Sweet ramiro pointed peppers roasted with coriander seeds, pinenuts and almonds to give the dish an interesting texture.
● SERVES 2 ● page 167

MUSTARD-SEEDED OKRA
This heavily seasoned vegetable makes a tasty side dish especially with grilled meat.
● SERVES 8 ● page 166

GLAZED SHALLOTS WITH BALSAMIC VINEGAR
Sweet and golden tender onions with their flavour enhanced by a splash of vinegar.
● SERVES 8–10 ● page 168

WINTER VEGETABLE ROAST
Seasonal root vegetables cooked slowly for a wholesome winter supper.
● SERVES 6 ● page 169

BROAD BEANS WITH ARTICHOKES AND CUMIN
A wonderful combination of spices, broad beans, ham and artichokes.
● SERVES 6 ● page 170

VEGETABLES AND SALADS

CHINESE BRAISED VEGETABLES
Vegetables, ginger and soy sauce capture an authentic taste of China.
● SERVES 8 ● *page 172*

FRENCH BEANS WITH TOMATOES AND HERBS
Ripe tomatoes, basil, parsley, garlic and onion bring out the flavour of freshly picked French beans making an interesting accompaniment to grilled meat or fish.
● SERVES 6 ● *page 171*

CORIANDER ROSTI
Grated potatoes mixed with onions and a generous amount of herbs.
● SERVES 6–8 ● *page 173*

RATATOUILLE
This traditional French dish combines all the finest Mediterranean flavours.
● SERVES 6 ● *page 174*

CHICKPEAS WITH SPINACH
A tasty combination of chickpeas, spices and spinach for a side dish or main meal.
● SERVES 4–6 ● *page 175*

VEGETABLES AND SALADS

CHICKPEAS WITH GINGER AND TOMATOES
Spices and chickpeas make an excellent accompaniment to potatoes and sausages as well as a range of Indian dishes.
● SERVES 6 ● *page 178*

OKRA TAGINE
A spicy vegetable casserole from North Africa, best served with couscous or rice.
● SERVES 4–6 ● *page 176*

GRILLED VEGETABLE SALAD
A highly colourful salad including the sweetest Mediterranean vegetables.
● SERVES 4–6 ● *page 179*

ROASTED PEPPER SALAD
Sweet roasted peppers with spring onions and a chilli, ginger and soy sauce dressing.
● SERVES 4 ● *page 180*

GRILLED AUBERGINES
Simply grilled baby aubergines with chilli, rosemary and garlic and basted with olive oil.
● SERVES 4 ● *page 182*

VEGETABLES AND SALADS

ASPARAGUS OR SAMPHIRE SALAD

A pretty salad using tender asparagus or the delicate seaweed, samphire.

● SERVES 6 ● *page 188*

STIR-FRIED SUMMER VEGETABLES

A colourful stir-fry of whatever tender young vegetables are available – baby carrots and courgettes, beans, mangetout, baby corn or sugar-snap peas.

● SERVES 4–6 ● *page 184*

AUBERGINES STUDDED WITH GARLIC AND ROSEMARY

Aromatic aubergines roasted until deliciously soft inside, to serve hot or cold.

● SERVES 6–8 ● *page 183*

SWEDE AND CARROTS WITH MUSTARD SEEDS AND GINGER

Swede and carrots cooked to a creamy mash and flavoured with mustard and ginger.

● SERVES 4 ● *page 186*

SUGAR-SNAP PEAS IN A MINTED-LEMON DRESSING

A classic flavour combination of peas and mint in a crème fraîche dressing.

● SERVES 4 ● *page 187*

VEGETABLES AND SALADS

MESCLUN WITH TOASTED SEEDS
Assorted salad greens mixed with toasted seeds and nuts. This is the perfect side salad and also makes a good basis for a more substantial dish.
● SERVES 4 ● *page 189*

CARROT SALAD
A simple, pretty salad with carrots, oranges and chives.
● SERVES 4–6 ● *page 192*

TOMATO AND PEACH SALAD WITH AVOCADO SALSA
A highly attractive fruity salad, excellent for a summer buffet.
● SERVES 4 ● *page 190*

THREE TOMATO SALAD
A colourful combination of ripe tomatoes with a sweet vinaigrette garnished with basil leaves and slivers of cheese.
● SERVES 4–6 ● *page 191*

CHILLED MELON AND GINGER SALAD
A simple summer salad with the well-loved combination of melon and ginger – a refreshing way to begin or end a meal.
● SERVES 6 ● *page 193*

VEGETABLES AND SALADS   VEGETARIAN DISHES

ORIENTAL CHICKEN SALAD
Chicken marinated in citrus juices, soy sauce, honey and garlic, with crunchy vegetables.
● SERVES 4 ● *page 194*

INDONESIAN FRUIT AND PRAWN SALAD WITH CHILLI DRESSING
A tasty combination of prawns and fruit.
● SERVES 4 ● *page 195*

TUSCAN BEAN STEW
A classic Italian stew with a mixture of beans, herbs, garlic and tomatoes – ideal for those with a hearty appetite.
● SERVES 4 ● *page 199*

VEGETARIAN DISHES

LEMON DAL
Split red lentils flavoured with lemon and turmeric and cooked to a smooth, creamy purée – the perfect accompaniment to a curry.
● SERVES 4–6 ● *page 198*

MIXED LENTIL CASSEROLE
Red and brown lentils combined with vegetables to make a rich and filling stew.
● SERVES 6 ● *page 200*

VEGETABLE CHILLI
A spicy red kidney bean and vegetable chilli, delicious with low-fat yogurt.
● SERVES 8 ● *page 201*

CURRIED TOFU BURGERS
Tofu flavoured with curry spices and made into moist little burgers.
● SERVES 4 ● *page 202*

QUORN KEBABS WITH TOMATO SALSA
Grilled Quorn and corn kebabs served with a spicy tomato and chilli salsa.
● SERVES 4 ● *page 203*

VEGETARIAN DISHES

STUFFED PEPPERS
Peppers with rice, mushrooms, ginger and soy sauce are packed with flavour.
● SERVES 6 ● *page 204*

VEGETABLE COUSCOUS
A traditional North African dish, this wholesome couscous can be cooked with whatever seasonal vegetables are available.
● SERVES 4 ● *page 208*

JACKET POTATOES WITH CHILLI
A hearty, tasty and filling dish that is quick and easy to prepare.
● SERVES 4 ● *page 205*

BAKED BLACK-EYED BEAN CASSEROLE
Beans cooked slowly in a rich sauce of cider, tomatoes, treacle and mustard.
● SERVES 4 ● *page 206*

SPICY VEGETABLE COUSCOUS WITH HARISSA
A spicy version of vegetable couscous, not for the faint-hearted.
● SERVES 4–6 ● *page 207*

DESSERTS

PEAR GALETTES WITH CHOCOLATE SAUCE
Impressive little galettes topped with pears flavoured with cinnamon and chocolate sauce – an indulgent treat for chocoholics on a special occasion.
● MAKES 6 ● *page 216*

SPICED PEACHES
Gently poached peaches in syrup make a highly attractive dessert oozing with flavour.
● SERVES 8 ● *page 212*

GINGER-GLAZED PINEAPPLE
Succulent pieces of pineapple glazed with honey and ginger, and grilled until golden.
● SERVES 8 ● *page 213*

BAKED PEARS WITH APRICOTS AND ALMONDS
Luscious ripe pears baked with a soft, sweet, almond topping.
● SERVES 4 ● *page 214*

POACHED PEARS WITH FUDGE SAUCE
Whole pears gently poached and served with a rich fudge sauce.
● SERVES 4 ● *page 215*

DESSERTS

PEARS IN MALMSEY MADEIRA
Pears poached in a rich syrup of Malmsey Madeira, lemon and vanilla.
● SERVES 6 ● *page 217*

WARM TROPICAL FRUITS WITH SABAYON SAUCE
Soft tropical fruits, baked then grilled with a heavenly sweet sabayon sauce – a delicious way to cook any type of fresh fruit.
● SERVES 4 ● *page 220*

FRUIT KEBABS WITH SPICED PEAR DIP
Skewers of figs, mango and pineapple grilled and served with a sweetly spiced pear dip.
● MAKES 6 ● *page 218*

RHUBARB AND RASPBERRY MERINGUES
A smooth pulp of rhubarb and ginger topped with sweet raspberry meringue.
● SERVES 4 ● *page 219*

HOT MANGO SOUFFLÉS WITH PAPAYA SAUCE
Exotic fruit-flavoured soufflés offset beautifully by a slightly sharp papaya sauce.
● SERVES 6 ● *page 221*

DESSERTS

APRICOT AND CARDAMOM CRUMBLE

A nice and light crumble made with fresh apricots and a delightfully aromatic cardamom-flavoured topping.

● SERVES 6 ● *page 223*

PLUMS WITH CARAMELISED FRUIT BREAD

Freshly stewed plums served on slices of fruit bread that soaks up the juice.

● SERVES 4 ● *page 222*

APPLE AND BLACKBERRY SNOW

A refreshing, light dessert of juicy blackberries and sweet autumn apples.

● SERVES 6 ● *page 236*

RASPBERRY CHEESECAKES

Delicious individual cheesecakes – a mixture of raspberries and ricotta on Madeira cake.

● SERVES 6 ● *page 237*

BLACK FOREST ROULADE

A classic roulade with chocolate and cherries, a rich sponge and light cream filling.

● SERVES 10 ● *page 226*

DESSERTS

RASPBERRIES WITH CHOCOLATE MALLOW
A wonderfully light, chocolate meringue with a sweet raspberry base.
● SERVES 6 ● *page 228*

PRUNE AND ARMAGNAC SOUFFLÉ WITH CARAMELISED WALNUTS
An impressive dessert for a special occasion with alcohol-soaked prunes beneath the light soufflé – it takes a little time to prepare but tastes delicious.
● SERVES 6 ● *page 229*

CHOCOLATE PANCAKES
Delicate pancakes made with a light batter and filled with chocolate and bananas.
● MAKES 12 ● *page 227*

CARROT AND CARDAMOM PUDDINGS
Individual puddings scented with cardamom and decorated with caramel flowers.
● SERVES 6 ● *page 230*

RED FRUIT TERRINE
An extremely elegant fruit-filled dessert, with redcurrants, strawberries and raspberries.
● SERVES 6 ● *page 232*

DESSERTS

FRUIT TERRINE WITH STRAWBERRY SAUCE
Alternate layers of ruby red and vivid orange jellies with raspberries complemented by a peppery strawberry sauce.
● SERVES 6 ● *page 234*

SPICED WINTER FRUIT COMPOTE
Dried fruits poached in apple and wine syrup scented with star-anise and cinnamon.
● SERVES 6 ● *page 225*

ORANGES IN CARAMEL
Oranges poached in a lightly alcoholic caramel syrup and served with crunchy caramel.
● SERVES 6 ● *page 235*

SUMMER PUDDING
Summer fruits packed into a breaded mould that oozes the taste of summer.
● SERVES 8 ● *page 224*

MELON WITH SUMMER FRUITS
Galia and ogen melons with summer fruits in a heady melon sauce.
● SERVES 4 ● *page 238*

DESSERTS

FRAGRANT FRUIT SALAD

Spicy stem ginger and ginger syrup bring out the flavours of these exotic fruits.

● SERVES 8 ● *page 239*

WARM SALAD OF SUMMER FRUITS WITH PORT

The glorious fruits of summer warmed through and softened in a wine and port syrup, served while they are still warm.

● SERVES 4 ● *page 241*

FRUIT SALAD

A cardamom and mint-scented syrup makes this simple fruit salad delicious.

● SERVES 6 ● *page 240*

EXOTIC FRESH FRUIT SALAD

A medley of mango, melon, papaya, pineapple and bananas in a jasmine syrup.

● SERVES 4 ● *page 242*

PEACHES WITH A HOT ZABAGLIONE SAUCE

Luscious ripe peaches served simply with a frothy sweet wine sauce.

● SERVES 4 ● *page 244*

DESSERTS

RASPBERRY AND COCOA SORBETS
Cocoa gives a wonderfully intense, chocolate taste and provides a glorious contrast with the raspberry sorbet served alongside.
● SERVES 6 ● *page 248*

MANGO, GINGER AND CITRUS SORBET
A smooth-textured sorbet with ginger and lime for a refreshing dessert.
● SERVES 4–6 ● *page 249*

THREE CLASSIC SORBETS
Mouthwatering sorbets of melon, orange and strawberry.
● SERVES 4–6 ● *page 245*

LEMON SORBET
A light and refreshing sorbet alive with a citrus tang – perfect to serve at the end of a meal or as a palate cleanser between courses.
● SERVES 3–4 ● *page 246*

SOUPS

The key to making delicious soup is to use fresh, seasonal ingredients and the best stock possible. A good, homemade stock makes all the difference to the soup's final taste, but if you haven't got the time or inclination to make your own, you will still get good results if you use one of the 'fresh' stocks available from the chilled cabinets in most supermarkets.

Soups can be a meal in themselves, served with fresh bread (keep the fat down by eating it without butter) or if they include chunky vegetables or noodles. And they can be the perfect starter for both informal suppers or more formal entertaining. Choose the best of each season's produce, whether it be tender baby spring vegetables, pungent fresh summer herbs, autumn's harvest of pumpkins and late tomatoes, or the glorious, earthy root vegetables of the winter months. Of course, the soup should look visually attractive, too, so remember to add a garnish of fresh herbs, a sprinkling of spice or a dollop of low-fat yogurt to make the dish more interesting.

This chapter includes a huge range of soups to suit every occasion and taste, from the hot and spicy Mushroom Tom Yam and hearty Italian soups, such as Minestrone, to the lighter, clear Chicken Consommé. Many of these soups are suitable for freezing, so if you are cooking for two, make up the full quantity and freeze half so that you have an emergency supply of homemade soup ready in the freezer whenever you need it.

CHILLED MELON AND GINGER SOUP

What could be more refreshing on a hot summer's day than a bowl of iced melon soup? The gingered cucumber relish sets off the flavour of the melon to perfection and adds an exotic element to the soup. For a special occasion serve the soup in the hollowed-out melon shells.

● SERVES 4 ● PREPARATION TIME: 35 MINUTES, PLUS CHILLING ● 145 CALS PER SERVING ● 3.2G FAT, OF WHICH 0.4G SATURATED FAT

4 small charentais or cantaloupe melons
4 spring onions, trimmed
60ml (4 tbsp) ginger wine
15ml (1 tbsp) chopped fresh dill
150ml (¼ pint) 0% fat Greek yogurt
salt and ground black pepper
lime juice, to taste
Cucumber relish:
125g (4oz) cucumber
15ml (1 tbsp) extra virgin olive oil
5ml (1 tsp) lime juice
15ml (1 tbsp) chopped fresh dill
5ml (1 tsp) chopped preserved stem ginger, plus
5ml (1 tsp) syrup from jar
fresh dill sprigs, to garnish

1 Cut a very thin slice from the base of each melon so it will stand upright. Then cut another slice about 2.5cm (1 inch) from the top. Place a sieve over a bowl and, holding the melon over the sieve to catch any juices, scoop out and discard the seeds. Scoop out and reserve the flesh along with the juices. Keep the melon shells for serving, if wished.

2 Place the melon flesh in a blender or food processor. Finely chop the spring onions and add to the melon with the ginger wine, dill and Greek yogurt. Purée until smooth, then blend in up to 300ml (½ pint) of the reserved melon juice to give the required consistency. Season with salt and pepper, and add a little lime juice to taste. Chill in the refrigerator for 1 hour.

3 Meanwhile, make the cucumber relish. Peel and halve the cucumber, scoop out the seeds and very thinly slice the flesh. Sprinkle the slices of cucumber with salt and set aside for 30 minutes.

4 Wash the cucumber to remove the salt and pat dry on kitchen paper. Place in a bowl and stir in the remaining ingredients, seasoning with pepper to taste.

5 Divide the soup between the reserved melon shells or soup bowls and top each portion with a little of the cucumber relish. Drizzle over extra virgin olive oil and serve garnished with dill sprigs.

VARIATION

● Add 225g (8oz) cooked peeled prawns and process with the melon flesh, increasing the yogurt to 300ml (½ pint).

NOTE

● Suitable for freezing: without cucumber relish.

CHILLED ASPARAGUS SOUP

This velvety-textured soup with tender spears of young asparagus captures the essence of summer.

● SERVES 6 ● PREPARATION TIME: 15 MINUTES, PLUS CHILLING ● COOKING TIME: 40–55 MINUTES
● 92 CALS PER SERVING ● 4.6G FAT, OF WHICH 2.6G SATURATED FAT

700g (1½ lb) asparagus
salt and ground black pepper
2 onions, peeled
25g (1oz) butter or margarine
1.4 litres (2½ pints) chicken stock
150ml (¼ pint) semi-skimmed milk
finely grated lemon rind, to garnish

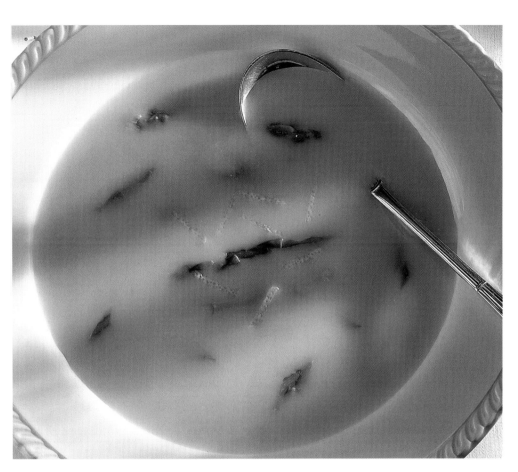

1 Cut the tips from the asparagus. Simmer gently in salted water for 3–5 minutes, until tender. Drain and refresh in cold water.

2 Scrape the asparagus stalks with a potato peeler or knife and cut off the woody ends; thinly slice the stalks. Chop the onions.

3 Melt the butter in a large saucepan. Add the asparagus stalks and onions, cover and cook for 5–10 minutes, until beginning to soften.

4 Add the stock and seasoning to taste. Bring to the boil, cover and simmer for 30–40 minutes, until the asparagus stalks and onions are tender.

5 Allow to cool slightly, then purée in a blender or food processor until smooth. Pass the soup through a sieve into a bowl, then stir in the milk.

6 Chill in the refrigerator for 2–3 hours. Serve garnished with the reserved asparagus tips and finely pared lemon rind.

NOTE

● *Suitable for freezing.*

CHILLED TOMATO SOUP WITH AVOCADO CREAM

A chilled, fresh soup of puréed ripe tomatoes and mint, topped with a smooth cream flavoured with avocado. This sophisticated soup needs no cooking and is best made with flavourful Italian plum tomatoes, which provide lots of colour too. Beef tomatoes would be a good substitute, but they must be very ripe.

● SERVES 6 ● PREPARATION TIME: 20 MINUTES, PLUS CHILLING ● 131 CALS PER SERVING ● 7G FAT, OF WHICH 1.6G SATURATED FAT

1.4kg (3lb) ripe red tomatoes
750ml (1¼ pints) tomato juice
pinch of sugar
dash of Tabasco sauce
15ml (1 tbsp) lemon juice
30ml (2 tbsp) chopped fresh mint
salt and ground black pepper
Avocado cream:
1 large ripe avocado
10–15 ml (2–3 tsp) lemon juice
½ small onion
30ml (2 tbsp) chopped fresh mint
90ml (6 tbsp) natural yogurt
mint sprigs, to garnish

1 Halve the tomatoes, then squeeze out the seeds into a bowl. Cut four tomato halves into fine dice, cover and refrigerate. Strain the tomato seeds through a small sieve to extract any juice; discard the seeds.

2 Place the remaining tomatoes in a blender or food processor with all the tomato juice, the sugar, Tabasco sauce, lemon juice, chopped mint and salt and pepper to taste. Liquidise or process until smooth, then pass through a sieve into a clean bowl. Taste and adjust the seasoning.

3 Cover, place in the refrigerator and leave for at least 2 hours to allow the flavours to develop and the soup to become thoroughly chilled.

4 Half an hour before serving, halve the avocado, remove the stone, then peel. Mash the avocado flesh in a bowl, using a fork, adding lemon juice to taste. Peel and finely grate the onion and mix into the avocado with the chopped mint and yogurt.

5 Stir the reserved diced tomato into the chilled soup. Ladle the soup into individual serving bowls and add a dollop of the avocado cream to each one. Garnish with mint sprigs to serve.

VARIATION

● Substitute fresh basil for the mint. Dice the avocado and stir into the soup, leaving out the grated onion. Serve topped with spoonfuls of soured cream.

NOTE

● Suitable for freezing: soup only (with the diced tomato); stir well when thawed. Do not freeze the avocado cream.

CARROT AND CORIANDER SOUP

This is a classic combination of flavours that never fails to please. The sweetness of the carrots blends perfectly with the distinct, fragrant taste of the coriander.

● SERVES 6 ● PREPARATION TIME: 15 MINS
● COOKING TIME: 25–30 MINS ● 185 CALS PER SERVING ● 6G FAT, OF WHICH 3.8G SATURATED FAT

175g (6oz) leeks
450g (1lb) carrots, peeled
40g (1½oz) butter or margarine
10ml (2 tsp) ground coriander
5ml (1 tsp) plain flour
1.1 litres (2 pints) vegetable stock
salt and ground black pepper
150ml (¼ pint) low-fat natural yogurt
chopped fresh coriander leaves, to garnish
low-fat natural yogurt, to serve (optional)

1 Slice the leeks and carrots. Heat the butter in a large saucepan. Add the vegetables, cover the pan and cook gently for 5–10 minutes or until the vegetables begin to soften, but not colour.

NOTE

● Suitable for freezing from step 3.

2 Stir in the coriander and flour and cook for 1 minute. Add the stock and bring to the boil, stirring. Season, reduce the heat, cover and simmer for 20 minutes or until all the ingredients are tender.

3 Leave the soup to cool slightly, then purée in a blender or food processor until quite smooth.

4 Return the soup to the pan and stir in the yogurt. Check the seasoning and reheat gently; do not boil. Serve garnished with the coriander leaves and a swirl of low-fat natural yogurt, if wished.

LEEK AND POTATO SOUP

A most satisfying soup that requires no stock. The recipe is based on the Portuguese method for making cabbage soup, in which potato and garlic are mashed into their cooking water and the greenery added to cook down. Use the best olive oil you can muster for the vital finishing splash of flavour.

● SERVES 4 ● PREPARATION TIME: 10 MINUTES ●
COOKING TIME: 15 MINUTES ● 226 CALS PER SERVING
● 11.7G FAT, OF WHICH 1.6G SATURATED FAT

575g (1¼ lb) floury potatoes
2–3 garlic cloves
salt and ground black pepper
350g (12oz) trimmed leeks
celery salt (optional)
60ml (4 tbsp) coarsely chopped fresh parsley
60ml (4 tbsp) extra virgin olive oil
sun-dried tomato bread, to serve

1 Peel and thinly slice the potatoes and garlic. Place in a saucepan and add 1.2 litres (2 pints) cold water. Bring to the boil and add a little salt. Cover and simmer for about 10 minutes until the potatoes are soft.

2 Meanwhile, slice the leeks. Add them to the potatoes and simmer for a further 5 minutes or so to soften the leeks.

3 Roughly mash the potatoes into the soup, using a potato masher. Correct the seasoning with celery salt, if using, and pepper, to taste. Stir in the parsley.

4 Ladle the soup into warmed soup plates and drizzle 15ml (1 tbsp) olive oil in a slash over the surface of each serving. Serve with chunks of sun-dried tomato bread.

NOTE

● Never use a food processor or blender to mash potatoes, as it will make the texture gluey.

VARIATION

● Use coarsely chopped watercress instead of parsley.

CHICKEN CONSOMMÉ

Consommé is a concentrated clarified stock made by reducing chicken, beef or veal stock, and clarifying it by adding egg whites. A consommé may be served as a soup, with other flavourings added, or it may be used as the basis of another dish.

● SERVES 4 ● PREPARATION TIME: 30 MINUTES
● COOKING TIME: 1 HOUR 15 MINUTES ● 140 CALS
PER SERVING ● 4.5G FAT, OF WHICH 1.3G
SATURATED FAT

1.7 litres (3 pints) well-flavoured, fat-free chicken stock
2 leeks
2 celery sticks
2 carrots, peeled
2 shallots, peeled
350g (12oz) chicken meat, minced
2 egg whites, lightly whisked
2 egg shells, crushed
salt and ground black pepper
dash of sherry or Madeira (optional)

NOTE

● *Suitable for freezing.*

VARIATIONS

● *Beef Consommé: Use well-flavoured, fat-free beef stock and lean minced steak in place of chicken.*
● *Consommé with Herbs: Flavour the consommé with 30–45 ml (2–3 tbsp) chopped fresh tarragon, parsley, chives or mint.*
● *Consommé Julienne: Cut small quantities of vegetables such as carrot, turnip and celery into thin strips and boil separately; rinse well and add to the soup before serving.*
● *Jellied Consommé: Cold consommé should be lightly jellied. Leave the consommé to cool, then chill until set. Chop roughly and serve in individual dishes.*

1 Heat the stock gently in a large pan. Meanwhile thinly slice the leeks, celery and carrots. Dice the shallots.

2 Mix the chicken and vegetables together in a large saucepan, then mix in the egg whites and shells.

3 Gradually pour in the stock, whisking all the time, then bring to the boil, still whisking. Immediately boiling point is reached, stop whisking, lower the heat and simmer very gently for 1 hour.

4 Carefully make a hole in the scum on the surface of the liquid and ladle the liquid out into a sieve lined with muslin over a large bowl. Reheat the consommé, check the seasoning and flavour with a little sherry or Madeira, if using.

RED PEPPER AND SWEET POTATO SOUP

The Mediterranean roasted red pepper blends perfectly with the Caribbean sweet potato in this flavourful soup. The peppers are roasted to enhance the flavour and freshly shredded basil leaves add extra taste. Serve the soup with plenty of fresh crusty bread as a warming starter.

● SERVES 4 ● PREPARATION TIME: 10–15 MINUTES ● COOKING TIME: 30 MINUTES ● 150 CALS PER SERVING ● 3.8G FAT, OF WHICH 0.7G SATURATED FAT

2 large red peppers, total weight about 450g (1lb)
225g (8oz) sweet potato
squeeze of lemon juice
1 onion
2 garlic cloves
225g (8oz) tomatoes, or 200g (7oz) can
plum tomatoes
15ml (1 tbsp) extra virgin olive oil
900ml (1½ pints) vegetable stock
coarse sea salt and ground black pepper
To serve:
60ml (4 tbsp) low-fat natural yogurt
30ml (2 tbsp) finely shredded fresh basil
fresh basil leaves, to garnish

1 Preheat the grill to hot, or preheat the oven to 190°C (375°F) Mark 5. Grill or roast the peppers on a rack, turning frequently, for 15–20 minutes until the skin is blistered and blackened. Cover with a damp cloth and leave to cool slightly (the steam helps to lift the skin).

2 Peel the sweet potato, cut into small pieces and immediately immerse in a bowl of cold water with a little lemon juice added to prevent discoloration. Add the sweet potato to a saucepan of boiling water and simmer for 10–15 minutes until tender. Drain.

3 Meanwhile, peel the roasted peppers, reserving some strips of blackened skin for garnish. Holding them over a bowl to catch the juices, halve the peppers, remove the core and seeds, then cut the pepper into slices. Peel and finely chop the onion and garlic.

4 Immerse the fresh tomatoes in a bowl of boiling water for 10–15 seconds, allow to cool slightly, then peel away the skins.

5 Heat the oil in a large saucepan and fry the onion and garlic until softened. Add the peppers and reserved juices, tomatoes, sweet potatoes and two-thirds of the stock. Season with salt and pepper to taste and cook for 5–10 minutes.

6 Transfer the soup to a blender or food processor and process until smooth. Return to the cleaned saucepan and reheat, adding more vegetable stock as required to achieve the desired consistency. Adjust the seasoning as necessary and add a squeeze of lemon juice, to taste.

7 To serve, divide the soup between warmed serving bowls and add a swirl of yogurt to each portion. Sprinkle with the shredded basil, and tiny pieces of blackened pepper skin if desired. Add a generous grind of pepper and garnish with basil leaves.

NOTES

● *You can use ordinary potato in place of sweet potato, if you prefer, though the soup will lose its sweetness.*
● *Suitable for freezing.*

CURRIED CARROT AND SPLIT PEA SOUP

There is undoubtedly something particularly warming about a curried lentil or split pea soup – the perfect remedy for a cold winter's night. Here split yellow peas are used to make a really thick and tasty soup.

● SERVES 4 ● PREPARATION TIME: 35 MINUTES, PLUS SOAKING ● COOKING TIME: 1–1¼ HOURS ● 125 CALS PER SERVING ● 3.5G FAT, OF WHICH 0.4G SATURATED FAT

50g (2oz) split yellow peas, soaked overnight in double their volume of cold water
1 small onion
1 garlic clove
225g (8oz) carrots
1 potato
1 red chilli
15ml (1 tbsp) sunflower oil
5ml (1 tsp) grated fresh root ginger
7.5ml (1½ tsp) hot curry paste
salt and ground black pepper
chopped fresh coriander, to serve

1 Drain the split peas, rinse well and place in a large saucepan with 1.5 litres (2½ pints) cold water. Bring to the boil and boil rapidly for 10 minutes. Reduce the heat, cover and simmer gently for 30 minutes.

2 Peel and chop the onion, garlic, carrots and potato. Halve, deseed and chop the chilli. Heat the oil in a saucepan, add the onion, garlic, ginger and chilli and fry, stirring frequently, for 10 minutes until evenly browned. Stir in the curry paste, carrots and potato and fry for a further 5 minutes.

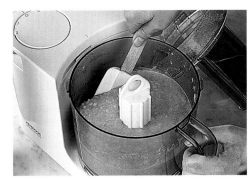

VARIATION

● *Replace the split peas with red lentils, which do not require pre-soaking. Add 125g (4oz) red lentils to the fried curried vegetables, together with 1.2 litres (2 pints) vegetable stock. Cook for 30 minutes until the vegetables and lentils are tender and cooked through.*

3 Add the curried vegetable mixture to the split peas. Return to the boil, cover and simmer for a further 35 minutes until the vegetables and peas are tender. Transfer to a blender or food processor and work until fairly smooth. Return to the saucepan, season to taste and heat through. Sprinkle with chopped coriander, to serve.

MUSHROOM AND ARTICHOKE SOUP WITH WALNUTS

Jerusalem artichokes can easily be confused with just another funny looking potato, but don't be fooled. These knobbly root vegetables have a distinctive flavour of their own. The intensity of the mushroom stock combines well with the artichokes, and the walnuts add texture to the finished soup.

● SERVES 4 ● PREPARATION TIME: 20 MINUTES, PLUS SOAKING ● COOKING TIME: 1½ HOURS ● 242 CALS PER SERVING ●15G FAT, OF WHICH 1.5G SATURATED FAT

15g (½oz) dried ceps
150ml (¼ pint) boiling water
1 small onion, peeled
450g (1lb) chestnut mushrooms
15ml (1 tbsp) olive oil
15ml (1 tbsp) chopped fresh thyme
90ml (6 tbsp) dry sherry
1.2 litres (2 pints) vegetable stock
450g (1lb) Jerusalem artichokes
1 garlic clove
30ml (2 tbsp) walnut oil
salt and ground black pepper
To serve:
25g (1oz) walnuts, chopped and toasted
extra walnut oil
fresh thyme sprigs, to garnish

1 Put the dried ceps into a bowl, pour over the boiling water and let soak for 30 minutes. Drain, reserving the liquid, and set the ceps aside.

2 Chop the onion and mushrooms. Heat the oil in a saucepan, fry the onion and thyme gently for 10 minutes until soft. Raise the heat, add the chestnut mushrooms and ceps and stir-fry for 2 minutes. Add the sherry and boil rapidly until well reduced.

3 Add the vegetable stock and reserved cep stock and bring to the boil. Cover and simmer gently for 20 minutes until the stock is rich tasting and the mushrooms have lost all their flavour.

4 Meanwhile, scrub the artichokes and cut away the knobbly bits. Peel, then dice the flesh. Peel and chop the garlic. Heat the walnut oil in a large saucepan, add the artichokes and garlic and fry for 10 minutes, stirring, until evenly browned.

5 Strain the mushroom liquid through a fine sieve and add to the artichokes. Bring to the boil, cover and simmer for 35–40 minutes until the artichokes are cooked. Purée in a blender or food processor until smooth.

6 Return the soup to the saucepan and heat gently for 5 minutes. Season with salt and pepper to taste and spoon into warmed soup bowls. Scatter the toasted nuts over the soup and drizzle with walnut oil. Serve at once, garnished with thyme.

NOTES

● It is essential that the mushrooms impart all their flavour to the stock. Before straining the stock, check that they are quite tasteless.
● Suitable for freezing.

BUTTERNUT SQUASH SOUP WITH PARMESAN CROSTINI

Butternut is the club-shaped squash with a pale yellow skin and bright orange flesh. Its natural sweet buttery flavour needs little to enhance it and it should be cooked simply. The creamy flesh is ideal for puréeing, and both the sharpness of the Parmesan and the crisp bite of the crostini set it off beautifully – a really special soup to serve when entertaining.

● SERVES 4 ● PREPARATION TIME: 40 MINUTES ● COOKING TIME: 50 MINUTES ● 185 CALS PER SERVING ● 8.3G FAT, OF WHICH 2.2G SATURATED FAT

1 large leek, trimmed
1 celery stick
1 garlic clove, peeled
1 small red chilli
350g (12oz) peeled and deseeded butternut squash
(see Note)
30ml (2 tbsp) olive oil
15ml (1 tbsp) chopped fresh sage
1 litre (1¾ pints) vegetable stock
pinch of cayenne pepper
salt and ground black pepper
Parmesan Crostini:
4 thin slices day-old ciabatta or French bread
2 garlic cloves, peeled
extra virgin olive oil, for drizzling
25g (1oz) Parmesan

1 Preheat the oven to 200°C (400°F) Mark 6. Slice the leek and celery; chop the garlic. Halve, deseed and chop the red chilli (wearing rubber gloves to avoid skin irritation). Cut the squash into cubes.

2 Heat the oil in a saucepan, add the leek, celery and garlic and fry gently for 10 minutes. Add the sage, chilli and squash, and stir-fry for 5 minutes until the squash just begins to colour.

3 Pour in the stock, add the cayenne pepper and bring to the boil. Cover and simmer for 35 minutes, then transfer to a food processor and blend until smooth. Return to the pan, adjust the seasoning and heat through.

4 Meanwhile, make the crostini. Place the bread on a baking sheet and bake in the oven for 10 minutes. Rub each side with garlic, drizzle with a little oil and return to the oven for a further 10 minutes or until the bread is crisp and golden.

5 Spoon the soup into warmed bowls, and top with the crostini. Grate over the Parmesan and drizzle over a little more olive oil. Serve at once.

VARIATION

● *For a curried version, add 30ml (2 tbsp) hot curry paste to the onion, garlic and sage, omitting the chilli. Serve the soup topped with a spoonful of 0% fat Greek yogurt and scattered with chopped fresh coriander.*

NOTE

● *To give this prepared weight of squash you will need about 450g (1lb) squash.*

MINESTRONE

This is a typically Italian soup; delicious, filling and packed with interesting textures. Most children love this soup, too.

● SERVES 6–8 ● PREPARATION TIME: 30 MINUTES, PLUS SOAKING ● COOKING TIME: 2 HOURS 45 MINUTES ● 321–241 CALS PER SERVING ● 9–7G FAT, OF WHICH 1.3–1G SATURATED FAT

175g (6oz) dried cannellini beans, soaked overnight in cold water
2 onions, peeled
2 carrots, peeled
2 celery sticks
350g (12oz) floury potatoes (such as King Edward or Maris Piper), peeled
175g (6oz) French beans
225g (8oz) dark green cabbage
30ml (2 tbsp) olive oil
3 garlic cloves, crushed
400g (14oz) can chopped tomatoes
2.3 litres (4 pints) vegetable stock or brown onion stock
125g (4oz) small pasta shapes
125g (4oz) shelled fresh or frozen peas
75ml (5 tbsp) chopped fresh parsley
60ml (4 tbsp) pesto
salt and ground black pepper

To serve:
pesto
freshly grated Pecorino or Parmesan

2 Meanwhile prepare the vegetables. Dice the onions, carrots, celery and potatoes. Slice the French beans and roughly chop the cabbage, discarding the tough stalks.

4 Stir in the beans, tomatoes, stock, potatoes, pasta and fresh peas, if using. Bring to the boil, then reduce the heat, half cover and simmer for 1 hour.

5 Add the frozen peas, if using, French beans, cabbage, parsley and pesto. Season with salt and pepper and simmer for 30 minutes or until the vegetables are tender. Serve immediately, as a main course, with the pesto and cheese in separate bowls for guests to stir into their soup.

1 Drain the beans, put them in a very large saucepan and cover with fresh water. Bring to the boil and boil rapidly for 10 minutes, then cover and simmer for 50 minutes; drain.

3 Heat the oil in a large saucepan, add the onions and garlic and fry for 5–10 minutes or until golden brown. Add the carrots and celery and cook for 2 minutes.

NOTE

● Suitable for freezing.

SPICED BEEF AND NOODLE SOUP

This hearty soup takes its influence from fragrant Asian flavours. If you can't find lemongrass, add grated lemon rind and juice to taste.

● SERVES 4 ● PREPARATION TIME: 10 MINUTES PLUS SOAKING TIME FOR MUSHROOMS ● COOKING TIME: 10 MINUTES ● 190 CALS PER SERVING ● 9.8G FAT, OF WHICH 2G SATURATED FAT

30ml (2 tbsp) oil
225g (8oz) fillet steak, cut into thin strips
1.1 litres (2¼ pints) beef stock
30ml (2 tbsp) Thai fish sauce (nam pla)
15g (½oz) dried porcini or shiitake mushrooms
1 large red chilli, deseeded and finely chopped
1 lemongrass stem, trimmed and thinly sliced
2.5cm (1 inch) piece fresh root ginger, peeled and finely chopped
6 spring onions, halved lengthways and cut into 2.5cm (1 inch) lengths
1 garlic clove, crushed
1.25ml (¼ tsp) caster sugar
50g (2oz) medium egg noodles
125g (4oz) spinach leaves, roughly chopped
60ml (4 tbsp) chopped fresh coriander
ground black pepper

1 First soak the mushrooms. Break them into small pieces and place them in a small bowl. Pour over 150ml (¼ pint) boiling water and leave to soak for 15–20 minutes.

2 Heat the oil in a large saucepan, brown the meat in two batches and set aside. Pour the stock into the pan with the fish sauce, mushrooms and their soaking liquor, chilli, lemongrass, ginger, spring onions, garlic and sugar. Bring to the boil.

3 Break the noodles up slightly and add to the pan, then stir gently until they begin to separate. Simmer gently for 4–5 minutes or until the noodles are just tender, stirring occasionally.

4 Stir in the spinach, coriander and reserved steak. Adjust the seasoning, adding a little more fish sauce if necessary. Serve immediately in warmed bowls.

VEGETABLE, NOODLE AND TOFU BROTH

The flavours of this soup are light, refreshing and quite delicate. Its success depends on the quality of the stock, which is used to poach a selection of vegetables and the tofu. The following recipe gives an authentic Thai vegetable stock.

● SERVES 4 ● PREPARATION TIME: 20 MINUTES
● COOKING TIME: 1¼ HOURS, INCLUDING STOCK
● 135 CALS PER SERVING ● 3G FAT, OF WHICH
0.5G SATURATED FAT

Thai Vegetable Stock:

1 onion, peeled and roughly chopped
2 carrots, roughly chopped
2 celery sticks, roughly chopped
2 garlic cloves, peeled and roughly chopped
2 lemongrass stems, roughly chopped
15g (½ oz) fresh root ginger, peeled and roughly chopped
4 kaffir lime leaves
4 coriander roots, scrubbed
5ml (1 tsp) white peppercorns
5ml (1 tsp) salt

Broth:

25g (1oz) dried black or shiitake mushrooms
120ml (4fl oz) boiling water
1 large carrot
50g (2oz) cauliflower florets
50g (2oz) baby sweetcorn
125g (4oz) plain tofu
30ml (2 tbsp) dark soy sauce
15ml (1 tbsp) lemon or lime juice
50g (2oz) dried thread egg noodles

To serve:

fresh mint leaves
chilli oil

1 Start by making the stock. Place 1.2 litres (2 pints) water in a large saucepan. Add all the ingredients. Bring to the boil, cover and simmer gently for 1 hour.

2 For the broth, first prepare the dried mushrooms. (Black dried mushrooms are the commonest variety used in Thai cooking.) Put the mushrooms in a bowl, pour over the boiling water and leave to soak for about 30 minutes. Strain and reserve the liquid; chop the mushrooms.

3 Prepare the remaining vegetables. Cut the carrot into matchsticks; cut the cauliflower into small florets; halve the sweetcorn lengthways; set aside.

4 Drain the tofu from its liquid and cut into 2.5cm (1 inch) cubes. (Note that you will not need a full packet of tofu so keep the remainder in a bowl of water in the refrigerator and eat within four days.)

5 Strain the stock into a clean pan and stir in the soy sauce, lemon or lime juice and reserved mushroom liquid. Return to the boil and stir in the vegetables, tofu and soaked mushrooms. Simmer for 5 minutes.

6 Plunge in the noodles and simmer for a further 5–6 minutes until the noodles and vegetables are tender. Ladle the soup into large warmed soup bowls. Serve at once, scattered with mint leaves and drizzled with a little chilli oil.

VARIATION

● *If you haven't time to prepare the stock, make up the required amount of liquid using a vegetable stock cube and add 15ml (1 tbsp) each of lime and lemon juice and a pinch of sugar. Alternatively, use a good quality chicken stock instead.*

PRAWN BROTH WITH ORIENTAL MUSHROOMS

Oyster and brown cap mushrooms are used in this broth for their distinct flavours. If you want to spice up the broth, add some chopped fresh ginger, a little Tabasco and chopped fresh coriander.

● SERVES 6 ● PREPARATION TIME: 40 MINUTES
● COOKING TIME: 2 HOURS 25 MINUTES ● 90 CALS
PER SERVING ● 1 G FAT, OF WHICH 0.4 G SATURATED FAT

Broth:
2 large onions, peeled and cut in half
1.1 kg (2½ lb) whole, large, raw prawns, with shells, or
1.4 kg (3 lb) langoustines, with shells
2 garlic cloves, crushed
1 thyme sprig
1 bay leaf
finely pared rind of 1 lemon and 1 orange
1 ripe tomato, seeds removed and roughly chopped

Stock:
450g (1lb) fish bones, such as sole, plaice or cod
1 onion, quartered
5ml (1 tsp) peppercorns
1 glass white wine (optional)

To serve:
100g (3½oz) brown cap mushrooms, quartered
100g (3½oz) oyster mushrooms, sliced
4 tomatoes, deseeded and diced
60ml (4 tbsp) chopped fresh chives
salt and ground black pepper
lemon juice, to taste

NOTE

● *Suitable for freezing: stock only.*

1 To make the broth, place the onions under a hot grill and cook for 10 minutes on each side or until well browned all over.

2 Remove the heads and shells from the prawns (reserve the shells); cover and chill in the refrigerator.

3 Place the prawn shells in a saucepan with the onions, the remaining ingredients and 1.5 litres (2½ pints) water. Bring slowly to the boil, then simmer for 2 hours. Strain, reserving the liquid. You should have 1 litre (1¾ pints) broth.

4 Meanwhile make the stock. Place the fish bones in a saucepan with the remaining ingredients. Add 1 litre (1¾ pints) water. Bring to the boil, reduce the heat then simmer gently for 20 minutes. Strain, reserving the liquid. You should have 900ml (1½ pints) stock.

5 To serve, place the broth in a saucepan with 600ml (1 pint) stock, bring to the boil and add the brown cap and oyster mushrooms, plus the reserved prawns. Simmer gently until the prawns turn pink. Add the tomatoes and chives. Check the seasoning, add lemon juice to taste and serve.

MUSHROOM AND OMELETTE SOUP

Thais frequently use eggs in their cooking and here an omelette is cut into pieces and stirred into a mushroom broth just before serving. A selection of fresh and dried mushrooms are required, available from larger supermarkets and Oriental stores. If you can't find fresh oyster mushrooms, use button or field mushrooms instead.

● SERVES 4 ● PREPARATION TIME: 25 MINUTES
● COOKING TIME: 1 HOUR, PLUS STOCK ● 145 CALS
PER SERVING ● 11g FAT, OF WHICH 2G SATURATED FAT

1.2 litres (2 pints) Thai Vegetable Stock (see page 68,
Vegetable, Noodle and Tofu Broth)
15g (½ oz) each dried black and dried shiitake
mushrooms, or 25g (1oz) dried shiitake mushrooms
300ml (½ pint) boiling water
1 bunch spring onions, trimmed
1–2 garlic cloves, peeled
2 small green chillies, seeded
grated rind and juice of 1 lime
15ml (1 tbsp) sunflower oil
10ml (2 tsp) sesame oil
125g (4oz) oyster mushrooms
25g (1oz) canned bamboo shoots, drained
15ml (1 tbsp) light soy sauce
Omelette:
15ml (1 tbsp) sunflower oil
2 eggs
salt and ground black pepper

1 Start by making the Thai vegetable stock. When cooked, drain the stock into a clean saucepan and set aside.

2 Place the dried mushrooms in a bowl, pour over the boiling water and leave to soak for 30 minutes. Strain and reserve the liquid; finely slice the shiitake mushrooms and chop the black mushrooms.

3 Slice the spring onions and set aside. Roughly chop the garlic and chillies, then pound with the lime rind, using a pestle and mortar or a spice grinder, until well crushed.

4 Heat both the oils in a wok or frying pan and fry the garlic and chilli paste with the spring onions for 5 minutes until softened. Stir into the strained stock with the lime juice, soaked mushrooms and reserved liquid. Cover and simmer for 20 minutes.

5 Meanwhile, make the omelette. Heat the oil in a small frying pan. Beat the eggs with salt and pepper, then pour the mixture into the hot oil. Cook over a low heat, stirring occasionally, until the omelette is just set. Remove from the pan with a spatula and cut into thick strips or squares.

6 Add the oyster mushrooms, bamboo shoots and soy sauce to the soup and simmer for 4–5 minutes until all the mushrooms are tender. Stir in the omelette pieces and serve at once.

VARIATION

● *Instead of making an omelette, simply beat 2 eggs together and whisk into the just simmering soup at the end of cooking. Immediately remove from the heat and serve.*

HOT AND SOUR PRAWN SOUP

An exquisite soup generously laden with prawns, with the wonderful contrast of hot and sour flavours, typical of Asian-style soups. A hint of fire from the chilli is offset by the sour flavours of the lemongrass and white wine vinegar.

- SERVES 4 ● PREPARATION TIME: 10 MINUTES
- COOKING TIME: 20 MINUTES ● 134 CALS PER SERVING ● 4.7G FAT, OF WHICH 0.8G SATURATED FAT

1 onion, peeled
1 small green chilli
2.5cm (1 inch) piece fresh root ginger
15ml (1 tbsp) oil
50g (2oz) small oyster mushrooms
1.2 litres (2 pints) chicken stock
1 lemongrass stem
15ml (1 tbsp) white wine vinegar
1 small bunch watercress
350g (12oz) large cooked, peeled prawns
salt and ground black pepper

1 Chop the onion. Halve, deseed and finely chop the chilli (wearing rubber gloves to avoid skin irritation). Peel and finely chop the ginger.

VARIATION

- *Replace the watercress with 60ml (4 tbsp) chopped fresh coriander.*

2 Heat the oil in a large saucepan, add the onion, chilli and ginger and fry, stirring, for 4–5 minutes. Add the mushrooms and sauté for 1–2 minutes.

3 Stir in the stock, lemongrass and vinegar. Bring to the boil, cover and simmer for 10–12 minutes. Meanwhile roughly chop the watercress, discarding the stalks. Add to the soup with the prawns and simmer for 2 minutes. Remove the lemongrass and adjust the seasoning before serving.

HOT AND SOUR SOUP WITH CRAB-STUFFED WONTONS

Although wontons are often associated with Chinese soups they are also found in traditional Thai dishes. Wonton wrappers can be bought in Oriental stores and supermarkets, but you can try making them yourself (see below); they are simple and satisfying to prepare.

● SERVES 4 ● PREPARATION TIME: 30 MINUTES
● COOKING TIME: 15 MINUTES, PLUS STOCK
● 115 CALS PER SERVING ● 3.7G FAT, OF WHICH
0.7G SATURATED FAT

1.2 litres (2 pints) Thai Vegetable Stock (see page 69)
4 small red chillies, bruised
15ml (1 tbsp) Thai fish sauce (nam pla)
30ml (2 tbsp) rice vinegar
15ml (1 tbsp) chilli sauce (optional)

Crab wontons:
125g (4oz) white crab meat, fresh or frozen and thawed
50g (2oz) cooked, peeled prawns
2 spring onions, trimmed
1 garlic clove, crushed
5ml (1 tsp) chopped preserved stem ginger, plus
5ml (1 tsp) syrup from the jar
1.25ml (¼ tsp) chilli powder
15ml (1 tbsp) light soy sauce
30ml (2 tbsp) chopped fresh coriander
16 wonton wrappers
1 small egg, beaten

To garnish:
chilli oil (optional)
fresh coriander leaves

1 To prepare the wonton filling, drain the crab meat thoroughly (if frozen) and place in a bowl. Roughly chop the prawns and spring onions and add to the crab meat with the garlic, stem ginger, ginger syrup, chilli powder, soy sauce and coriander. Stir well until evenly combined.

2 Lightly brush a wonton wrapper with a little beaten egg and place a heaped teaspoon of crab mixture in the centre. Draw up the edges of the wrapper and press together at the top to seal. Repeat to make 16 wontons. Cover and set aside.

3 Strain the vegetable stock into a clean pan and add the chillies, fish sauce, rice vinegar and chilli sauce, if using. Return to the boil and simmer gently for 10 minutes.

4 Bring the soup to a rolling boil, then add the wontons. Return to the boil, then lower the heat and simmer gently for 3–4 minutes until the wontons are softened and heated through.

5 Ladle into warmed soup bowls and serve at once, drizzled with a little chilli oil if wished, and garnished with coriander leaves.

HOMEMADE WONTON WRAPPERS

Sift 150g (5oz) plain flour with 2.5ml (¼ tsp) salt into a bowl. Gradually work in 1 egg and enough cold water to form a stiff dough. Knead for 5 minutes. Wrap and chill for 30 minutes. Roll out the dough in batches as thinly as possible, using a pasta machine if possible. Cut into 7.5cm (3 inch) squares. Use immediately or freeze for future use.

MUSHROOM TOM YAM

With only 80 calories per serving, this spicy Thai soup would also make a wonderfully light lunch dish served with a steaming bowl of aromatic rice.

● SERVES 4 ● PREPARATION TIME: 35 MINUTES, PLUS 20 MINUTES SOAKING ● COOKING TIME: 35–40 MINUTES ● 80 CALS PER SERVING ● 6G FAT, OF WHICH 0.7G SATURATED FAT

25g (1oz) dried shiitake mushrooms
150ml (¼ pint) boiling water
30ml (2 tbsp) groundnut oil
2 shallots, peeled and finely chopped
2 small red chillies, deseeded and chopped
2 garlic cloves, peeled and crushed
2 ripe tomatoes, roughly chopped
30ml (2 tbsp) lemon juice
5ml (1 tsp) sugar
1.2 litres (2 pints) vegetable stock
1 lemongrass stem, finely sliced
4 kaffir lime leaves, finely shredded, or grated rind of 1 lime
225g (8oz) fresh oyster or button mushrooms, sliced (see Note)
15ml (1 tbsp) light soy sauce
30ml (2 tbsp) chopped fresh coriander

NOTE

● Always choose firm-textured mushrooms with stalks that look fresh. Wipe the mushrooms with a clean damp cloth before slicing.

1 Put the dried mushrooms in a bowl, pour over the boiling water and leave to soak for 20 minutes. Strain and reserve the liquor; chop and reserve the mushrooms.

2 Heat the groundnut oil in a saucepan, add the shallots, chillies and garlic and fry gently for 5 minutes. Add the tomatoes to the pan with the lemon juice and sugar. Fry for a further 5 minutes until the tomatoes are soft and pulpy.

3 Pour in the vegetable stock and reserved mushroom liquor, then add the lemon grass and kaffir lime leaves or grated lime rind. Bring to the boil, then cover and simmer for 20 minutes.

4 Add the shiitake and fresh oyster or button mushrooms and the soy sauce. Return to the boil and simmer gently for a further 5–10 minutes until tender. Remove from the heat, Stir in the coriander and serve.

TURKEY, HAM AND SPINACH BROTH WITH SPLIT PEAS

A thoroughly nutritious and satisfying starter which can also be served as a filling main course for lunch or supper.

● SERVES 6; MAKES ABOUT 2 LITRES (3½ PINTS)
● PREPARATION TIME: 20 MINUTES, PLUS SOAKING
● COOKING TIME: 1 HOUR 15 MINUTES ● 300 CALS
PER SERVING ● 14G FAT, OF WHICH 6.5G SATURATED
FAT

125g (4oz) green or yellow split peas, soaked
overnight in double their volume of cold water
25g (1oz) butter
225g (8oz) onion, chopped
15ml (1 tbsp) ground coriander
40g (1½oz) pearl barley
2 litres (3½ pints) ham or turkey stock
1 bay leaf
1 stick celery
fresh thyme sprig
225g (8oz) potatoes, peeled and cut into chunks
400g (14oz) carrots, peeled and cut into chunks
salt and ground black pepper
150g (5oz) each cooked turkey and ham, cut
into chunks
150g (5oz) baby spinach leaves, washed and dried
To garnish:
fresh coriander sprigs
ground black pepper
50g (2oz) Parmesan, finely grated (optional)

1 Drain the split peas and place in a saucepan with cold water to cover. Bring to the boil and simmer for 10 minutes. Drain the peas and discard the liquid.

NOTE

● Suitable for freezing: complete the recipe, omitting the spinach, then cool, pack and freeze. When ready to use, thaw overnight at cool room temperature. Reheat, then add the spinach. Simmer for 2–3 minutes. Garnish and serve.

2 Meanwhile, melt the butter in a saucepan, add the onion and cook for 5 minutes or until soft. Add the ground coriander and cook for 30 seconds.

3 Add the split peas, pearl barley and stock. Tie the bay leaf, celery and thyme sprig together and add to the pan. Bring to the boil and simmer for 40 minutes or until the peas and barley are tender. Add the potatoes and cook for 5 minutes; add the carrots and cook for 5–10 minutes. Season well.

4 Add the turkey, ham and spinach and bring back to the boil. Simmer for 2–3 minutes. Garnish with coriander and pepper and serve with grated Parmesan, if using.

STARTERS

The main purpose of a starter is to whet the appetite and tantalise the tastebuds for the courses to come. A well-planned meal is one of contrasting flavours and textures, so a balance has to be struck between serving light and heavy dishes, hot and cold courses and to find flavours that marry well together. Or perhaps you might want to put together a complete authentic meal, in which case the starter should definitely complement the courses that are to follow. Think about the colour of the food as well, so that you avoid serving dishes that look the same. Similarly, it is generally best not to serve a fish starter if the main course is to be fish, or a meat starter if the main dish is meat.

This chapter includes a variety of starters and finger foods, most of which can be made well in advance. Marinated salmon melts in the mouth while Spanish tapas are a useful starter that can also be served with drinks before a meal. It is best to keep starter portions quite small, so that you don't spoil your guests' appetites. On the other hand, if you increase the size of the portions, many of these recipes are suitable for a light lunch.

FATTOUSH

This glorious flavourful Arabic salad is reminiscent of a rather solid Gazpacho. It's good eaten on its own as a starter or light lunch. Alternatively, it can be topped with a fried egg and served as a supper dish.

● SERVES 4 ● PREPARATION TIME: 15 MINUTES
● COOKING TIME: 2–3 MINUTES ● 150 CALS PER SERVING ● 7G FAT, OF WHICH 1.3G SATURATED FAT

4 tomatoes
½ cucumber
4 spring onions
1 small green pepper
1 garlic clove, crushed
juice of ½ lemon
30ml (2 tbsp) finely chopped fresh parsley
45ml (3 tbsp) olive oil
salt and ground black pepper
1 pitta bread
To garnish:
roughly torn fresh mint leaves
black olives

NOTE

● You can make this salad by hand if you prefer – chopping all the vegetables finely – but it will take a little longer to prepare.

1 Preheat the grill. Immerse the tomatoes in boiling water for 1 minute, drain, cool slightly, then peel away the skins. Cut them up roughly and place in a food processor or blender. Cut the cucumber roughly and place in the food processor, too.

2 Trim and roughly chop the spring onions. Halve, core and deseed the green pepper, then roughly chop the flesh. Add the spring onions and green pepper to the food processor with the garlic and lemon juice. Process to a chunky purée.

3 Turn the mixture into a bowl and stir in the parsley, olive oil, salt and pepper so they are thoroughly mixed.

4 Toast the pitta bread briefly on both sides. Break into small pieces and scatter over the salad.

5 Transfer the salad to a serving dish. Tear the mint leaves over the salad and stud with black olives.

MINTED CITRUS SALAD

This is the perfect appetiser for a balmy summer evening supper or lunch. The flavours of the fragrant exotic fruits are enhanced by the addition of the fresh mint.

● SERVES 4 ● PREPARATION TIME: 20 MINUTES, PLUS CHILLING ● 60 CALS PER SERVING ● 3.0G FAT; NO SATURATED FAT

1 pomelo
1 ugli fruit
1 small melon
2 papayas
45ml (3 tbsp) chopped fresh mint
fresh mint sprigs, to garnish

1 Holding the pomelo over a bowl to catch the juices, peel and segment discarding all the pith, using a sharp serrated knife. Prepare the ugli fruit in the same way. Place both in the bowl with their juices.

2 Halve the melon and scoop out the seeds. Scoop out the flesh using a melon baller, or cut away the skin and slice or cube the flesh neatly. Add to the bowl.

3 Peel the papayas. Halve, then remove the seeds and slice or cube the flesh neatly and add to the bowl.

4 Carefully toss the salad with the mint; cover and chill for 1 hour to let the flavours blend. Place in individual bowls and serve garnished with mint sprigs.

ZESTY ORANGE AND ASPARAGUS SALAD

This colourful salad is a deliciously light starter that is also a perfect lunch dish for two in early summer when asparagus is in season. If you want to reduce the fat, omit the nuts and go easy on the dressing.

● SERVES 4 ● PREPARATION TIME: 10 MINUTES
● COOKING TIME: 6 MINUTES ● 153 CALS PER SEVING ● 10G FAT, OF WHICH 1.3G SATURATED FAT

450 g (1 lb) asparagus
2 oranges, peel and pith removed, and thinly sliced
25 g (1 oz) pecans or walnuts, toasted and roughly chopped
125 g (4 oz) frisée or other salad leaves
2 tbsp fresh tarragon sprigs
Dressing:
1 tsp Dijon mustard
1 tbsp sherry vinegar
2 tbsp olive oil
1 tbsp orange juice
salt and ground black pepper

1 To make the dressing, whisk together the mustard, vinegar, oil and orange juice, then season with salt and pepper. Set aside.

2 Using a vegetable peeler, remove the tough woody ends of the asparagus and pare a little of the tough outer skin from the base. If necessary, shave the length of each stalk from just below the tip. Trim the spears to roughly the same length.

3 Tie in a bundle and place upright in a tall pan (hold in place with scrunched-up foil, if necessary). Pour in enough boiling water to come about three-quarters of the way up the stems. The heads should be above the water level.

4 Cover with foil or a lid and boil gently for 6 minutes or until just tender.

5 Drain the asparagus and toss in the dressing while still hot. Toss together the oranges, pecans, salad leaves and tarragon and divide between four individual serving plates. Top with the asparagus and dressing and serve immediately.

ROASTED GARLIC AND TOMATO TAPAS

Bursting with the flavours of the Mediterranean, this Spanish appetiser, or tapas as they are called, makes for a more unusual and informal starter. Simply serve on a large plate with bread or crackers on the side and leave guests to help themselves.

● SERVES 6 ● PREPARATION TIME: 5 MINUTES
● COOKING TIME: 40 MINUTES ● 71 CALS PER SERVING ● 6.5G FAT, OF WHICH 1G SATURATED FAT

1 large garlic head
30ml (2 tbsp) olive oil
250g (9oz) cherry tomatoes
salt and ground black pepper
150g (5oz) Kalamata olives
30ml (2 tbsp) caper berries
bread or crackers, to serve

1 Place the garlic head in a small saucepan of cold water, bring to the boil and simmer for 5 minutes. Drain and place in a small ovenproof dish, drizzle with 15ml (1 tbsp) olive oil and cook at 200°C (400°F) Mark 6 for 40 minutes or until the garlic is very soft.

2 Meanwhile, in a separate ovenproof dish, toss the cherry tomatoes with 15ml (1 tbsp) olive oil, then season with salt and pepper and cook until the skins just begin to burst (about 10–15 minutes).

3 Arrange on a serving plate with the olives and caper berries. Squeeze the cooked, soft garlic cloves on to the bread or crackers and serve using cocktail sticks to spear the olives, cherry tomatoes and caper berries.

NOTE

● Choose ripe, flavourful cherry or vine-ripened tomatoes for best results.

LIME AND GIN MARINATED SALMON

Use Japanese sushi rice for this recipe – when cooked, its high starch content gives just the right amount of stickiness. Sushi rice and pickled ginger are available from supermarkets and Oriental stores.

● MAKES 15 ● PREPARATION TIME: 30 MINUTES, PLUS MARINATING AND 45 MINUTES COOLING ● COOKING TIME: 12 MINUTES ● 55 CALS PER CANAPÉ ● 1.3G FAT, OF WHICH 0.2G SATURATED FAT

30ml (2 tbsp) gin
grated rind of 1 lime
15ml (1 tbsp) sea salt flakes
15ml (1 tbsp) pink peppercorns, lightly crushed
150g (5oz) raw salmon fillet, skin and bones removed
150g (5oz) Japanese sushi rice, washed and drained
30ml (2 tbsp) rice vinegar
15ml (1 tbsp) caster sugar
15 slices pickled ginger
15ml (1 tbsp) wasabi paste (see Note)
snipped fresh chives, to garnish

NOTE

● *Wasabi is a condiment made from Japanese horseradish, available from leading supermarkets. You can buy it ready-made in a tube or as a powder that you mix with water to make a paste. Use sparingly as it is very hot!*

1 In a bowl, mix together the gin, lime rind and sea salt flakes and peppercorns. Place the salmon in the marinade, cover and chill overnight in the refrigerator.

2 Pour 350ml (12fl oz) water into a large saucepan and add the rice. Bring to the boil, then cover and simmer for 10–12 minutes. Remove from the heat and stir in the rice vinegar and the caster sugar. Leave until cool, then cover.

3 Using a sharp carving knife, cut the salmon into 30 very thin slices (there's no need to remove the seasonings).

4 Wet your hands and mould the rice into 15 walnut-sized balls and flatten to form discs. Top each disc with two slices of marinated salmon, a slice of pickled ginger and a little wasabi paste. Garnish with a sprinkling of snipped fresh chives.

SMOKED SALMON AND SCALLOP PARCELS

This is full of the punchy flavours of chilli, lime and coriander. You can omit the scallops, if you prefer, as the avocado mixture makes a delicious filling on its own. Keep any leftover dressing in the refrigerator and use as a salad dressing.

● SERVES 6 ● PREPARATION TIME: 40 MINUTES
● COOKING TIME: 6 MINUTES ● 235 CALS PER
SERVING ● 15G FAT, OF WHICH 2.2G SATURATED
FAT

Coriander dressing:

25g (1oz) fresh coriander sprigs
1 small garlic clove, crushed
50ml (3½ tbsp) grapeseed oil
15ml (1 tbsp) lime juice
salt and ground black pepper
pinch of caster sugar

Salmon parcels:

6 large scallops or 12 small queen scallops with
corals attached, 225g (8oz) total weight
1 large ripe avocado
1 garlic clove, crushed
4 small spring onions, finely chopped
1 green chilli, deseeded and finely chopped
15ml (1 tbsp) grapeseed oil
grated rind and juice of 1 lime
6 large slices of smoked salmon, about 300g (11oz)
total weight and 23cm (9 inches) in length
a squeeze of lime to taste

To garnish:

salad leaves, such as rocket
ground black pepper

1 To make the coriander dressing, place all the dressing ingredients in a blender and process until smooth. Set aside.

2 For the parcels, first remove any tough membrane (the little muscle at one side of the white meat) from the scallops. Season with salt and pepper.

3 Place in a steamer and cook for about 5 minutes or until the flesh is just white. Alternatively, put the scallops on a heatproof plate, cover with another plate and steam over a pan of simmering water for about 3 minutes on each side. Drain and set on kitchen paper to cool.

4 Meanwhile, place the avocado, garlic, spring onions, chilli, oil, grated lime rind and juice in a bowl. Crush the avocado with a fork, then mix together. Season well.

5 Lay the salmon slices on a work surface, place a large scallop or two small ones on each slice and spoon the avocado mixture on top. Roll the salmon around the filling.

6 To serve, place the salmon parcels on serving plates and squeeze a little lime juice over each. Drizzle with the coriander dressing and garnish with salad leaves and a sprinkling of ground black pepper.

MARINATED SALMON

Although you have to prepare the salmon two days in advance, the actual preparation is relatively simple and the result is a delicately flavoured fish that simply melts in the mouth.

● SERVES 8 ● PREPARATION TIME: 15 MINUTES, PLUS MARINATING ● 335 CALS PER SERVING ● 21G FAT, OF WHICH 4G SATURATED FAT

30ml (2 tbsp) sea salt
30ml (2 tbsp) caster sugar
10ml (2 tsp) crushed ground black peppercorns
60ml (4 tbsp) chopped fresh dill
120ml (8 tbsp) fresh lime juice
1.4–1.8kg (3–4lb) salmon or sea trout, filleted, with skin intact
To serve:
lime slices
brown bread

1 Mix all the ingredients except the salmon together in a small bowl. Spoon a quarter of the marinade mixture over the base of a non-metallic dish.

2 Lay one salmon fillet, skin-side down, in the dish. Spoon over half of the remaining marinade. Cover with the second fillet, skin-side up. Pour over the remaining marinade.

3 Cover with greaseproof paper, then clingfilm. Weigh down with a 900g (2lb) weight and leave in a cool place for two days, turning the fish occasionally.

4 To serve, drain the salmon well and trim off any hard edges. Cut the salmon into wafer-thin slices. Serve with lime slices and brown bread, if wished.

NOTE

● Suitable for freezing.

MUSSELS WITH GINGER, CHILLI AND CORIANDER

This is a deliciously spicy alternative to moules marinières, which uses the same method of cooking but includes ginger and chilli, and substitutes freshly chopped parsley with sprigs of coriander. Adding crème fraîche instead of butter (see Variation) gives the dish a creamier sauce.

● SERVES 4 ● PREPARATION TIME: 20 MINUTES
● COOKING TIME: 10 MINUTES ● 175 CALORIES PER SERVING ● 9.8G FAT, OF WHICH 5.7G SATURATED FAT

1kg (2¼lb) mussels
1 bunch spring onions
2 garlic cloves
25g (1oz) piece fresh root ginger
1 small red chilli
15g (½oz) fresh coriander
150ml (¼ pint) white wine
40g (½oz) butter
fresh coriander sprigs, to garnish

1 Scrub the mussels thoroughly under cold running water; pulling away the beards from the sides of the shells. Discard mussels with damaged shells, or any that refuse to close when tapped with the back of a knife. Put the mussels in a colander and set aside.

VARIATION

● Stir in 60–75ml (4–5 tbsp) low-fat crème fraîche instead of the butter.

2 Trim and shred the spring onions; peel and finely chop the garlic. Peel the ginger and chop finely. Halve the chilli lengthways and remove the seeds, then cut into fine slivers (wearing rubber gloves to avoid skin irritation). Strip the leaves from the coriander and set aside; reserve the stalks.

3 Put the spring onions, garlic, ginger, chilli and coriander stalks in a saucepan which is large enough to hold the mussels. Add the wine and 150ml (¼ pint) water. Bring to the boil and simmer for 2 minutes.

4 Add the mussels to the saucepan, cover with a tight-fitting lid and cook over a moderate heat, shaking the pan occasionally, until the shells open. This will take about 4–5 minutes. Turn the mussels into a colander set over a bowl. Discard the coriander stalks and any unopened mussels. Pour the liquid from the bowl back into the saucepan. Place over a low heat and whisk in the butter a piece at a time. Lastly add the coriander leaves.

5 Transfer the mussels to warmed, individual serving dishes and pour over the sauce. Serve immediately, garnished with coriander sprigs.

GRILLED KING PRAWNS WITH CHILLI SOY SAUCE

This is a dish that definitely requires finger bowls. It's a messy business, but what could be better than dipping succulent grilled prawns into a rich, tangy soy dip? If preferred, the prawns can be threaded onto bamboo skewers and grilled or barbecued.

● SERVES 4 ● PREPARATION TIME: 20 MINUTES, PLUS MARINATING ● COOKING TIME: 6–8 MINUTES ● 115 CALS PER SERVING ● 3G FAT, OF WHICH 0.6G SATURATED FAT

12 large raw tiger prawns
Marinade:
1 garlic clove, peeled
1 red chilli, deseeded
15ml (1 tbsp) sesame oil
30ml (2 tbsp) dark soy sauce
grated rind and juice of 2 limes
15–30ml (1–2 tbsp) soft brown sugar
Chilli soy sauce:
5ml (1 tsp) crushed chilli flakes
15ml (1 tbsp) lime juice
30ml (2 tbsp) dark soy sauce
15ml (1 tbsp) Thai fish sauce (nam pla)
30ml (2 tbsp) soft brown sugar
To serve:
chopped fresh coriander
lime wedges

1 Wash and dry the prawns and place in a shallow non-metallic dish. To make the marinade, finely chop the garlic and chilli and mix with the remaining ingredients. Pour the marinade over the prawns and stir well to coat. Cover the dish and leave in a cool place for at least 4 hours, preferably overnight.

2 For the chilli soy sauce, place all the ingredients in a small pan with 30ml (2 tbsp) cold water and bring to the boil, stirring until the sugar is dissolved. Remove the pan from the heat and leave to cool.

3 Just before serving, preheat the grill. Transfer the prawns to the grill pan and grill as close to the heat as possible for 6–8 minutes, turning and basting frequently with the marinade juices, until the prawns are pink and lightly charred.

4 Transfer the prawns to a warmed serving platter and scatter over some chopped fresh coriander. Serve with lime wedges and the chilli sauce for dipping. Don't forget the finger bowls!

VARIATION

● *Pre-soak 4 bamboo skewers in water for 30 minutes, drain and thread 3 marinated prawns onto each skewer. Grill as close to the heat as possible for 2–3 minutes on each side until charred and cooked through. Serve with the chilli soy sauce.*

MUSHROOM PÂTÉ WITH MADEIRA

This is a rich mushroom pâté flavoured with dried porcini and a variety of fresh mushrooms. You can use any combination, but try to include some flavourful wild mushrooms or cultivated dark field ones. Don't be tempted to use all button mushrooms as the end result will lack colour and flavour. Serve the pâté with hot olive bread, ciabatta, French bread or toast.

● SERVES 6 ● PREPARATION TIME: 15 MINUTES, PLUS SOAKING ● COOKING TIME: 20–25 MINUTES ● 100 CALS PER SERVING ● 6.4G FAT, OF WHICH 4G SATURATED FAT

15g (½oz) dried porcini mushrooms (see Note)
150ml (¼ pint) milk
1 small onion
1 garlic clove (optional)
25g (1oz) butter
coarse sea salt and ground black pepper
350g (12oz) selection fresh mushrooms
125g (4oz) ricotta cheese
15ml (1 tbsp) Madeira
dash of balsamic vinegar or squeeze of lemon juice
5ml (1 tsp) mushroom ketchup
freshly grated nutmeg, to taste
15–30ml (1–2 tbsp) chopped fresh parsley or coriander (optional)
chopped fresh parsley or coriander, to garnish

1 Rinse the porcini under cold running water to wash away the grit, then place in a bowl. Pour on the warm milk and leave to soak for 20 minutes. Drain the porcini well and chop finely.

2 Peel and finely chop the onion and garlic, if using. Melt the butter in a saucepan, add the onion and garlic and fry gently for 5–10 minutes until softened and transparent. Season with salt and pepper.

3 Meanwhile, wipe the fresh mushrooms with a damp cloth to clean them, then chop them finely.

4 Add the porcini and fresh mushrooms to the onion and garlic in the saucepan, increase the heat a little and cook, stirring occasionally, for about 15 minutes until the mushrooms are tender and reduced to a thick pulp. Leave to cool slightly.

5 Transfer the mushroom mixture to a food processor or bowl. Add the ricotta, Madeira, balsamic vinegar, mushroom ketchup and nutmeg and process very briefly or stir until evenly mixed; the pâté should retain a coarse texture. Stir in the chopped parsley or coriander, if using. Adjust the seasoning.

6 Turn into a serving dish or individual ramekins and garnish with chopped parsley or coriander.

NOTE

● *If dried porcini are unobtainable, use an extra 125g (4oz) flavourful fresh mushrooms, such as dark field mushrooms.*

LEEK TERRINE WITH WARM LEMON AND CAPER DRESSING

This light and delicious terrine becomes easier to slice if it's made up to two or three days in advance. Allow the terrine to come to room temperature before serving. It's delicious served with rye bread.

● SERVES 8 ● PREPARATION TIME: 30 MINUTES, PLUS CHILLING ● COOKING TIME: 40–45 MINUTES ● 170 CALS PER SERVING ● 13.5G FAT, OF WHICH 2G SATURATED FAT

3.2–3.4kg (7–7½lb) medium leeks
salt and ground black pepper
60ml (4 tbsp) capers
10ml (2 tsp) caraway seeds
45ml (3 tbsp) lemon juice
100ml (4fl oz) olive oil
To garnish:
grated lemon rind
finely sliced spring onion tops,

1 To clean the leeks, remove the root base, the tough green ends and outer leaves of the leeks, leaving the root ends intact.

2 Hold the leeks by the root ends and place in a bowl of cold water. Shake thoroughly to loosen any dirt.

3 Finally, rinse the leeks by holding them under cold running water to remove any remaining grit. You may need to cut very long leeks into about 23 cm (9 inch) lengths so that they will fit into the terrine.

4 Bring a large saucepan or large oval casserole of salted water to the boil. Add half the leeks and cook for about 20 minutes or until all the leeks are tender (if they are under-cooked they won't compress enough which can make the terrine difficult to slice). Drain and plunge into ice-cold water to prevent further cooking.

5 Repeat with the remaining leeks, then drain well and place on wire cooling racks for at least 10 minutes to remove excess water. Pat the leeks dry using a clean tea towel or kitchen paper.

6 To assemble the terrine, line a 900g (2lb) loaf tin with a double layer of clingfilm. Trim the leeks to fit and arrange a layer in the base so they fit tightly and the white ends are facing the same way; season. Cover with another layer of leeks so the green ends are on top of the white ones. Repeat until the leeks are slightly higher than the top of the tin. Cover with clingfilm and weigh down (see Note). Place in a roasting tin to catch any juices and chill overnight.

7 To make the dressing, place the lemon juice and seasoning in a small pan, then whisk in the oil, capers and caraway seeds.

8 Turn the terrrine out and carefully remove the clingfilm. Slice, using an electric carving knife or a sharp knife in a gentle sawing action. Arrange each slice on a plate, set aside and allow to return to room temperature. Warm the dressing slightly, spoon around the terrrine and garnish with the grated lemon rind and sliced onion tops.

NOTE

● Use a wooden board and weights, or a second tin filled with full cans of food, to weigh down the terrine. This will extract liquid from the leeks. Drain the terrine regularly.

FISH AND SHELLFISH

People are buying more fish and shellfish these days, both as an alternative to meat and because they are packed with protein, vitamins and minerals and are low in calories, too. Although some fish dishes are relatively high in fat, you can still eat them on a low-fat diet, provided that you are careful about what else you eat during the day.

There are two important things to remember with fish and shellfish: buy them as fresh as possible, and take care not to overcook them.

The recipes in this chapter show just how versatile fish and shellfish dishes can be. Included are recipes for a variety of seafood, from fresh swordfish steaks, succulent monkfish, delicate plaice and the stronger-flavoured halibut to wonderful dishes for scallops, prawns, mussels and squid. A number of the recipes are inspired by Thai cuisine, which works particularly well with fish and seafood, but there are also many other favourites – from all-time classics such as Dressed Crab to the more unusual like Grilled Scallops in Basil Leaves with colourful coats of grilled red and yellow peppers. For the barbecue try the Seafood Kebabs or Sweet and Sour Monkfish Kebabs or, for a more substantial meal, Roasted Monkfish with Mediterranean Vegetables. There is something here to suit everyone's taste in fish and shellfish, whether they prefer hot and spicy or light and simple dishes.

SPICED FRIED FISH

For this dish, look for firm fish fillets that won't break up during cooking. Monkfish is the best choice but it is quite expensive. Although a little more delicate, cod and haddock fillet – cut from the thickest part of the fish – will also work well.

● SERVES 4 ● PREPARATION TIME: 20 MINUTES
● COOKING TIME: 10 MINUTES ● 223 CALS PER SERVING ● 9.5G FAT, OF WHICH 1.3G SATURATED FAT

700g (1½ lb) firm white fish fillets
1–2 hot red chillies
1 bunch fresh coriander
1 garlic clove
10ml (2 tsp) plain flour
large pinch of salt
5ml (1 tsp) cumin seeds
10ml (2 tsp) coriander seeds
finely grated rind of 1 lime
oil for shallow-frying
To garnish:
lime wedges
banana leaves (optional)

1 Skin the fish fillets and cut into large chunks. Chop the chillies (wearing rubber gloves to avoid skin irritation), discarding the seeds if you prefer a mild flavour. Trim off the roots (if still attached) and most of the tough stems from the coriander, then finely chop the leaves. Peel the garlic and chop finely.

2 Put the chillies, coriander leaves and garlic in a large mixing bowl and stir in the flour and salt.

3 Heat a small heavy-based frying pan. Add the cumin and coriander seeds and dry-fry for 2 minutes, stirring all the time so they don't burn. Remove from the pan and allow to cool, then finely crush the spices using a pestle and mortar or a heavy bowl and the end of a rolling pin. Add to the flour mixture with the grated lime rind.

4 Add the prepared fish to the spiced flour mixture and toss carefully to ensure each piece is coated on all sides.

5 Heat the oil in a frying pan. Cook the fish, a few pieces at a time, until browned and crisp on the outside and cooked through, this should take about 5 minutes. Drain well and keep warm while cooking the remaining fish. Garnish with the lime wedges and banana leaves, if using.

GREMOLATA SWORDFISH WITH LEMON AND MINT BULGHAR WHEAT

Swordfish can be quite filling so the colourful lemon and mint bulghar wheat salad is all you need as an accompaniment, The salad also goes well other firm-fleshed white fish.

- ● SERVES 4 ● PREPARATION TIME: 15 MINUTES
- ● COOKING TIME: 10 MINUTES ● 279 CALS PER SERVING ● 8G FAT, OF WHICH 1.5G SATURATED FAT

4 swordfish steaks, each about 125 g (4 oz)
olive oil, for brushing
Bulghar wheat salad:
125 g (4 oz) bulghar (cracked) wheat
grated rind and juice of 1 large lemon
4 spring onions, trimmed and finely sliced
125 g (4 oz) cherry tomatoes, halved
2 tbsp chopped fresh mint
40 g (1½oz) Kalamata olives, stoned
salt and ground black pepper
Gremolata:
2 garlic cloves
grated rind of 1 lemon
2 tbsp finely chopped fresh parsley

1 To make the bulghar wheat salad, put the wheat in a sieve and rinse under cold running water. Transfer to a saucepan, cover with water and bring to the boil. Simmer for 3–4 minutes, then remove from the heat; stand for 15 minutes.

2 Drain the wheat well and pat dry with kitchen paper. Tip into a large bowl and add the remaining salad ingredients. Season to taste with salt and pepper, then toss together. Cover and chill.

3 To make the gremolata, blanch the garlic in boiling water for 3 minutes, then crush. Mix with the lemon rind and parsley, season to taste and set aside.

4 To cook the fish, lightly brush the swordfish steaks with olive oil, then grill for 2–3 minutes on each side, depending on thickness of the steaks.

5 To serve, divide the bulghar wheat salad between four individual serving plates, arrange the swordfish steaks on top and sprinkle with the gremolata. Serve immediately.

SEAFOOD WITH GARLIC, PARSLEY AND LEMON

This delicious seafood dish is wonderful in its simplicity. Very few ingredients are needed, just herbs and lemon juice, which are combined with the juices from the fish.

● SERVES 6 ● PREPARATION TIME: 15 MINUTES
● COOKING TIME: 10 MINUTES ● 195 CALS
PER SERVING ● 9.8G FAT, OF WHICH 1.6G
SATURATED FAT

60ml (4 tbsp) vegetable oil
3 garlic cloves, peeled and finely chopped
450g (1lb) prepared raw squid or octopus, sliced into rings (see Note)
12–18 large raw prawns, peeled and deveined
rind and juice of ½ lemon
30ml (2 tbsp) chopped fresh flatleaf parsley
salt and ground black pepper
fresh herbs, such as thyme and basil, to garnish

NOTE

● If you can't find squid or octopus, use cooked seafood in jars. Jars of Antipasto Seafood are available from some supermarkets and delicatessens. Drain and toss this in the olive oil, cooked garlic, lemon rind and juice and the parsley. Season and serve.

1 Heat the oil in a frying pan; cook the garlic until slightly golden. Fry the squid or octopus quickly in batches, keeping it warm. Fry the prawns until they are just pink, then set aside with the squid.

2 Place the lemon rind and juice in a pan, adding any juices from the squid and prawns. Bring to the boil, then bubble for 3–4 minutes or until syrupy. Return the squid and prawns to the pan with the parsley and toss together. Season and serve warm, garnished with fresh herbs.

GRILLED COD WITH SWEET CHILLI GLAZE

Grilling is one of the best methods of cooking fish and this is such an easy way to perk up a simple supper. Not only is it wonderfully quick, it also produces delicious, moist fish with a crisp skin. Most varieties of fish cook in much the same time, so you can use any type of fish with this sweet, spicy glaze. Thick cut cod fillet is hard to beat, with its large flakes and firm texture, but an oil-rich fish such as mackerel is fine, too.

● SERVES 4 ● PREPARATION TIME: 10 MINUTES
● COOKING TIME: 5 MINUTES ● 259 CALS PER
SERVING ● 1G FAT, OF WHICH 0.2G SATURATED FAT

1 red chilli, deseeded and finely chopped
10ml (2 tsp) dark soy sauce
grated rind and juice of 1 lime
1.25ml (¼ tsp) ground allspice or six allspice berries,
crushed (see Note)
50g (2oz) soft light brown sugar
4 thick cod fillets, with skin, each weighing about
175g (6oz)
Saffron Mash, to serve (see below)
To garnish:
fried chilli
lime rind and lime wedges

NOTES

● *As a general rule, the smaller the chilli the hotter it is, but removing the seeds and membrane cuts down the heat. Look for birds-eye chillies which are tiny and fiery, but just one is enough to add a pleasant heat to most recipes. Remember to protect your hands when handling chillies: the smallest amount of chilli just can cause severe irritation to the skin.*
● *The allspice berries are soft enough to crush on a board with the flat of a large knife.*
● *You can now get thick cod fillets from some supermarkets or ask your fishmonger to cut thick fillets. They work better for this recipe.*

SAFFRON MASH

● SERVES 4 ● 215 CALS PER SERVING ● 5G FAT, OF WHICH 3.5G SATURATED FAT

For a delicious, creamy mash, cook 900g (2lb) maincrop, peeled potatoes in boiling, salted water. Meanwhile, soak a pinch of saffron strands in 30ml (2 tbsp) boiling water. Drain and mash the potatoes with 25g (1oz) butter and beat in the saffron with its soaking liquid. Sprinkle with coarse sea salt and serve.

1 Put the chilli, soy sauce, lime rind and juice, allspice and sugar in a bowl and mix together until well combined.

2 Grill the cod for about 1 minute, flesh-side up. Turn skin-side up and grill for 1 minute more. Spoon the chilli glaze over. Return to the grill for a further 2–3 minutes until the skin is crisp and golden. Serve with Saffron Mash. Garnish with fried chilli and lime rind and lime wedges.

GRILLED TURBOT WITH CHERVIL AND TOMATO SAUCE

Simply grilled turbot steaks are served with a delicate, creamy tomato and chervil sauce made with infused milk.

● SERVES 4 ● PREPARATION TIME: 20 MINUTES
● COOKING TIME: 10–12 MINUTES ● 280 CALS
PER SERVING ● 11.3G FAT, OF WHICH 5.4G
SATURATED FAT

300 ml (½ pint) semi-skimmed milk
1 onion slice
1 mace blade
4–6 black peppercorns
2 tomatoes
25g (1oz) butter
scant 15g (½oz) plain flour
salt and ground black pepper
5ml (1 tsp) tomato purée
1 large bunch chervil, chopped
4 turbot steaks, each weighing about 175g (6oz)
lemon juice, to taste

1 Put the milk in a small saucepan with the onion, mace and peppercorns. Bring to the boil and remove from the heat. Leave to infuse for 10 minutes, then strain.

2 Immerse the tomatoes in boiling water for 15–30 seconds, then remove and peel away the skins. Cut the flesh into strips, discarding the seeds.

3 Melt 15g (½oz) butter in a small pan. Stir in the flour and cook for 1 minute. Remove from the heat, then gradually stir in the strained milk. Season.

4 Bring to the boil, stirring constantly. Simmer gently for a few minutes. Whisk in the tomato purée and about 60ml (4 tbsp) chopped chervil.

5 Melt the remaining butter. Halve the turbot steaks, brush with melted butter and grill for about 5–6 minutes each side.

6 Add the tomato strips to the sauce. Reheat gently, stirring in the lemon juice to taste. Garnish the turbot with the remaining chopped chervil and serve with the sauce.

PARCHMENT BAKED FISH

This method of cooking fish, wrapped in parchment paper, ensures maximum flavour as the fish cooks in its own juices. Here the juices are flavoured with fennel and wine. Unwrap the fish at the table to allow the guests to enjoy the aromas as each parcel is opened.

● SERVES 4 ● PREPARATION TIME: 15 MINUTES, PLUS SOAKING ● COOKING TIME: 15 MINUTES
● 195 CALS PER SERVING ● 8.7G FAT, OF WHICH 3.8G SATURATED FAT

50ml (2fl oz) dry white wine
125g (4oz) cucumber, thinly sliced
4 fish steaks (cod, halibut or turbot) each weighing about 150g (5oz)
5ml (1 tsp) fennel seeds
25g (1oz) butter or margarine
salt and ground black pepper
fresh fennel sprigs, to garnish

1 Cut four pieces of non-stick baking parchment or greaseproof paper, each about 28cm (11 inches) square, and crumple them together into a small bowl. Pour over the wine and leave to soak for 1 hour; push the paper down into the wine occasionally.

2 Separate and open out each parchment sheet. Arrange a circle of cucumber rounds in the centre of each sheet. Place a fish steak on top. Sprinkle with fennel seeds, dot with a small piece of butter and season with salt and pepper. Drizzle over any remaining wine.

3 Lift up the opposite sides of the parchment and fold together. Twist and tuck under the two shorter ends. Place the parcels on a baking sheet. Bake at 200°C (400°F) Mark 6 for about 15 minutes. Serve at once, garnished with fennel sprigs.

ROLLED PLAICE WITH PESTO

An elegant and nutritious dish which takes hardly any time to cook. The fish remains moist and contrasts beautifully with the crunchy steamed vegetables.

● SERVES 4 ● PREPARATION TIME: 20 MINUTES
● COOKING TIME: 10 MINUTES ● 153 CALS PER SERVING ● 4G FAT, OF WHICH 0.6G SATURATED FAT

8 small plaice fillets, about 550g (1¼lb) total weight
3 spring onions
125g (4oz) fine asparagus or French beans
1 carrot, peeled
15ml (1 tbsp) pesto
30ml (2 tbsp) lemon juice
100ml (4fl oz) fish stock
salt and ground black pepper
75g (3oz) oyster or button mushrooms
125g (4oz) baby corn, halved
125g (4oz) mangetout

1 Skin the plaice fillets and divide each one along the centre line into two fillets. Roll the fish up loosely (skinned side in).

2 Using a sharp knife, cut the spring onions, asparagus and carrot into 6cm (2½ inch) lengths diagonally.

3 Place the fish in a sauté pan. Mix the pesto with the lemon juice and stock. Pour over the fish and season. Bring to the boil, cover tightly with damp greaseproof paper and the lid. Simmer gently for 10 minutes or until cooked. Meanwhile, steam the vegetables or sauté in oil until tender. Serve the vegetables topped with the fish and the juices.

SWEET AND SOUR MONKFISH KEBABS

Tender pieces of monkfish are wrapped in bacon, so the fish retains its succulence, then marinated in a rich sweet and sour sauce, evoking a taste of Asia.

● SERVES 4 ● PREPARATION TIME: 25 MINUTES, PLUS MARINATING ● COOKING TIME: 10–12 MINUTES
● 258 CALS PER SERVING ● 7G FAT, OF WHICH 2.5G SATURATED FAT

450g (1lb) monkfish fillet, skinned
12 lean back bacon rashers
1 small aubergine, about 125g (4oz), thinly sliced
2 small red onions, peeled
2 lemons or limes, sliced
15ml (1 tbsp) lemon juice
30ml (2 tbsp) clear honey
15ml (1 tbsp) soy sauce
15ml (1 tbsp) tomato purée
salt and ground black pepper
frisée leaves, to garnish

1 Cut the monkfish into 2.5cm (1 inch) cubes. Stretch the bacon rashers with the back of a knife and cut in half. Wrap a piece of bacon around each fish cube.

2 Blanch the aubergine slices in boiling water, drain and dry on absorbent kitchen paper.

3 Quarter the onions, then separate each quarter into two, to give thinner pieces.

4 Thread the fish, onions, aubergines and lemon or lime slices on to eight wooden skewers. Place the kebabs side by side in a non-metallic dish.

5 Whisk together the lemon juice, honey, soy sauce, tomato purée and seasoning. Spoon over the kebabs.

6 Cover and leave to marinate in the refrigerator for at least 12 hours, turning once. Preheat the grill. Place the kebabs in a grill pan. Brush all over with a little of the marinade and grill for 10–12 minutes, turning the kebabs occasionally, until the fish and vegetables are tender. Serve the kebabs garnished with frisée.

SEAFOOD KEBABS

This is a great summer barbecue dish, with pieces of seafood interspersed with lime slices and cucumber. Grill or barbecue and serve alfresco.

● SERVES 4 ● PREPARATION TIME: 20 MINUTES
● COOKING TIME: 8–10 MINUTES ● 90 CALS PER
SERVING ● 0.7G FAT, OF WHICH 0.2G SATURATED FAT

450g (1lb) monkfish or cod fillet
125g (4oz) cucumber
50g (2oz) large cooked prawns in shells
1 lime or lemon, thinly sliced
75ml (3fl oz) ready-made low-fat vinaigrette
15ml (1 tbsp) chopped dill or 2.5ml (½ tsp) dried
salt and ground black pepper
selection salad leaves, to serve
fresh dill sprigs, to garnish

1 Skin the fish if necessary, then cut into 2.5cm (1 inch) cubes. Halve the cucumber lengthways and cut it into thick, chunky slices.

2 Peel the prawns, leaving the tail shell on. Preheat the grill.

3 Soak four wooden skewers in cold water for 20 minutes. Thread the prawns and lime slices onto the skewers, alternating with the cubes of fish and cucumber. Place the kebabs in a flameproof dish.

4 Spoon the vinaigrette and dill over the kebabs. Grill for about 8–10 minutes, turning and basting occasionally. Season and serve immediately on a bed of salad leaves. Garnish with dill sprigs.

GRILLED SCALLOPS IN BASIL LEAVES

Tender scallops are wrapped in fresh basil leaves, then in strips of grilled red and yellow peppers, and threaded onto skewers with chunks of courgette. When grilled the scallops remain moist, protected from the fierce heat by their colourful coats. Choose scallops of a uniform size, each with the coral still attached if possible. Serve the skewers on a bed of couscous, or a mixture of wild and long-grain rice.

● SERVES 4 ● PREPARATION TIME: 15 MINUTES
● COOKING TIME: 15 MINUTES ● 300 CALS
PER SERVING ● 13.4G FAT, OF WHICH 2.2G
SATURATED FAT

2 red peppers
2 yellow peppers
16 large fresh scallops, shelled and cleaned
60ml (4 tbsp) olive oil
salt and ground black pepper
3 courgettes
16 large basil leaves
lemon wedges, to serve

1 Cut the peppers into quarters, and remove the core and seeds. Preheat the grill. Place the peppers, skin-side up, on the grill rack and cook until the skins are charred and blackened. Cover the peppers with a damp cloth and leave to cool slightly; the steam created will help to loosen the skins. When the peppers are cool enough to handle, peel away the skins.

2 Place the scallops in a bowl, add 30ml (2 tbsp) of the olive oil and season with salt and pepper. Toss the scallops in the oil.

3 Cut the courgettes into chunks. Blanch in boiling water for 3 minutes. Drain.

4 Wrap each scallop in a basil leaf, then a piece of grilled pepper. Thread the scallops, alternately with the courgettes, onto eight metal or wooden skewers. Brush with the remaining olive oil, and season with salt and pepper.

5 Preheat the grill and place the skewers on the grill rack. Grill for about 8 minutes, turning the skewers occasionally and baste with any oil and juice in the pan. Serve immediately, with lemon wedges.

VARIATION

● Alternatively, cook the scallops on a barbecue. Lay some herb sprigs on the grid to impart flavour and aroma.

NOTE

● If using wooden skewers, soak them in cold water for 20 minutes before threading on the ingredients. This prevents them from charring quickly under the grill.

MUSSELS WITH GARLIC AND PARSLEY

Mussels are readily available from larger supermarkets and your fishmonger. Here they are cooked simply with the minimum of ingredients. Serve with warm, fresh French bread.

- SERVES 4–6 ● PREPARATION TIME: 20 MINUTES
- COOKING TIME: 15 MINUTES ● 312–208 CALS
PER SERVING ● 13G–8.7G FAT, OF WHICH 3G–2G
SATURATED FAT

1.1–1.4kg (2½ –3lb) mussels, cleaned
150ml (10 tbsp) fresh white breadcrumbs
150ml (10 tbsp) chopped fresh parsley
2 garlic cloves, finely chopped
ground black pepper
45ml (3 tbsp) olive oil
30ml (2 tbsp) freshly grated Parmesan
lemon wedges, to serve

1 Place the mussels in a large saucepan containing 1cm (½ inch) boiling water. Cover and cook over a high heat for about 5 minutes until the mussels are open, shaking the pan frequently. Discard any mussels that do not open.

2 Discard the empty half-shell from each mussel. Strain the cooking liquid through a sieve lined with absorbent kitchen paper and reserve the liquid. Arrange the mussels in their half-shells on two baking sheets.

3 Mix together the breadcrumbs, parsley, garlic and plenty of pepper. Add the oil and 60ml (4 tbsp) of the strained cooking liquid. Mix until well combined, then adjust the seasoning to taste.

4 With your fingers, pick up a good pinch of the breadcrumb mixture and press it down on each mussel to cover it well, filling the shell. Sprinkle with Parmesan and bake at 230°C (450°F) Mark 8 for 10 minutes. Arrange the mussels on a serving plate with lemon wedges, to serve.

PRAWNS FRIED WITH GREENS

This is a good way to use those interesting greens sold in Chinese food stores. Pak choi is the one with the long, ribbed white stalks and dark green leaves which grow from a central root, rather like a head of celery. Baby pak choi – the mini variety – is good in this dish as it can be left whole for maximum visual impact. Chinese flowering cabbage has thin white stems, bright green leaves and tiny yellow flowers. Many supermarkets now stock a good selection of these Chinese vegetables.

● SERVES 4–6 ● PREPARATION TIME: 20 MINUTES ● COOKING TIME: ABOUT 10 MINUTES ● 195-130 CALS PER SERVING ● 7.9G–5.3G FAT, OF WHICH 1.1G–0.7G SATURATED FAT

1–2 hot red chillies
1 lemongrass stem
450g (1lb) large raw prawns (see Note)
1 small head of pak choi or Chinese flowering cabbage, or 2–3 baby pak choi (or a mixture)
30ml (2 tbsp) vegetable oil
2 garlic cloves, peeled and thinly sliced
2 kaffir lime leaves, torn in small pieces
2 red shallots, or 1 small red onion
4cm (½ inch) piece fresh root ginger, peeled and cut into long shreds
15ml (1 tbsp) coriander seeds, crushed
75g (3oz) green beans
175g (6oz) mangetout
30ml (2 tbsp) Thai fish sauce (nam pla)
juice of 1 lime, or to taste
lime halves, to garnish

NOTE

● *If raw prawns are unobtainable, use cooked ones instead. Add with the lime juice; heat through for 1 minute only.*

1 Slice the chillies (wearing rubber gloves to avoid skin irritation), discarding the seeds if a milder flavour is preferred. Cut the lemongrass in half and bruise with a rolling pin.

2 Peel the prawns, leaving the tail end attached. Grip the head between your thumb and forefinger. Gently pull until the shell comes off (leaving the tail in your other hand).

3 Using a small sharp knife, make a shallow slit along the outer curve from the tail to the head end and remove the dark intestinal vein. Rinse under cold running water; drain and pat dry with kitchen paper.

4 Trim the pak choi or Chinese flowering cabbage, removing any discoloured leaves or damaged stems. Leave baby pak choi whole; tear other leaves into small pieces.

5 Heat the oil in a wok or large frying pan. Add the garlic, lemongrass, lime leaves, shallots, chillies, ginger and coriander seeds, and stir-fry for 2 minutes. Add the green beans and cook for 2 minutes. Add the prawns, mangetout and pak choi or the Chinese flowering cabbage and stir-fry for 2–3 minutes or until the vegetables are cooked, but still crisp and the prawns are pink and opaque.

6 Add the fish sauce and lime juice, and heat through for 1 minute. Serve immediately, while the vegetables are crisp. Garnish with the lime halves.

VARIATION

● *Replace the prawns with skinless chicken breast fillets, cut into wafer-thin slices. Stir-fry with the beans at step 4.*

FISH BAKED WITH HOT SPICES

Make this simple dish with your favourite fish – it works well with any firm white fish. While the fish is marinating, make a tabbouleh salad to serve with it.

● SERVES 4 ● PREPARATION TIME: 15 MINUTES, PLUS MARINATING ● COOKING TIME: 10–15 MINUTES
● 223 CALS PER SERVING ● 9.5G FAT, OF WHICH 1.3G SATURATED FAT

4 large white fish fillets, (such as cod, haddock, monkfish or sea bass) each weighing about 175g (6oz)

Spice Mixture:

3 garlic cloves, crushed
grated rind and juice of 1 lemon
grated rind of 1 lime
30ml (2 tbsp) chopped fresh coriander
30ml (2 tbsp) chopped fresh parsley
large pinch of powdered saffron
large pinch of turmeric
5ml (1 tsp) ground cumin
2.5ml (½ tsp) ground cinnamon
5–10ml (1–2 tsp) hot chilli sauce
10ml (2 tsp) brown sugar
15ml (1 tbsp) sweet paprika
45ml (3 tbsp) olive oil
salt and ground black pepper
Tabbouleh Salad, to serve (see below)

TABBOULEH SALAD

Put 175g (6oz) bulghar wheat in a bowl and pour on boiling water to cover and come about 1cm (½ inch) above. Leave to soak for about 20 minutes or until all the water has been absorbed and the wheat has softened. Meanwhile, finely chop about 4 ripe juicy tomatoes, 6 spring onions or 1 small red onion, a large handful of fresh parsley and a large handful of fresh mint. Add these to the soaked wheat and season generously with salt, ground black pepper and ground allspice. Add olive oil and lemon juice to taste. Toss lightly to mix.

1 Combine all the ingredients for the spice mixture in a glass bowl, adding plenty of salt and pepper. Whisk together with a fork.

2 Spoon the spice mixture onto the fish fillets, then rub it in well, making sure that each piece is completely coated. Cover and leave to marinate in a cool place for 30 minutes to 1 hour. Don't be tempted to leave it much longer than this, or the acid in the marinade will begin to 'cook' the fish.

3 Preheat the oven to 200°C (400°F) Mark 6. Wrap each fish fillet in a piece of foil and place on a baking sheet. Bake in the oven for about 10–15 minutes or until the fish flakes easily when tested with a fork. The cooking time will depend on the thickness of the fillets: if using chunky fillets like monkfish or cod they will take longer than thinner, more delicate fillets.

4 Unwrap and transfer each fillet to a warmed serving plate. Pour the liquid from each parcel over the fish. Serve at once, with the tabbouleh salad.

ROASTED MONKFISH WITH MEDITERRANEAN VEGETABLES

This colourful, strongly flavoured dish evokes tastes of the Mediterranean. Monkfish is a close-textured fish that is perfect for roasting in this manner. Buy ready-prepared monkfish from your fishmonger. Serve with rice or new potatoes.

● SERVES 4 ● PREPARATION TIME: 30 MINUTES, PLUS MARINATING ● COOKING TIME: 25 MINUTES ● 330 CALS PER SERVING ● 14G FAT, OF WHICH 2.2G SATURATED FAT

2 monkfish fillets each weighing about 350g (12oz)
3 fresh bay leaves
5ml (1 tsp) fennel seeds
60ml (4 tbsp) olive oil
few fresh thyme sprigs
salt and ground black pepper
2 medium red peppers
3 ripe plum tomatoes (or other flavourful tomatoes)
1 medium aubergine
2 medium courgettes
30ml (2 tbsp) capers, drained
45ml (3 tbsp) chopped fresh parsley
4 garlic cloves, unpeeled
45ml (3 tbsp) lemon juice

1 Sandwich the two monkfish fillets together with the bay leaves and fennel seeds wrapped inside and tie at 5cm (2 inch) intervals with cotton string to secure.

NOTE

● Roasted garlic is soft and tastes sweetly nutty. Allow guests to squeeze it out of the skin and spread it on the fish themselves.

2 Put the olive oil, thyme and a little pepper in a shallow non-metallic dish and add the monkfish, turning well to coat. Cover and leave to marinate in the refrigerator for at least 1 hour.

3 Preheat the oven to 220°C (425°F) Mark 7. Halve the red peppers and remove the core and seeds; cut each half into eight pieces. Halve the tomatoes lengthways, deseed and cut the flesh into large dice. Trim the aubergine and cut into 2cm (¾ inch) cubes. Cut the courgettes into similar-sized cubes. Chop the capers and mix with the parsley; cover and set aside.

4 Remove the fish from the marinade and pat dry. Pour 30ml (2 tbsp) of the marinade into a heavy-based frying pan and

heat until almost smoking. Add the monkfish and brown over a brisk heat for 2–3 minutes to seal. Transfer to a roasting rack.

5 In the same pan, quickly brown the unpeeled garlic and all of the vegetables except the tomatoes, using the remaining marinade. Transfer to a heavy-based shallow baking dish and set the monkfish on top. Pour over the lemon juice. Bake in the oven for about 20 minutes, basting occasionally and turning the vegetables from time to time; add the tomatoes after 10 minutes.

6 Remove the string from the monkfish, discard the bay leaves and cut the fish in thick slices. Season the vegetables with salt and pepper to taste. Serve the fish on the vegetables, garnished with capers and parsley.

SQUID AND VEGETABLES IN A BLACK BEAN SAUCE

Don't be put off by the rather lengthy preparation time for this dish as it's quite delicious and has a particularly authentic flavour. Remember the great thing about Thai meals is that most of the preparation can be done ahead of time, and the cooking times are wonderfully short.

● SERVES 4 ● PREPARATION TIME: 55 MINUTES
● COOKING TIME: 10–15 MINUTES ● 360 CALS PER SERVING ● 17G FAT, OF WHICH 2.7G SATURATED FAT

900g (2lb) squid (see Note)
50g (2oz) broccoli florets
50g (2oz) mangetout
50g (2oz) carrots
75g (3oz) cauliflower
1 small green or red pepper, deseeded
50g (2oz) Chinese cabbage or pak choi
25g (1oz) beansprouts
30ml (2 tbsp) sunflower oil
15ml (1 tbsp) sesame oil
2 garlic cloves, peeled
2 dried red chillies
Sauce:
30ml (2 tbsp) black bean sauce
15ml (1 tbsp) Thai fish sauce (nam pla)
10–15 ml (2-3 tsp) clear honey
90ml (3fl oz) fish or vegetable stock
15ml (1 tbsp) tamarind paste
10ml (2 tsp) cornflour
To garnish:
30ml (2 tbsp) toasted sesame seeds
30ml (2 tbsp) roughly torn fresh coriander

NOTE

● If you don't like the idea of preparing the squid yourself, you can buy ready-cleaned and prepared squid from the fish counters of some larger supermarkets; in this case you will need 500g (1lb 2oz) prepared weight.

1 First prepare the sauce. In a small bowl, mix together the black bean sauce, fish sauce, honey and stock. Add the tamarind paste and cornflour and whisk until smooth. Set aside.

2 To prepare the squid, hold the body in one hand and firmly pull the tentacles and body apart. The contents of the body will emerge with the tentacles attached. Squeeze out the plastic-like quill from the body of the squid and discard.

3 Turn the squid pouch inside out and wash thoroughly under cold running water. Dry the cleaned squid, and halve the tentacles if they are large.

4 Cut each clean pouch along one side and open out flat, with the inside turned uppermost. Using a sharp knife score the flesh diagonally, without cutting all the way through, then cut into large squares; set aside.

5 Prepare the vegetables. Cut the broccoli into small florets; top and tail the mangetout; peel and thinly slice the carrots; cut the cauliflower into small florets; thinly slice the green or red pepper; roughly shred the Chinese cabbage or pak choi; wash and dry the beansprouts.

6 Heat the two oils together in a large wok or frying pan, add the garlic and whole chillies and fry gently for 5 minutes. Remove the garlic and chillies with a slotted spoon and discard.

7 Add the vegetables to the oil and stir-fry for 3 minutes. Then add the squid, increase the heat and stir-fry for a further 2 minutes until the squid curls up and turns opaque. Add the sauce and allow to simmer for 1 minute. Scatter over the sesame seeds and coriander and serve at once.

FISH STEW WITH ARTICHOKES AND OYSTER MUSHROOMS

Chunky pieces of haddock, tender artichoke hearts and subtle-tasting oyster mushrooms are cooked together in a white wine sauce, flavoured with lemon. Serve this special occasion fish stew with mixed wild and long-grain rice, or boiled new potatoes.

● SERVES 4–6 ● PREPARATION TIME: 15 MINUTES
● COOKING TIME: ABOUT 25 MINUTES ● 351–234
CALS PER SERVING ● 10.6–7G FAT, OF WHICH 3–2G
SATURATED FAT

1kg (2.2lb) thick-cut skinless haddock fillet
salt and ground black pepper
45–60ml (3–4 tbsp) plain flour
2 onions
2 garlic cloves
30ml (2 tbsp) olive oil
15g (½oz) butter
300 ml (½ pint) white wine
175ml (6fl oz) fish stock
225g (8oz) oyster mushrooms
1 bay leaf
30ml (2 tbsp) chopped fresh parsley
1 lemon
12 artichoke hearts, in water, drained
30ml (2 tbsp) chopped fresh basil
fresh basil leaves, to garnish

3 Heat the oil and butter in a deep sauté pan. When foaming, add the fish and cook until browned all over. Remove the fish with a slotted spoon and set aside.

4 Add the onions to the pan and cook until browned and softened. Add the garlic and cook for 2 minutes. Stir in the wine and stock, the mushrooms, bay leaf and parsley. Bring to the boil and simmer for a further 5 minutes.

1 Cut the haddock into 5cm (2 inch) pieces, removing any bones. Season with salt and pepper and dust with flour.

5 Cut the lemon into thin slices. Add the fish and artichokes to the sauce, then lay the lemon slices on top. Cover and cook for 10–15 minutes. Stir in the chopped basil. Serve immediately, garnished with basil leaves.

VARIATION

● Use cod in place of haddock, and replace the oyster mushrooms with brown cap or open cap mushrooms.

2 Peel the onions and cut each one into eight wedges, retaining the root to hold the layers together. Peel and chop the garlic.

DILL-GLAZED SALMON

This method of cooking salmon is by far the best way of producing a moist, perfectly cooked fish every time — an elegant dish for a cold buffet. The larger the fish the more liquid required and therefore the longer the liquid takes to heat up and cool down again.

● SERVES 8 ● PREPARATION TIME: 30 MINUTES, PLUS CHILLING ● COOKING TIME: 2 MINUTES, PLUS STANDING ● 375 CALS PER SERVING ● 22G FAT, OF WHICH 3.9G SATURATED FAT

1 salmon or sea trout, about 1.8kg (4lb), cleaned
100ml (3½fl oz) dry white wine
few carrot and onion slices
few black peppercorns
1 bay leaf
1 small bunch fresh dill
2.5ml (½ tsp) powdered gelatine
To garnish:
salad leaves
lemon and lime slices

1 Rinse the salmon or sea trout well under cold running water. Remove the head and tail if wished. Place the fish in a fish kettle or large roasting tin. Pour over the white wine and just enough water to cover the fish. Add the onion and carrot slices, peppercorns, bay leaf and dill stalks. Divide the feathery dill tops into small sprigs; cover and refrigerate.

2 Cover the fish kettle with the lid, or the roasting pan tightly with foil. Bring the liquid slowly to the boil. Simmer for 2 minutes. Turn off the heat and leave the salmon (still covered) in the liquid until quite cold.

3 Carefully lift the salmon out of the poaching liquid. Strain and reserve 150ml (¼ pint) liquid. Carefully skin the salmon or trout, gently scraping away any dark brown flesh to reveal the pink underneath.

4 Place the fish on a flat serving platter. If the head and tail are still on, cut a 'v' shape into the tail to neaten it. Cover and chill for at least 30 minutes.

5 Place the reserved poaching liquid in a small bowl. Sprinkle over the powdered gelatine and leave to soak for 3–4 minutes. Place the bowl in a saucepan of simmering water and heat gently until the gelatine has completely dissolved. Cool until just beginning to thicken. Brush a little of the poaching liquid gelatine over the salmon.

6 Press the reserved dill sprigs onto the exposed salmon flesh. Brush all over with more liquid. Chill in the refrigerator until set. Garnish with salad leaves and lemon and limes slices to serve.

THAI SEAFOOD SALAD

Perhaps the most delicious and exciting of all Thai salads is a combination of seafood tossed with a sweet and sour dressing. The flavours are wonderfully refreshing and this dish is visually stunning.

● SERVES 4 ● PREPARATION TIME: 45–50 MINUTES
● COOKING TIME: ABOUT 10 MINUTES ● 262 CALS
PER SERVING ● 8G FAT, OF WHICH 3G SATURATED FAT

8 large raw tiger prawns
225g (8oz) small squid
12 scallops, shelled
20 fresh mussels in shells, cleaned (see Note)
2 shallots, peeled
1 carrot
10cm (4 inch) piece cucumber
75g (3oz) Chinese cabbage
2 kaffir lime leaves, shredded
30ml (2 tbsp) chopped fresh coriander
15ml (1 tbsp) chopped fresh mint
25g (1oz) dried grated coconut, toasted
Dressing:
2–3 small red chillies, deseeded
15ml (1 tbsp) lime juice
15ml (1 tbsp) rice vinegar
15ml (1 tbsp) Thai fish sauce (nam pla)
10ml (2 tsp) sesame oil
pinch of sugar

NOTE

● *Scrub the mussels thoroughly under cold running water and remove their beards. Discard any with damaged shells or any that remain opened when sharply tapped with the back of a knife.*

VARIATION

● *Use other types of seafood, such as clams instead of mussels, or you can use cubes of white fish – such as cod or haddock – in place of squid and/or scallops.*

1 Cut the heads off the prawns and peel away the shells. Make a shallow slit down the back of each prawn and remove the dark intestinal vein; rinse well. Clean the squid (see page 108, Squid and Vegetables in a Black Bean Sauce), scoring the body pouches with a sharp knife, but leaving the tentacles whole. Clean the scallops and separate the white meat from the coral if preferred; slice the white meat into rounds.

2 Place the mussels in a large saucepan with just the water clinging to the shells. Cover with a tight-fitting lid and steam for 4–5 minutes until the shells have opened. Discard any that remain closed. Drain, reserving the poaching liquid, and refresh the mussels under cold running water. Set aside.

3 Return the mussel liquid to the boil. Add the prawns and poach for 3 minutes, then add the squid and scallops and cook for 2–3 minutes until all the seafood is cooked. Remove with a slotted spoon and refresh under cold running water. Reserve 30ml (2 tbsp) of the poaching liquid.

4 Thinly slice the shallots and carrot. Halve, deseed and slice the cucumber. Shred the cabbage. Place the vegetables in a large bowl and toss in the seafood, lime leaves, coriander and mint.

5 For the dressing, finely dice the chillies and mix with the rest of the ingredients. Add to the salad, toss well and divide between individual serving plates. Top each salad with the toasted grated coconut and serve at once.

CRAB SALAD

There is nothing quite like the taste of freshly cooked crab meat and this salad is the perfect way to appreciate it. If you are lucky enough to obtain freshly cooked crabs you will need two, each weighing about 1.4kg (3lb). The dark meat is not included in this dish, but it can be frozen for future use. You can use frozen white crab meat instead, but ensure it is well drained.

● SERVES 6 ● PREPARATION TIME 20 MINUTES, PLUS CRAB IF NECESSARY ● COOKING TIME: 15 MINUTES, PLUS STOCK ● 145–109 CALS PER SERVING ● 7.7–5.7G FAT, OF WHICH 1–0.75G SATURATED FAT

450g (1lb) white crab meat, fresh (see Note) or
frozen and thawed and well drained
6 spring onions, trimmed
30ml (2 tbsp) chopped fresh coriander
15ml (1 tbsp) chopped fresh chives
pinch of cayenne pepper
2 garlic cloves, peeled
2.5cm (1 inch) piece fresh root ginger, peeled
30ml (2 tbsp) sunflower oil
2 kaffir lime leaves, shredded
2.5ml (½ tsp) dried crushed chilli flakes
60ml (4 tbsp) lime juice
15ml (1 tbsp) sugar
5ml (1 tsp) shrimp paste (optional)
15ml (1 tbsp) Thai fish sauce (nam pla) or soy sauce
1–2 heads of radicchio or red chicory
50g (2oz) cucumber
25g (1oz) beansprouts
To garnish:
lime wedges
coriander sprigs

NOTE

● *If you are unsure of preparing fresh crab yourself then ask your fishmonger to do it for you, or at least to separate the body from its shell and pull off the legs and claws. Remember to discard the stomach sac and inedible feathery gills or 'dead man's fingers'.*

1 If preparing the crab yourself, crack open the claws and legs and use a skewer to pick out all the meat. Flake the white crab meat into shreds and place in a bowl. Finely chop the spring onions and add to the crab with the coriander, chives and cayenne pepper. Mix together gently, then cover and chill until required.

2 Crush the garlic and ginger together, using a pestle and mortar or spice grinder. Heat the oil in a small saucepan, add the garlic, ginger, lime leaves and chilli flakes and fry over a gentle heat for 3 minutes until softened but not brown. Add the lime juice, sugar, shrimp paste, if using, and the fish sauce. Stir well, then remove from the heat. Leave until cold.

3 Drizzle the cooled dressing over the crab mixture and toss lightly until evenly combined. Arrange the radicchio or chicory leaves on serving plates and spoon in the crab mixture. Thinly slice the cucumber and arrange on top of each serving with the beansprouts. Garnish with lime wedges and coriander sprigs to serve.

SEAFOOD AND MELON SALAD WITH GINGER LIME DRESSING

For this clean, fresh-tasting salad, prawns, mussels and squid are combined with fragrant melon in a piquant dressing of lime juice, fresh ginger and chilli. Serve it on a bed of pretty mixed salad leaves as part of a buffet, or piled into scallop shells as a starter.

● SERVES 4 ● PREPARATION TIME: 15 MINUTES, PLUS MARINATING ● 154 CALS PER SERVING ● 6G FAT, OF WHICH 0.9G SATURATED FAT

250g (9oz) packet mixed seafood (fresh or frozen and thoroughly thawed)
1 ripe charentais melon
2 ripe tomatoes
15–30ml (1–2 tbsp) chopped fresh coriander or parsley

Dressing:
1 red chilli
15g (½oz) fresh root ginger
25ml (1fl oz) sunflower or peanut oil
juice of 2 limes
grated rind of ½ lime
pinch of salt
15ml (1 tbsp) chopped fresh coriander

To garnish:
lettuce leaves
fresh coriander sprigs
lime wedges

1 First make the dressing. Halve the chilli lengthwise, deseed (wearing rubber gloves to avoid skin irritation), then cut into very fine strips. Peel the ginger and shred finely or cut into very fine julienne strips. In a bowl, whisk together the oil and lime juice until thoroughly combined. Stir in the lime rind, ginger, chilli, salt and coriander.

2 Place the seafood in a shallow dish and pour over the dressing. Mix gently, cover and leave to marinate in the refrigerator for 1–2 hours.

3 Halve the melon, scoop out and discard the seeds. Cut the melon into eight wedges, then cut the flesh away from the skin and slice into chunks.

4 Immerse the tomatoes in a bowl of boiling water for 30 seconds, then refresh in cold water. Peel away the skins. Quarter the tomatoes, remove the seeds, then cut the flesh into strips.

5 Add the melon, tomato and coriander or parsley to the marinated seafood and toss gently to combine all the ingredients thoroughly. Serve garnished with lettuce leaves, coriander and lime wedges.

NOTE

● If you want to make the salad in advance, prepare up to step 4, keeping the melon and tomato separate. Add these just before serving.

PRAWN AND GLASS NOODLES SALAD

A very pretty dish, this Thai salad includes glass noodles, or cellophane noodles as they are sometimes called, made from mung beans. They are as thin as pasta vermicelli and have a transparent quality, which makes them an attractive and unusual addition to a salad. Serve as a starter, or as a light lunch dish.

● SERVES 4 ● PREPARATION TIME: 15 MINUTES
● COOKING TIME: 1 MINUTE ● 170 CALS PER
SERVING ● 9G FAT, OF WHICH 0.9G SATURATED FAT

50g (2oz) glass noodles or cellophane noodles
75g (3oz) shiitake mushrooms
1 large carrot
1 large courgette
12 large cooked prawns, shelled
Dressing:
2 garlic cloves
15ml (1 tbsp) light soy sauce
30ml (2 tbsp) sugar
15ml (1 tbsp) wine vinegar
15ml (1 tbsp) sesame oil
1 red chilli
To garnish:
15ml (1 tbsp) toasted sesame seeds
30ml (2 tbsp) chopped fresh coriander

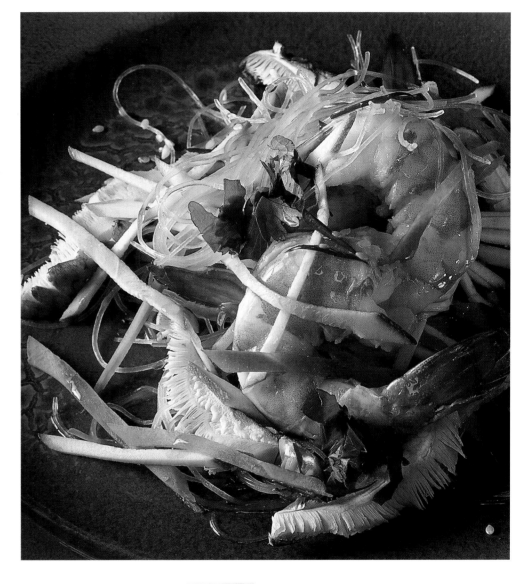

1 First make the dressing. Crush the garlic and mix with the soy sauce, sugar, wine vinegar and sesame oil in a small bowl. Cut the chilli in half lengthways, deseed (wearing rubber gloves to avoid skin irritation), then cut into very fine strips. Mix into the dressing.

2 Cut the noodles into 10cm (4 inch) lengths. Cook in boiling water for 1 minute or according to packet instructions. Drain thoroughly and refresh under cold running water. Drain again.

3 Trim the mushrooms and slice finely. Add to the dressing and mix thoroughly.

4 Cut the carrot and courgette into fine julienne strips, or small matchsticks using a sharp knife.

5 Place the noodles in a bowl and add the mushrooms with the dressing, the julienne of carrot and courgette, and the prawns. Toss the salad well to combine all the ingredients. Sprinkle with the sesame seeds and garnish with chopped coriander to serve.

VARIATIONS

● Use other cooked seafood such as squid, mussels or crab meat, instead of prawns.
● For a warm salad, do not refresh the cooked noodles with cold water. Simply drain and toss the hot noodles with the other ingredients.

LIME MARINATED HALIBUT WITH AVOCADO AND RED ONION SALSA

This recipe is based on the famous Mexican dish of ceviche – raw fish marinated in citrus juices. The acid from the fruit 'cooks' the fish, but retains the texture, keeping it moist. Most white fish can be used, and scallops work well too. This recipe relies on the freshest of fish for its success. It makes a splendid light lunch or starter, served with toasted corn bread or warm soft tortillas.

● SERVES 4 ● PREPARATION TIME: 10 MINUTES, PLUS MARINATING ● 210 CALS PER SERVING ● 8G FAT, OF WHICH 1.5G SATURATED FAT

575g (1¼lb) halibut
juice of 1 orange
juice of 5 limes
Salsa:
1 red pepper
1 red chilli
1 small red onion
1 beef tomato
1 small avocado
60ml (4 tbsp) chopped fresh coriander
30ml (2 tbsp) chopped fresh parsley
1.25ml (¼ tsp) salt
ground black pepper

1 Remove any skin and bones from the fish, and cut into bite-size pieces. Place in a bowl with the orange juice and lime juice. Turn the fish and make sure that it is all covered with the juice. Cover the bowl and leave to marinate in the refrigerator for at least 8 hours, or preferably overnight.

2 To make the salsa, halve the pepper, remove the core and seeds, then dice the flesh. Cut the chilli in half lengthways, deseed (wearing rubber gloves to prevent skin irritation), then chop very finely. Peel and dice the red onion. Mix all these ingredients together in a bowl.

3 Immerse the beef tomato in a small bowl of boiling water, leave for 30 seconds, refresh in cold water, then peel away the skin; it should lift off very easily. Cut the tomato into quarters, remove the seeds, then dice the flesh.

4 Cut the avocado in half, remove the stone and peel away the skin. Cut the flesh into dice. Add to the onion mixture with the tomato, coriander, parsley, salt and pepper to taste. Mix well.

5 Serve the marinated fish mounded up on individual plates and topped with a large spoonful of salsa.

NOTE

● If a smoother sauce is preferred, the salsa ingredients can be puréed to the required consistency in a blender or food processor.

MARINATED SALMON WITH LIME AND CORIANDER DRESSING

This salad can be served as a starter, light lunch or supper dish. The acidity of the marinade will 'cook' the salmon, giving it an opaque appearance.

● SERVES 4 ● PREPARATION TIME: 20 MINUTES, PLUS CHILLING ● 435 CALS PER SERVING ● 18G FAT, OF WHICH 3G SATURATED FAT

Marinade:
grated rind and juice of 3 limes
60ml (4 tbsp) olive oil
2 tomatoes, peeled, deseeded and diced
60ml (4 tbsp) chopped fresh coriander
10ml (2 tsp) caster sugar
salt and ground black pepper
Salad:
225g (8oz) salmon fillet, skinned and chilled
mixed salad leaves, such as rocket, lamb's lettuce or frisée
50g (2oz) cucumber, peeled, deseeded and finely chopped
1 bunch spring onions, roughly chopped
1 large green chilli, deseeded and finely chopped
finely grated lime rind, to garnish

1 For the marinade, combine the grated lime rind and juice, oil, tomatoes, coriander, caster sugar and seasoning in a small bowl. Cover and set aside.

2 To make the salad, using a sharp knife, cut the salmon fillet on the diagonal into wafer thin slices. Place in a large, shallow non-metallic dish, pour over the marinade, then cover and chill in the fridge for up to 3 hours or until the salmon is pink and has an opaque appearance.

3 To serve, arrange the salmon with the marinade juices on the mixed salad leaves and top with cucumber, spring onions and chilli. Garnish with the grated lime rind.

MEAT DISHES

The healthy eating trend is to eat less meat, especially red meat, but it can still play an important part in a well-balanced diet. When shopping for meat, choose the leanest cuts possible or trim the meat well when you are preparing it. Generally, try to limit the amount of fat you use when cooking meat and remember that you don't need to serve large portions – it's healthier to increase the amount of accompanying vegetables. Chicken is increasingly popular, due to its lower fat content compared to other meat, its relatively cheap price, and the ease with which it can be prepared. On a low-fat diet the important thing is to avoid eating the skin.

All these recipes are healthy yet full of flavour, concentrating mainly on chicken, lamb and pork cooked in a variety of interesting ways. You will also find suggestions for cooking beef, venison and duck. Some recipes include a marinade which makes all the difference to the end taste and texture of the meat and also how long it will need to be cooked. Marinades tenderise the meat as well as giving it flavour. Stir-fried Pork and Grilled Chicken with a Spiced Yogurt Crust are just two of the dishes that taste delicious for very little effort. If you prefer, in many of the chicken recipes you could substitute turkey, but avoid goose and poussins which are high in fat.

AROMATIC CHICKEN PARCELS

For this recipe the spices are ground to release their aromatic flavours. However, if you don't have time to do this, omit the cardamom pods and cloves. In step 2, simply dry-fry the cinnamon sticks and orange rind then go straight to step 3 and dust the chicken breasts with 5ml (1 tsp) each dried cloves and mixed spice, instead. Harissa is a fiery chilli paste from North Africa.

● SERVES 8 ● PREPARATION TIME: 1 HOUR, PLUS COOLING ● COOKING TIME: 1 HOUR ● 290 CALS PER SERVING ● 10.5g FAT, OF WHICH 2g SATURATED FAT

350g (12oz) small shallots
1 garlic bulb
450g (1lb) each celery and carrots (see Note)
2 large oranges
2 eating apples, such as Granny Smith, Braeburn or Cox's
4 cinnamon sticks
4 vanilla pods
5ml (1 tsp) cardamom pods
6–8 cloves
salt and ground black pepper
8 skinless chicken breast fillets, 1.2kg (2¼lb) total weight
15ml (1 tbsp) vegetable oil
15ml (1 tbsp) tomato paste
300ml (½ pint) unsweetened apple juice
2 x 400g (14oz) cans chopped tomatoes
5ml (1 tsp) harissa (see page 207)
extra oil, for brushing
Mustard-seeded Okra, to accompany (see page 166)

NOTES
● The carrots and celery could be replaced with celeriac, parsnips or turnips.
● To test if the chicken is cooked, pierce through the neck of the parcel deep into the chicken flesh with a sharp skewer. Leave the skewer for 30 seconds – it should feel very hot when it comes out; if not, the chicken needs longer.

1 Peel the shallots and garlic; slice the celery and carrots; set aside. Pare the rind of the oranges and squeeze the juice. Peel, core and roughly chop the apples, then stir them into the orange juice. Split the cinnamon sticks and the vanilla pods in half lengthways.

2 Place the cinnamon sticks in a heavy-based frying pan with the orange rind, cardamom pods and cloves. Heat, stirring all the time until the cardamom pods darken and the spices start to smell aromatic. Cool, lift out the cinnamon sticks and orange rind and set aside with the vanilla pods. Remove the seeds from the cardamom pods. Crush the seeds to a fine powder, with the cloves in a pestle and mortar or in a heavy bowl using the end of a rolling pin.

3 Season the chicken breasts and dust with the ground spices. Place a piece of orange rind, cinnamon stick and vanilla pod in the centre of each breast. Fold the chicken around the orange rind and spices and cover with cling film; chill for 30 minutes.

4 To make the sauce, heat the oil, fry the shallots for 5–10 minutes until browned. Add the celery and carrots, garlic and apples. Cook on a high heat, stirring, for 10 minutes until browned and caramelised.

5 Add the tomato paste and cook for 1 minute, then add the apple juice and orange juice. Boil until reduced by half. Add the tomatoes and harissa, bring back to the boil and bubble, stirring, for 10 minutes. Cool.

6 Cut out eight 35.5cm (14 inch) squares of greaseproof paper. Brush each with oil. Place two tablespoonfuls of the tomato sauce in the middle of each, place a chicken breast on top. Spoon one tablespoonful of tomato sauce over. Bring the edges of the paper together to make a parcel, then tie it securely with fine string.

7 Place the parcels in a roasting tin and cook at 200°C (400°F) Mark 6 for 30 minutes until cooked through (see Note).

CHICKEN CASSEROLE WITH HERB DUMPLINGS

This is a warming, filling dish with a hint of sweetness supplied by the prunes. Omitting the dumplings reduces the calories and fat considerably.

● SERVES 6 ● PREPARATION TIME: 50 MINUTES
● COOKING TIME: 1 HOUR 40 MINUTES ● 295 CALS PER SERVING ● 12.5G FAT, OF WHICH 5.5G SATURATED FAT

1.4kg (3lb) oven-ready chicken
225g (8oz) onions, roughly chopped
1 medium carrot, roughly chopped
50g (2oz) celery, roughly chopped
1 bay leaf
salt and ground black pepper
15ml (1 tbsp) olive oil
900g (2lb) leeks, trimmed
125g (4oz) self-raising flour
2.5ml (½ tsp) baking powder
50g (2oz) butter
15ml (1 tsp) each chopped flatleaf parsley and fresh thyme
125g (4oz) ready-to-eat pitted prunes
chopped fresh chives, to garnish
cooked baby carrots, to serve

1 Place the chicken in a pan. Add the onions, carrot, celery, bay leaf and 5 ml (1 tsp) salt. Add 1.7 litres (3 pints) cold water, bring to the boil, then cover and simmer for 45 minutes–1 hour or until the chicken is cooked.

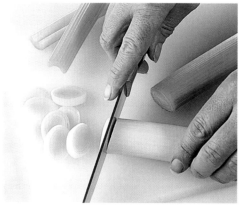

2 Meanwhile, cut the leeks into 1cm (½ inch) slices. Heat the oil and cook the leeks for 5–6 minutes or until lightly golden. Add the leeks to the casserole for the last 20 minutes of the cooking time.

3 Remove and discard the skin and bones from the chicken, roughly shred the meat and return to the saucepan with the stock.

4 Sift the flour, baking powder and a pinch of salt into a bowl. Rub in the butter, herbs and stir in 60ml (4 tbsp) water to form a dough, then shape into twelve 2.5cm (1 inch) balls. Place on a baking sheet lined with greaseproof paper and cook at 200°C (400°F) Mark 6 for 15–20 minutes or until golden.

5 Bring the casserole to the boil, season well, then add the prunes and simmer gently for 5 minutes. Garnish with chives and serve hot with the dumplings and carrots.

CHICKEN, BEAN AND SPINACH CURRY

This is a substantial supper that you can make in just 30 minutes. Use a good quality, ready-made curry sauce which you can buy in supermarkets or delicatessens.

● SERVES 4 ● PREPARATION TIME: 10 MINUTES
● COOKING TIME: 20 MINUTES ● 404 CALS
PER SERVING ● 12.7G FAT, OF WHICH 1.8G
SATURATED FAT

15ml (1 tbsp) sunflower oil
350g (12oz) skinless chicken breasts, cut into strips
1 garlic clove, crushed
300–350g (10–12oz) tub or jar of curry sauce
400g (14oz) can cooked aduki beans, drained and rinsed
175g (6oz) ready-to-eat dried apricots
150g carton natural bio yogurt
125g (4oz) ready-prepared fresh spinach

1 Heat the oil in a large saucepan and fry the chicken strips with the crushed garlic until golden. Add the curry sauce, beans and apricots, then cover and simmer gently for 15 minutes or until the chicken is tender.

2 Over a low heat, stir in the yogurt, keeping the curry hot without boiling, then stir in the spinach over the heat until it just begins to wilt. Serve immediately.

TANDOORI-STYLE CHICKEN

The best way to emulate the intense direct heat of a tandoor oven at home is by grilling or barbecuing. It's essential to preheat the grill until very hot, and to keep the food fairly close to the heat source so that it gets well browned. Ideally, serve the tandoori chicken with a fresh chutney.

● SERVES 4 ● PREPARATION TIME: 15 MINUTES, PLUS MARINATING ● COOKING TIME: 25 MINUTES
● 204 CALS PER SERVING ● 7.2G FAT, OF WHICH 2.1G SATURATED FAT

2–3 garlic cloves
2.5cm (1 inch) piece fresh root ginger
1–2 hot green chillies
600ml (1 pint) 0% fat Greek yogurt
15ml (1 tbsp) ground coriander
15ml (1 tbsp) ground cumin
10ml (2 tsp) tandoori or curry paste
30ml (2 tbsp) chopped fresh coriander
30ml (2 tbsp) chopped fresh mint (optional)
salt
few drops each of red and yellow food colouring (optional)
4 chicken suprêmes, skinned
melted ghee or oil, for basting
lemon or lime juice, to taste
lime or lemon wedges, to garnish

1 Peel and crush the garlic. Peel and finely chop the ginger. Chop the chillies, discarding the seeds if a milder flavour is preferred.

2 Put the yogurt in a large non-metallic dish and add the garlic, ginger and chillies. Add the ground spices and tandoori or curry paste and mix thoroughly. Add the chopped coriander and mint, if using. Season with salt and add a few drops of food colouring to enhance the colour, if desired.

3 Make 3–4 deep cuts in each chicken portion, being careful not to cut right through. Add the chicken to the marinade and turn to ensure that each piece is thoroughly coated in the marinade. Rub the mixture well into the cuts. Cover the bowl and leave the chicken to marinate in the refrigerator overnight.

4 Preheat the grill (or barbecue) until it is very hot. Remove the chicken from the marinade and place on the grill (or barbecue) rack and cook for about 25 minutes, basting with melted ghee or oil and turning frequently to ensure that it cooks evenly. Don't be afraid to let it get really brown in places; a few crispy bits add to the flavour. To check that the chicken is cooked through, pierce the thickest part with a skewer; the juices should run clear – if they are at all pink cook for a little longer.

5 Serve the tandoori chicken straight away, brushed with a little more melted ghee or oil and sprinkled with lime or lemon juice. Serve garnished with lime or lemon wedges.

CHICKEN FAJITAS

Serve this Mexican-style dish with tortillas, guacamole and soured cream. If you have trouble buying ready-made corn tortillas you could always make your own wheat version (see below).

● SERVES 6 ● PREPARATION TIME: 30 MINUTES, PLUS MARINATING ● COOKING TIME: ABOUT 15 MINUTES ● 508 CALS PER SERVING ● 10.9G FAT, OF WHICH 2.6G SATURATED FAT

3 onions
2–3 hot chillies
2 garlic cloves, crushed
30ml (2 tbsp) chopped fresh coriander, plus leaves to garnish
grated rind and juice of 2 limes
6 skinless chicken breast fillets
8 red, yellow or orange peppers (or a mixture)
15–30ml (1–2 tbsp) olive oil
salt and ground black pepper
To serve:
12 tortillas
guacamole (optional)
soured cream

1 Peel and halve the onions, leaving most of the root end attached so that they will hold their shape during cooking. Cut each half into wedges, working from the root end to the top. Slice the chillies, discarding the seeds if a milder flavour is preferred.

HOMEMADE TORTILLAS

Put 300g (10oz) plain flour in a food processor with 7.5ml (1½ tsp) salt and 50g (2oz) white vegetable fat. Process briefly then, with the machine still running, gradually add 150–175ml (5–6fl oz) warm water or enough to make a fairly soft dough. Knead briefly on a floured surface, then divide into 12 pieces. Roll out each piece to an 18cm (7 inch) circle. Cook the tortillas one at a time on an ungreased griddle or frying pan for 1 minute each side.

2 Put the garlic, onions, chillies, coriander, lime rind and juice in a shallow non-metallic dish and mix thoroughly. Cut the chicken into large pieces and add to the dish. Stir well to coat the chicken thoroughly, cover and leave to marinate in a cool place for at least 1 hour or preferably overnight.

3 Halve the peppers and remove the cores and seeds, then cut into wedges.

4 Heat the oil in a heavy-based frying pan. Remove the chicken and onions from the marinade with a slotted spoon, reserving the marinade. Add the chicken and onions to the pan and cook, turning, over a high heat until thoroughly browned on the outside. Remove the chicken from the pan.

5 Add the peppers to the pan and cook, turning, over a high heat for about 5 minutes until the onions and peppers are just softened.

6 Return the chicken to the pan, add the marinade, lower the heat and cook for about 5 minutes, stirring occasionally, or until the chicken is cooked right through.

7 Season with salt and pepper to taste and sprinkle with the coriander leaves. Serve immediately, with the tortillas, guacamole if using, and soured cream.

GREEN CHICKEN CURRY

This dish – along with Thai red curry – is perhaps the most well-known of all Thai main meals. A basic spice paste mixture forms the basis of every Thai curry; this is often made up in larger quantities and stored in the refrigerator for future use. The colour of the curry paste depends on the chillies used – either green as here, or red. Reduce the amount of chillies for a milder flavour. Serve with boiled rice.

● SERVES 4 ● PREPARATION TIME: 30 MINUTES, PLUS STANDING ● COOKING TIME: 30 MINUTES
● 243 CALS PER SERVING ● 12G FAT, OF WHICH 5.4G SATURATED FAT

4 baby aubergines (see Note)
5ml (1 tsp) sea salt
4 shallots, peeled
2 garlic cloves, peeled
30ml (2 tbsp) sunflower oil
30ml (2 tbsp) green curry paste (see Note)
150ml (¼ pint) chicken stock
15ml (1 tbsp) Thai fish sauce (nam pla)
15ml (1 tbsp) lemon juice
350g (12oz) skinless chicken breast fillets
1 red pepper, deseeded
125g (4oz) French beans, trimmed
25g (1oz) creamed coconut
12 deep-fried basil leaves, to garnish (optional)

NOTES

● If baby aubergines are unobtainable, use 1 small aubergine, halved and cut into wedges instead.
● Ready-made Thai green curry paste is available from larger supermarkets and Oriental stores.

1 Quarter the aubergines and sprinkle over the sea salt. Place in a colander set over a plate and leave the bitter juices to drain for 30 minutes. Rinse the aubergines thoroughly to remove the salt and pat dry.

2 Halve or quarter the shallots if large and slice the garlic. Heat the oil in a large deep frying pan and fry the shallots and garlic for 3 minutes until lightly browned. Add the curry paste and stir-fry for 2–3 minutes.

3 Carefully stir in the stock, fish sauce and lemon juice. Bring to the boil and simmer, uncovered, for 10 minutes.

4 Meanwhile, cut the chicken breast into 3cm (1¼ inch) cubes. Slice the red pepper and halve the French beans. Add to the sauce with the aubergines and return to the boil. Simmer for 10–15 minutes until the vegetables and chicken are tender.

5 Add the creamed coconut and stir until melted and the sauce is thickened; do not reboil. Divide between warmed serving bowls and garnish with fried basil leaves, if using. Serve at once.

BARBECUE CHICKEN

This recipe works best with small potatoes – look out for ready-washed tiny ones, about the size of a large walnut. It also works well with baby onions, as they retain their shape when cooked, but as they're fiddly and time-consuming to prepare, sliced onions are used here instead.

● SERVES 4 ● PREPARATION TIME: ABOUT 15 MINUTES ● COOKING TIME: 40–50 MINUTES
● 450 CALS PER SERVING ● 12G FAT, OF WHICH 3G SATURATED FAT

450g (1lb) tiny potatoes, scrubbed clean
salt
8 chicken drumsticks, skinned, or 4 thighs and
4 drumsticks
2 onions
120ml (8 tbsp) tomato ketchup
30ml (2 tbsp) soft dark brown sugar
15ml (1 tbsp) mild mustard
30ml (2 tbsp) Worcestershire sauce
1 garlic clove, crushed
15ml (1 tbsp) vegetable oil

1 Preheat the oven to 220°C (425°F) Mark 7. Add the potatoes to a saucepan of cold salted water. Bring to the boil, lower the heat and cook for 5 minutes.

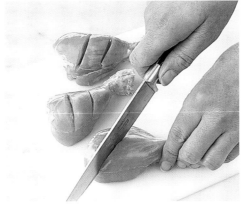

2 Meanwhile, make 2–3 deep cuts in each piece of chicken, using a sharp knife. This allows the sauce to penetrate and flavour the chicken well.

3 Peel the onions and cut into fairly thick rings. In a large bowl, mix the tomato ketchup, sugar, mustard, Worcestershire sauce and garlic. Add the chicken and onions, and stir until well coated with the sauce.

4 Drain the potatoes. Heat the oil in a roasting tin on the hob. Quickly tip the potatoes into the hot oil and shake the tin so that the potatoes are evenly coated with oil.

5 Turn off the heat, then add the chicken and onions, with the sauce. Mix thoroughly, then bake in the preheated oven for 40–50 minutes or until the chicken is cooked through and the potatoes are tender. Stir occasionally so everything browns evenly.

VARIATION

● *Replace half of the chicken portions with spicy sausages for guests or children not concerned about eating food with a higher fat content.*

GRILLED CHICKEN WITH A SPICED YOGURT CRUST

Yogurt makes a wonderful basis for a marinade, as it tenderises and flavours yet doesn't disappear during cooking. Instead it forms a delicious soft crust which protects the meat from the fierce heat of the grill. Serve with a crisp green salad.

● SERVES 4 ● PREPARATION TIME: 10 MINUTES, PLUS MARINATING ● COOKING TIME: 20 MINUTES
● 245 CALS PER SERVING ● 8G FAT, OF WHICH 2.7G SATURATED FAT

4 chicken breast fillets, skinned
15ml (1 tbsp) coriander seeds
5ml (1 tsp) ground cumin
10ml (2 tsp) mild curry paste
1 garlic clove, crushed
450ml (¾ pint) natural bio yogurt
salt and ground black pepper
45ml (3 tbsp) chopped fresh coriander (optional)

1 Prick the chicken breasts all over with a fork and flatten them out slightly at the same time.

2 Crush the coriander seeds, using a pestle and mortar (or put in a heavy bowl and crush with the end of a rolling pin). Mix with the cumin, curry paste, garlic and yogurt in a large shallow dish. Add seasoning, and the fresh coriander, if using.

3 Add the chicken and turn to coat thoroughly with the spiced yogurt mixture. Cover and leave to marinate for 30 minutes, or place in the refrigerator and marinate overnight.

4 Preheat the grill to high. Grill the chicken, turning occasionally, for about 20 minutes or until cooked through. To see if it is cooked, pierce the thickest part with a fork and check that the juices run clear; if they are pink cook for a little longer. Serve immediately.

NOTE

● You could use other cuts of chicken, but they will take longer to cook. Skin them first, then slash in several places to enable the heat to penetrate right through to the middle.

VARIATION

● For children, use chicken drumsticks and omit the cumin and coriander for a milder flavour.

CHICKEN BAKED WITH SPICES

This is a really easy, tasty supper dish. If you can, set the chicken to marinate the day before to allow plenty of time for it to absorb the flavours. It will then be ready to pop into the oven when required. Serve with a simple rice pilaff and a crisp green salad.

● SERVES 6 ● PREPARATION TIME: 15 MINUTES, PLUS MARINATING ● COOKING TIME: ABOUT 25 MINUTES ● 238 CALS PER SERVING ● 10G FAT, OF WHICH 4.6G SATURATED FAT

2 garlic cloves
30ml (2 tbsp) mild paprika
10ml (2 tsp) ground coriander
5–10ml (1–2 tsp) cayenne pepper
finely grated rind and juice of 1 large lemon
30ml (2 tbsp) chopped fresh mint
30ml (2 tbsp) chopped fresh coriander
45ml (3 tbsp) grated fresh coconut (optional)
200ml (7fl oz) low-fat thick yogurt
salt and ground black pepper
6 chicken suprêmes, or other portions
ghee or vegetable oil, for brushing

To serve:
mint and rocket leaves
grated fresh coconut (optional)
lemon or lime wedges

1 In a pestle and mortar, crush the garlic and mash with the paprika, coriander, cayenne pepper and lemon rind and juice. Put the herbs, and coconut, if using, in a bowl and stir in the yogurt. Beat in the garlic mixture. Add salt and pepper to taste.

2 Skin each chicken suprême or portion and make 2–3 deep cuts in the thickest part of the flesh.

3 Drop the chicken portions into the yogurt mixture and turn the portions in the mixture so that they are thoroughly coated on all sides. Make sure that the marinade goes well into the cuts. Cover and leave to marinate in a cool place for at least 30 minutes, or overnight if possible.

4 Preheat the oven to 200°C (400°F) Mark 6. Arrange the chicken in a single layer in a roasting tin and brush with ghee or oil. Roast in the oven, basting from time to time, for about 25 minutes until the chicken is cooked right through. To test it, pierce the thickest part with the point of a knife: if the juices run clear, the chicken is cooked; if there is any trace of pink, bake for a further 10 minutes or until cooked.

5 Serve garnished with mint and rocket leaves, grated coconut, if using, and lemon or lime wedges.

VENISON WITH POMEGRANATE

Venison is a good lean meat with great flavour. It doesn't need much cooking – here it is quickly sautéed and served in a mushroom sauce.

● SERVES 4 ● PREPARATION TIME: 15 MINUTES
● COOKING TIME: 15 MINUTES ● 346 CALS PER
SERVING ● 14G FAT, OF WHICH 2.6G SATURATED FAT

1 pomegranate
350g (12oz) venison fillet
15ml (1 tbsp) plain flour
salt and ground black pepper
30ml (2 tbsp) oil
50g (2oz) mushrooms, thickly sliced
200ml (7fl oz) mushroom or vegetable stock

1 Using a sharp knife, halve the pomegranate. Scoop out and reserve the seeds and juice. Discard the membrane.

2 Slice the venison fillet into 5mm (¼ inch) thick pieces. Place between sheets of dampened greaseproof paper and bat out until the meat is quite thin. Mix the flour in a bowl with the salt and pepper. Toss the venison in the seasoned flour to coat.

3 Heat the oil in a large sauté pan and brown the venison on both sides, in batches. Return all the meat to the pan, stirring in any remaining flour.

4 Add the mushrooms, stock and pomegranate seeds and juice. Bring to a simmer and cook for 2–3 minutes or until heated through. Serve immediately.

DUCK BREASTS WITH PICKLED PLUMS

These duck breasts are marinated, then quickly seared to seal in the flavour and finally cooked through in a rich Thai-style sauce. Home-pickled plums provide a nice sharp contrast to the richness of the duck and its sauce. Serve with rice or noodles.

● SERVES 6 ● PREPARATION TIME: 15 MINUTES, PLUS MARINATING ● COOKING TIME: 15 MINUTES
● 203 CALS PER SERVING ● 5G FAT, OF WHICH 1G SATURATED FAT

6 x duck breast fillets, each weighing about 225g (8oz)
15ml (1 tbsp) sunflower oil
150ml (¼ pint) chicken stock
30ml (2 tbsp) oyster sauce

Marinade:
2 garlic cloves, crushed
5ml (1 tsp) hot chilli sauce
pinch of salt
10ml (2 tsp) clear honey
10ml (2 tsp) dark muscovado sugar
30ml (2 tbsp) lime juice
15ml (1 tbsp) dark soy sauce

Pickled Plums:
6 large under-ripe plums
50g (2oz) caster sugar
50ml (2fl oz) distilled malt vinegar
1.25ml (¼ tsp) dried crushed chilli flakes
5ml (1 tsp) salt
pinch of ground cinnamon

VARIATION

● Replace the plums with 6 small oranges, peel and pith removed.

1 First mix together all the ingredients for the marinade. Skin the duck breasts, wash well and dry thoroughly. Cut a few deep slashes in each duck breast and place in a shallow, non-metallic dish. Spread evenly with the marinade, then cover and leave to marinate for at least 4 hours, turning the duck breasts several times.

2 Meanwhile, prepare the pickled plums. Wash and dry the plums, halve and remove the stones. Place the remaining ingredients in a saucepan with 50ml (2fl oz) water and heat gently, stirring until the sugar is dissolved. Add the plums, bring to the boil and simmer gently for 5 minutes or until the plums have just softened. Set aside to cool.

3 When ready to serve, remove the duck breasts from the marinade and pat dry, reserving the marinade juices. Heat the oil in a large non-stick frying pan and brown the duck quickly on both sides. Add the stock, marinade juices and oyster sauce and simmer gently, covered, for 5 minutes. Remove the duck breasts with a slotted spoon and keep warm.

4 Remove the plums from their liquid with a slotted spoon and carefully add the plums to the duck sauce. Bring to the boil and simmer, uncovered, for a further 5 minutes. Slice the duck breasts and arrange on warmed serving plates with the plum halves. Spoon over the sauce and serve at once.

LAMB AND BAMBOO SHOOT RED CURRY

Thai red curry paste is used to flavour this dish. It is quick and easy to make your own (see below), but you only need a tiny amount so you may prefer to use one of the red curry pastes available from larger supermarkets and Oriental stores. Serve with rice or noodles.

● SERVES 4 ● PREPARATION TIME: 10 MINUTES
● COOKING TIME: 45 MINUTES ● 325 CALS PER
SERVING ● 18G FAT, OF WHICH 5.4G SATURATED FAT

1 large onion
2 garlic cloves
450g (1lb) lean boneless lamb
30ml (2 tbsp) sunflower oil
30ml (2 tbsp) Thai red curry paste (see below)
150ml (¼ pint) lamb or beef stock
30ml (2 tbsp) Thai fish sauce (nam pla)
10ml (2 tsp) soft brown sugar
200g (7oz) can bamboo shoots, drained
1 red pepper
30ml (2 tbsp) chopped fresh mint
15ml (1 tbsp) chopped fresh basil
25g (1oz) raw peanuts, toasted
basil leaves, to garnish

1 Peel the onion and cut into wedges; peel and finely chop the garlic; cut the lamb into 3cm (1¼ inch) cubes.

2 Heat the oil in a wok or large frying pan, add the onion and garlic and fry over a medium heat for 5 minutes.

3 Add the lamb and the curry paste and stir-fry for 5 minutes. Add the stock, fish sauce and sugar. Bring to the boil, lower the heat, then cover and simmer gently for a further 20 minutes.

4 Meanwhile, slice the bamboo shoots into strips; core, deseed and slice the red pepper. Stir into the curry with the herbs and cook, uncovered, for a further 10 minutes. Stir in the peanuts and serve at once, garnished with basil leaves.

THAI RED CURRY PASTE

Halve, deseed and roughly chop 2 long thin fresh red chillies and 8 dried red chillies (wear rubber gloves to avoid skin irritation). Roughly chop 4 kaffir lime leaves. Peel and chop a 2.5cm (1 inch) piece of galangal, 4 shallots, and 4 garlic cloves. Peel and finely chop 2 lemon grass stalks. Purée all the prepared ingredients in a spice grinder or blender with 5ml (1 tsp) ground black pepper, 5ml (1 tsp) turmeric and 30ml (2 tbsp) sunflower oil to form a smooth paste. Store in a screw-topped jar in the refrigerator for up to one month.

LAMB CUTLETS WITH MINTED CUCUMBER SALSA

Juicy and tender spring lamb is roasted to golden crispness on the outside while rosy pink on the inside. The sauce is made from the pan juices, flavoured with orange and a hint of mint jelly. Serve with smooth mashed potatoes mixed with spring onions and black pepper, plus seasonal vegetables.

● SERVES 6 ● PREPARATION TIME: 35 MINUTES
● COOKING TIME: 20–30 MINUTES ● 300 CALS PER SERVING ● 14G FAT, OF WHICH 6G SATURATED FAT

3 x 7-bone racks of spring lamb
30ml (2 tbsp) brandy
salt and ground black pepper
a little sunflower oil, for brushing
Salsa:
1 medium cucumber
2 pickled dill cucumbers
1 small sweet red onion
45ml (3 tbsp) chopped fresh mint
Sauce:
150ml (¼ pint) medium-dry white wine
10ml (2 tsp) plain flour
finely grated rind and juice of 2 oranges
45ml (3 tbsp) mint jelly
fresh mint sprigs, to garnish

1 If the rack of lamb is not ready-trimmed, pull off the thick outer layer of fat, leaving a very fine layer on the outside to baste the meat during cooking (see Note). Rub with the brandy and seasoning. Cover and leave in a cool place for 30 minutes.

2 To make the salsa, peel the cucumber, if preferred. Halve the cucumber lengthways and scoop out the seeds. Cut the flesh into fine dice. Finely dice the dill cucumbers. Peel and finely dice the onion. Mix all these ingredients together and stir in the mint. Season with salt and pepper to taste. Cover and chill in the refrigerator.

3 Preheat the oven to 200°C (400°F) Mark 6. Stand the rack of lamb in a roasting tin. Brush with a little oil and roast in the preheated oven for 20–30 minutes, depending on how pink you like your lamb. Remove from the oven and transfer to a warm dish. Cover with foil and leave to rest in a warm place for 10 minutes before carving – this makes the lamb more juicy and easier to carve.

4 Meanwhile, make the sauce. Set the roasting pan over a medium heat and pour in the wine. Bring to the boil, scraping up the sediment off the bottom of the pan. Boil until well reduced, then whisk in the flour. Cook, stirring, for 1 minute then add the orange rind, juice and mint jelly. Bring to the boil, then simmer for 2–3 minutes until syrupy. If too thick add a little more wine or water. Season with salt and pepper to taste. Strain if you like, but the bits add character! Pour into a warmed jug.

5 Cut the lamb into cutlets, allowing three per person. Arrange on warmed dinner plates. Spoon a little salsa on top of each cutlet and pour a little sauce around them. Garnish with mint sprigs and serve the remaining sauce separately.

NOTE

● It is essential to use well-trimmed lamb for this recipe. If you don't remove the outer layer of fat the meat will take longer to cook.

GRILLED LAMB WITH COURGETTES AND ROSEMARY

By threading the meat with the sprigs of rosemary before grilling, the rosemary infuses the meat with its heady aroma. The garlic is roasted in its skin to give a soft buttery finish. The garlic can then be squeezed onto the cooked lamb as the finishing touch.

● SERVES 4 ● PREPARATION TIME: 10 MINUTES
● COOKING TIME: 15–20 MINUTES ● 293 CALS PER SERVING ● 15G FAT, OF WHICH 7G SATURATED FAT

12 large garlic cloves
450g (1lb) medium courgettes
olive oil, for brushing
salt and ground black pepper
4 lamb loin chops, each weighing about 175g (6oz)
4 long rosemary sprigs

1 Boil the unpeeled garlic cloves in water for 5 minutes; drain. Halve the courgettes lengthways and arrange on a grill rack with the garlic. Brush with oil and season.

2 Trim the fat from the chops and bend the tail of each chop around the eye of the meat.

3 Using a skewer, make holes through each chop and thread with rosemary sprigs to secure. Brush with oil.

4 Grill the garlic and courgettes for 5 minutes, turning after 2 minutes. Add the lamb and grill for 6–8 minutes on each side; the garlic skin will blacken but the flesh will be soft. Divide the garlic and courgettes equally between four serving plates, place a loin chop on each serving and serve immediately, allowing guests to squeeze the garlic onto the lamb themselves.

SPICED LAMB MEATBALLS

Reminiscent of the flavours of the Eastern Mediterranean these lightly spiced meatballs are simple to prepare and are ideal for a quick family supper. Serve with crusty bread and a cucumber and feta cheese salad.

● SERVES 4 ● PREPARATION TIME: 15 MINUTES, PLUS MARINATING ● COOKING TIME: 15 MINUTES
● 222 CALS PER SERVING ● 12G FAT, OF WHICH 4.7G SATURATED FAT

1 large onion, peeled
1 green chilli
450g (1lb) extra-lean minced lamb
2.5ml (½ tsp) mild chilli seasoning
7.5ml (1½ tsp) ground cumin
2 garlic cloves, crushed
2.5ml (½ tsp) salt
2.5ml (½ tsp) pepper
grated rind and juice of 1 lemon
olive oil, for brushing

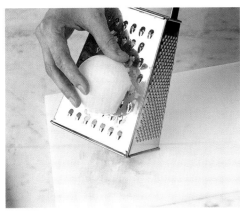

1 Grate the onions. Deseed and chop the chilli (wearing rubber gloves to avoid skin irritation).

2 Put all the ingredients (except the oil) in a bowl and mix thoroughly. Cover and refrigerate overnight.

3 Shape the mixture into 28 small balls, discarding any excess liquid that may result. Brush the grill rack and meatballs lightly with the olive oil.

4 Grill for 10–15 minutes under a high heat, turning and basting the meatballs frequently with oil.

LAMB FILLET AND PEPPER STIR-FRY

Tender slices of lamb and a colourful collection vegetables are quickly stir-fried so the vegetables remain crisp, then flavoured with a tangy garlic and onion sauce for a simple supper or quick lunch.

- SERVES 4 ● PREPARATION TIME: 10 MINUTES
- COOKING TIME: ABOUT 10 MINUTES
- 275 CALS PER SERVING ● 15G FAT, OF WHICH 5G SATURATED FAT

450g (1lb) lamb fillets
125g (4oz) carrots
2 celery sticks
1 red pepper
1 yellow pepper
30ml (2 tbsp) oil
125g (4oz) mangetout
1 large courgette, sliced
45ml (3 tbsp) garlic and spring onion sauce
(see Note)
15ml (1 tbsp) soy sauce
salt and ground black pepper

NOTE

- Bottled, ready-prepared garlic and spring onion sauce is available from large supermarkets and delicatessens. If you do not have any to hand, replace with 30ml (2 tbsp) sherry and 1 crushed garlic clove.

1 Thinly slice the lamb. Slice the carrots diagonally; thinly slice the celery. Halve, core and deseed the peppers, then slice.

2 Heat the oil in a large sauté pan or wok and quickly stir-fry the lamb for about 4 minutes, or until almost cooked through and golden brown. Remove from the pan with a slotted spoon and drain on kitchen paper.

3 Add the carrots, celery and peppers to the pan and stir-fry over a high heat for a further 3–4 minutes.

4 Add the remaining ingredients, together with the lamb, pouring over the garlic and spring onion sauce and soy sauce last. Cook for a further 2–3 minutes until the vegetables are just tender. Adjust the seasoning to serve.

SPICED LAMB ESCALOPES

Lean lamb escalopes marinated in a delicious combination of herbs, ginger, garlic, cloves, chilli and mint result in a delicately spiced and really tender dish.

● SERVES 4 ● PREPARATION TIME: 20 MINUTES, PLUS MARINATING ● COOKING TIME: 30 MINUTES
● 280 CALS PER SERVING ● 17G FAT, OF WHICH 6G SATURATED FAT

12 lean lamb escalopes, about 550g (1¼ lb) total weight
1 onion, peeled
30ml (2 tbsp) oil
2.5cm (1 inch) piece fresh root ginger
2 garlic cloves, peeled
pinch of ground cloves
30ml (2 tbsp) chopped mint
pinch of chilli powder
salt and ground black pepper
To garnish:
thinly sliced onions
lemon wedges
fresh mint sprigs

1 Place the lamb escalopes between two sheets of greaseproof paper and bat them out slightly with a rolling pin to tenderise and thin them.

NOTE
● Suitable for freezing from Step 4.

2 Finely chop the onion. Heat 15ml (1 tbsp) of oil in a small sauté pan and sauté the onion for about 10 minutes or until soft and golden brown. Set aside to cool.

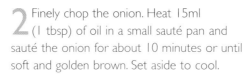

3 Peel and chop the ginger. Place in a blender or food processor with the garlic and 50ml (2fl oz) water. Blend to a smooth paste. Mix with the cloves, mint, chilli powder and cooled onion. Season with salt and pepper to taste.

4 Place the lamb escalopes in a large shallow non-metallic dish and spread with the onion mixture. Cover and leave to marinate for 1 hour.

5 Heat the remaining oil in a large sauté pan and brown the lamb escalopes well on both sides. Transfer to a shallow ovenproof casserole, cover with foil and a lid, and cook at 180°C (350°F) Mark 4 for 20 minutes. Serve garnished with onion slices, lemon wedges and mint sprigs.

PAN-FRIED LIVER WITH TOMATOES

Wafer-thin slices of liver are marinated in Marsala, cooked lightly, then served with a rich tomato and onion sauce in this dish where the meat melts in the mouth. Serve with noodles.

● SERVES 4 ● PREPARATION TIME: 15 MINUTES, PLUS MARINATING ● COOKING TIME: 10 MINUTES
● 300 CALS PER SERVING ●17.5G FAT, OF WHICH 4G SATURATED FAT

450g (1lb) lamb's liver
30ml (2 tbsp) Marsala or sweet sherry
salt and ground black pepper
225g (8oz) tomatoes
2 onions, peeled
30ml (2 tbsp) oil
pinch of ground ginger
150ml (¼ pint) lamb stock

1 Using a very sharp knife, cut the liver into wafer-thin strips. Place in a shallow bowl with the Marsala or sweet sherry. Sprinkle with pepper. Cover and leave to marinate for several hours.

2 Immerse the tomatoes in boiling water for 10–15 seconds; cool slightly, then peel away the skins. Cut the tomatoes into quarters and remove the seeds, reserving the juice. Slice the tomato flesh into fine strips and set aside. Finely slice the onions. Heat the oil in a sauté pan or non-stick frying pan. Add the onions and ginger and cook gently for about 5 minutes. Remove with a slotted spoon; set aside.

3 Add a quarter of the liver to the pan and shake briskly for about 30 seconds. Turn the slices and cook for 30 seconds. Remove with a slotted spoon; cook the remainder in batches. Return the onions and liver to the pan. Add the stock, tomatoes and juice, and seasoning; heat through, then serve.

LEMON-ROASTED PORK WITH GARLIC AND BASIL

This is an excellent way to cook pork – sealing in the flavour by searing the meat first, then roasting with garlic and fresh herbs so these impart their wonderful flavours further. Serve with sautéed shallots.

● SERVES 6 ● PREPARATION TIME: 20 MINUTES, PLUS MARINATING ● COOKING TIME: 40 MINUTES
● 105 CALS PER SERVING ● 6G FAT, OF WHICH 1.3G SATURATED FAT

2 lean pork fillets, each weighing about 350g (12oz)
finely grated rind and juice of 4 lemons
90ml (6 tbsp) chopped fresh basil or parsley
12 garlic cloves
salt and ground black pepper
2–3 bay leaves
30ml (2 tbsp) oil
To garnish:
fresh basil or parsley
lemon slices

2 Peel the garlic. Then blanch the cloves by immersing them briefly in fast boiling water. When cool enough to handle, halve any large cloves so that the pieces are of uniform size.

4 Close the pork fillets and tie loosely at 2.5cm (1 inch) intervals with cotton string. Place in a shallow, non-metallic dish with the bay leaves and strained lemon juice. Cover and leave to marinate in the refrigerator overnight.

1 Trim the pork fillets and split lengthways, without cutting right through. Open each fillet out flat. Sprinkle with the lemon rind and basil or parsley.

3 Halve any large garlic cloves. Lay the garlic cloves evenly along the middle of each fillet and season with salt and pepper.

5 Remove the pork and reserve the marinade. Heat the oil in a sauté pan and brown the meat all over. Transfer to a shallow roasting tin and pour over the marinade. Season and cook at 200°C (400°F) Mark 6 for 35 minutes, basting frequently. Serve sliced, garnished with herbs and lemon slices.

STIR-FRIED PORK WITH BABY CORN

An easy dish to make in the wok with a wonderful balance of crisp vegetables and succulent morsels of lean pork. Accompany with noodles tossed in a little oil and fresh herbs.

- SERVES 4 ● PREPARATION TIME: 10 MINUTES
- COOKING TIME: 10 MINUTES ● 240 CALS PER SERVING ● 10G FAT, OF WHICH 2.4G SATURATED FAT

450g (1lb) lean pork fillet
175g (6oz) carrots, peeled
175g (6oz) baby corn
175g (6oz) sugar-snap peas
salt and ground black pepper
30ml (2 tbsp) sunflower oil
60ml (4 tbsp) stir-fry chilli and tomato sauce
5ml (1 tsp) caster sugar
30ml (2 tbsp) wine vinegar
60ml (4 tbsp) light soy sauce

To garnish:
fresh chives
fresh parsley sprigs

1 Trim the pork fillet and cut across into 5mm (¼ inch) thick slices. Cut the carrots into matchsticks. Blanch the vegetables in boiling salted water for 2 minutes; drain and then refresh under cold running water. Drain thoroughly.

2 Heat the oil in a large wok or frying pan (preferably non-stick). Add the pork and stir-fry over a high heat for 2–3 minutes or until well browned and almost tender.

3 Add the vegetables and continue stir-frying over a high heat for 2–3 minutes until piping hot.

4 Mix in the remaining ingredients and bring to the boil, stirring well. Adjust the seasoning and serve, garnished with chives and parsley.

NOTE

- Bottled stir-fry chilli and tomato sauce is available from delicatessens and some larger supermarkets.

GLAZED BAKED GAMMON

This is a perfect joint to serve at larger gatherings as it looks very attractive, studded with cloves. The sweetness of the pork is heightened with the addition of a honey, mustard, ginger and orange glaze. Carve at the table for maximum impact.

● SERVES 8 ● PREPARATION TIME: 15 MINUTES, PLUS SOAKING ● COOKING TIME: 1 HOUR 45 MINUTES ● 400 CALS PER SERVING ● 12.4G FAT, OF WHICH 4.7G SATURATED FAT

1.8kg (4lb) smoked middle cut gammon joint
1 onion
about 16 cloves
1 bay leaf
6 peppercorns
300ml (½ pint) dry white wine
40g (1½oz) dark soft brown sugar
125ml (4fl oz) orange juice
15ml (1 tbsp) clear honey
2.5ml (½tsp) ground ginger
15ml (1 tbsp) Dijon mustard

1 Soak the gammon in sufficient cold water to cover for 3 hours, then discard the water. Place the gammon in a large saucepan.

2 Add the onion, stuck with 3 cloves, the bay leaf, peppercorns and 225ml (8fl oz) of the white wine. Add sufficient cold water to cover the joint. Bring to the boil, cover and simmer for 1 hour.

3 Meanwhile, make the glaze. Place the brown sugar, 30ml (2 tbsp) of the orange juice, the honey, ginger and mustard in a bowl and mix well. Drain the gammon and discard the onion, peppercorns and bay leaf. Remove the skin from the gammon and score the fat into a diamond pattern.

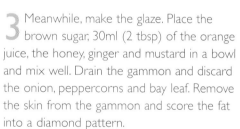

4 Stud with cloves and place in a baking dish. Pour the remaining wine and orange juice into the dish.

5 Spoon one-third of the glaze over the gammon. Bake at 200°C (400°F) Mark 6 for 45 minutes, basting with the pan juices and glaze 3–4 times during the cooking. Discard the pan juices and serve the gammon hot or cold, carved into slices.

BEEF SALAD WITH ROASTED VEGETABLE PASTE

This recipe is based on a Thai dish called larp which is similar to steak tartare. Here the beef is seared as a whole fillet, then sliced and served on a bed of tangy salad leaves. The dressing is a sweet and sour paste made from roasted vegetables; it has a distinctive Thai flavour that provides the perfect complement to the beef.

● SERVES 4 ● PREPARATION TIME: 35 MINUTES, PLUS MARINATING ● COOKING TIME: 30-35 MINUTES ● 210 CALS PER SERVING ● 13G FAT, OF WHICH 2.6G SATURATED FAT

225g (8oz) fillet steak
15ml (1 tbsp) Szechuan peppercorns
5ml (1 tsp) ground black pepper
5ml (1 tsp) ground coriander
1.25ml (¼ tsp) Chinese five-spice powder

Vegetable Paste:
225g (8oz) shallots, peeled
4–8 garlic cloves, peeled
2–3 large chillies, deseeded
2.5cm (1 inch) piece fresh root ginger, peeled
1 lemongrass stem
5ml (1 tsp) cumin seeds
45ml (3 tbsp) sunflower oil, plus extra for brushing
15ml (1 tbsp) tamarind paste (see below)
15ml (1 tbsp) light soy sauce or Thai fish sauce (nam pla)
10 ml (2 tsp) sugar

To serve:
125g (4oz) salad leaves
15ml (1 tbsp) sesame seeds
lime wedges

1 Preheat the oven to 200°C (400°F) Mark 6. Wash and dry the steak. Roughly grind the Szechuan peppercorns, using a pestle and mortar or spice grinder, and mix with the black pepper, ground coriander and five-spice powder. Spread on a board. Press the steak well down into the spice mixture, turning to coat well on both sides. Cover and set aside for 2 hours.

2 Meanwhile, prepare the vegetable paste. Halve any large shallots; roughly chop the garlic, chillies and ginger; finely chop the lemongrass. Place these ingredients in a small roasting pan with the cumin seeds. Pour over the oil and toss well until evenly combined. Transfer to the oven and roast for 30 minutes until browned and softened. Allow to cool slightly.

3 Transfer the roasted vegetables and spices to a food processor and add the tamarind paste, soy sauce or fish sauce, and the sugar. Purée to form a rough paste, adding a little water if too thick. Taste and add a little salt if necessary.

4 Brush a griddle or heavy-based frying pan with a little oil and heat. As soon as the oil starts to smoke, add the beef fillet and sear by pressing it down hard with a fish slice. Fry for 1 minute, turn the steak and repeat with the second side. Remove from the pan and leave to rest for 2 minutes.

5 Divide the salad leaves between individual serving plates. Thinly slice the beef fillet and arrange on the plates. Spoon on a little of the roasted vegetable paste and scatter over the sesame seeds. Serve at once, with lime wedges.

TAMARIND PASTE

This is a bean paste made from the tamarind plant, sold in block form. To make the paste, break 25g (1oz) off the block and blend in 45ml (3 tbsp) hot water. Press and use as required. Lemon juice is a suitable substitute.

VARIATION

● Replace the fillet steak with fresh tuna steak.

LAMB AND ROSEMARY RAGU

Ready-made pasta sauces are great to have on hand in the refrigerator or freezer, but some are far too heavily seasoned. Homemade, chilled tomato sauces freeze well and can be improved with clever additions, such as meat and herbs. This tasty ragu sauce can also be made with minced beef. Serve with salad and crusty bread.

● SERVES 4–6 ● PREPARATION TIME: 5 MINUTES
● COOKING TIME: 40 MINUTES ● 390–580 CALS
PER SERVING ● 14G–9G FAT, OF WHICH 6.3–4.5G
SATURATED FAT

450g (1lb) minced lamb
225g (8oz) large onion, finely chopped
1 sprig fresh rosemary or large pinch dried
200ml (7fl oz) red wine
350g (12oz) tub chilled fresh Napoletana sauce
salt and ground black pepper
350g (12oz) dried tagliatelle
Parmesan or feta cheese shavings, to serve
fresh rosemary sprigs, to garnish

1 Brown the minced lamb in a non-stick pan, stirring to break down any lumps. This will take a good 5–7 minutes. Remove the mince and set aside. Add the onion to the pan with the rosemary (you don't need to add any extra oil – there should be enough fat left over from the mince) and fry together until the onion is soft and golden – about 10 minutes.

2 Return the mince to the pan, keep over a high heat and stir in the wine. It should bubble immediately. Scrape the bottom of the pan to loosen any crusty bits then leave the wine to bubble for 1–2 minutes until reduced by half. Stir in the Napoletana sauce. Cover and simmer gently for 20 minutes. Season to taste.

3 Meanwhile, cook the tagliatelle in boiling salted water for about 10 minutes; drain. Stir in the lamb ragu, sprinkle the cheese over, garnish with rosemary and serve.

NOTE
● Suitable for freezing from step 2.

STIR-FRIED PORK WITH CHINESE GREENS

Unlike the fiddly preparation of some stir-fries, this one really is quick to make using the cheat's method of buying ready-prepared vegetables and pork that is already trimmed and cut in strips.

● SERVES 6 ● PREPARATION TIME: 5 MINUTES
● COOKING TIME: 10 MINUTES, PLUS MARINATING IF TIME ● 200 CALS PER SERVING ● 10G FAT PER SERVING, OF WHICH 2G SATURATED FAT

350g (12oz) stir-fry pork
60ml (4 tbsp) rice wine or dry sherry
30ml (2 tbsp) soy sauce
45ml (3 tbsp) stir-fry oil (see Note)
450g (1lb) Chinese greens
2 x 300g (11oz) bags fresh stir-fry vegetables
about 15ml (1 tbsp) Chinese five-spice paste

NOTE

● You can buy stir-fry oil which is a mix of sesame and sunflower oils with added garlic and ginger. It is ideal if you only cook stir-fries occasionally. Alternatively use a mix of sunflower and sesame oils.

1 Toss together the pork, rice wine or sherry and soy sauce with 15ml (1 tbsp) stir-fry oil (if there is time, leave the pork to marinate for 1 hour at this stage). Shred the Chinese greens and, together with the stir-fry vegetables, rinse in cold water.

2 Use a slotted spoon to lift the pork from the marinade; reserve the marinade. Heat a wok or large, deep frying pan until it's very hot. Add 15ml (1 tbsp) stir-fry oil to the wok, add half the pork (cook it in batches to ensure it fries and seals quickly) and stir-fry for about 1 minute or until beginning to brown at the edges. Set aside and stir-fry the remaining pork.

3 Wipe out the wok with kitchen paper, add the remaining oil and heat. Add the Chinese five-spice paste and all the vegetables and fry for a further 3–4 minutes. Return the pork and reserved marinade to the wok, bring to the boil and bubble for 1–2 minutes. Serve immediately.

SWEET AND SOUR SPICED PORK

Inspired by classic Chinese cookery, the combination of chilli, ginger and plum sauce is delicious with pork.

● SERVES 4 ● PREPARATION TIME: 30 MINUTES, PLUS CHILLING ● COOKING TIME: 50 MINUTES

● 410 CALS PER SERVING ● 15G FAT, OF WHICH 4G SATURATED FAT

2 garlic cloves
900g (2 lb) boneless loin of pork, rind removed
1 large red chilli
2.5cm (1 inch) piece fresh root ginger
150ml (¼ pint) plum sauce
15ml (1 tbsp) dark soy sauce
5ml (1 tsp) Chinese five-spice powder
30ml (2 tbsp) oil

To garnish:
½ cucumber
5 spring onions
1 red chilli

NOTE

● *To bat out the pork so that it is thin and tenderised, cover it with a sheet of greaseproof paper and flatten with a rolling pin to a thickness of about 6.5cm (2½ inches) – if it is any thicker the pork will take longer to cook.*
● *Take care not to brush too much plum sauce on the pork in the roasting tin as the sauce may burn the base.*

1 Thinly slice the garlic; trim the fat side of the loin of pork and lightly bat out (see Note). Turn the loin over and, using a small sharp knife, make deep slits in the meat then insert the slices of garlic.

2 Deseed and finely chop the chilli (wearing rubber gloves to avoid skin irritation); peel and finely chop the ginger. Place in a bowl with 15ml (1 tbsp) water, plum sauce, soy sauce and Chinese five-spice powder.

3 Heat the oil in a small roasting tin on the hob and brown the meat, fat-side down, for 5 minutes. Turn over and brown the other side for 2–3 minutes. Brush the surface of the pork with a little of the plum sauce mixture and transfer to the oven. Cook at 200°C (400°F) Mark 6 for about 40 minutes. Baste the pork occasionally, brushing with some of the plum sauce mixture (see Note) until the fat has caramelised and the pork is cooked.

4 For the garnish: cut the cucumber in half lengthways, remove the seeds with a teaspoon and discard, then cut the flesh into thin matchsticks.

5 Cut the trimmed spring onions into long thin strips. Deseed the red chilli and also cut into very fine matchsticks. Place the cucumber and onion in a large bowl of ice-cold water for about 15 minutes until the spring onions begin to curl. Drain and dry well.

6 Lift the pork from the roasting tin, cover loosely with foil; keep warm. Tilt the roasting tin and skim off the fat. Add the remaining plum sauce mixture to the juices in the roasting tin, bring to the boil and simmer for 1–2 minutes.

7 To serve, thickly slice the pork, spoon the sauce around it and garnish with the cucumber, spring onions and chilli.

PASTA AND RICE

P asta and rice are quick and easy to prepare, satisfying to eat and nutritionally balanced. High in fibre and low in fat and calories, they are the perfect fast food for all the family. Pasta sauces are where you have to be careful or else fat and calories can come creeping in, but the good news is that indulgent sauces can be achieved without being fattening. Choose low-fat cheeses, skimmed milk or low-fat yogurt in place of cream, make the most of vegetables and use herbs as seasoning. Always try to keep to a minimum the amount of oil and butter you cook with in sauces.

There are so many varieties of pasta now readily available it can be hard to choose, but the general rule is that fine spaghetti and noodles are good with delicate or creamy sauces, smaller shell shapes are suited to holding lots of sauce and larger pasta shapes are good with more chunky vegetable sauces. The best way to cook pasta until *al dente*, still with a little bite, is in fast boiling water according to the packet instructions.

Cooking rice isn't difficult – it just needs a little care and attention. Choose from the creamy, nutty-textured Italian risotto rice (arborio) to long-grain or wild rice. The recipes here also include other grains and noodles, all of which are easy to cook and low in fat. Many of these dishes can be served as starters, accompaniments or as meals in themselves.

WARM SEAFOOD AND PASTA SALAD

This dish is delicious served warm or cold. To save time, the recipe uses a jar of Seafood Antipasto, which comes in a dressing and is available from delicatessens and supermarkets, but it also works well with chicken or prawns (see Variations).

● SERVES 4 ● PREPARATION TIME: 10 MINUTES
● COOKING TIME: 10 MINUTES ● 360 CALS
PER SERVING ● 15.8G FAT, OF WHICH 2.8G
SATURATED FAT

175g (6oz) pasta shapes
285g (9oz) jar Seafood Antipasto
grated rind and juice of 2 limes
2 red chillies, deseeded and finely chopped
salt and ground black pepper
225g (8oz) yellow cherry tomatoes, halved
1 large avocado, thickly sliced
1 red onion, finely sliced
50g (2oz) large green olives, cut into quarters
45ml (3 tbsp) roughly chopped fresh coriander

VARIATIONS

● As an alternative, replace the seafood with either 300g (11oz) smoked chicken, cut into slices, or 350g (12oz) cooked peeled prawns. If you do this, make the dressing using 45ml (3 tbsp) olive oil and 15ml (1 tbsp) rice wine vinegar, then continue as from step 2.

1 Cook the pasta in a large pan of boiling water according to the packet instructions until al dente. Drain and transfer to a serving dish. Drain the seafood and set aside, reserving the dressing.

2 Whisk the lime rind, juice and chillies into the reserved seafood dressing. Season to taste with salt and pepper.

3 Stir the seafood, tomatoes, avocado, onion, olives and coriander into the pasta. Pour the dressing over, stir all the ingredients together well and serve immediately.

TAGLIATELLE WITH CHICKEN LIVERS AND SPINACH

The liver and spinach in this rich and highly nutritious pasta dish are high in iron and just one serving of this dish will provide over half a woman's recommended daily intake (14.8 mg).

● SERVES 6 ● PREPARATION TIME: 25 MINUTES
● COOKING TIME: 30 MINUTES ● 395 CALS PER
SERVING ● 13G FAT, OF WHICH 3G SATURATED FAT

45ml (3 tbsp) olive oil
*450g (1lb) chicken livers, rinsed and chopped, with
any fibrous bits discarded*
125g (4oz) mixed red and yellow cherry tomatoes
75g (3oz) smoked back bacon, cut into thin strips
2 red onions, sliced into thick wedges
4 garlic cloves, crushed
30ml (2 tbsp) sun-dried tomato paste
150ml (¼ pint) sherry
150ml (¼ pint) chicken stock
30ml (2 tbsp) balsamic vinegar
salt and ground black pepper
300g (11oz) dried tagliatelle
350g (12oz) fresh young spinach

1 Heat 15ml (1 tbsp) oil in a large non-stick frying pan. Once it's really hot, fry the livers in batches over a high heat, stirring, for 5 minutes or until just browned (take care as the pieces may splutter). Using a slotted spoon, remove the livers from the pan and set aside. Add the tomatoes and cook, stirring, for 1–2 minutes. Remove and set aside.

2 Add the remaining oil with the bacon and fry until it starts to become crisp. Add the onions and garlic and cook over a medium heat, stirring frequently, for 10–15 minutes or until the onion is soft.

3 Add the tomato paste, sherry, chicken stock and balsamic vinegar. Bring to the boil and bubble for 5 minutes or until syrupy. Return the chicken livers and tomatoes to the pan, season to taste with salt and pepper and stir gently for 1–2 minutes or until the mixture is heated through.

4 Meanwhile, cook the pasta according to the packet instructions until *al dente*, then drain well. Before serving, stir the spinach into the sauce and heat until it begins to wilt. Serve the pasta in warmed serving bowls and pour the sauce over.

ORECCHIETTE WITH PEPPERS, CAPERS AND ANCHOVIES

It really is worthwhile roasting the peppers in this instance because it concentrates their flavour, producing a mellow, smoky and sweet taste. Take care when seasoning the recipe as anchovies are already salty. Serve with crusty bread.

● SERVES 4 ● PREPARATION TIME: 20 MINUTES, PLUS STANDING ● COOKING TIME: 30 MINUTES
● 520 CALS PER SERVING ● 11.5G FAT, OF WHICH 1.2G SATURATED FAT

3 red peppers, halved and deseeded
2 yellow peppers, halved and deseeded
350g (12oz) orecchiette pasta
30ml (2 tbsp) olive oil
2 garlic cloves, crushed
½ level tsp dried, crushed red chillies
50g (2oz) can anchovy fillets in oil, drained and chopped
400g (15oz) can chopped plum tomatoes
30ml (2 tbsp) capers, drained and rinsed
salt and ground black pepper
lemon juice, to taste
anchovy fillets, to garnish

NOTES

● Orecchiette, which means 'tiny ears' in Italian, is available from some supermarkets, or specialist Italian delicatessens and food shops. You can use small pasta shells if you prefer.
● It's difficult to give specific quantity guidelines for pasta because of the nature of the sauce and whether the dish is to be served as a starter, light lunch or main meal. As a rough guide, allow about 75–125g (3–4oz) pasta (uncooked weight) per person, cooked in 600ml (1 pint) water.

1 Preheat the grill to high. Place the peppers on a baking sheet, skin-side up, and grill for 6–8 minutes or until the skins turn black all over. Put the peppers in a bowl, cover with a damp cloth and set aside for 15 minutes (the steam will help to loosen the skin). Peel the peppers and slice into thin strips.

2 Cook the pasta according to packet instructions until al dente. Meanwhile, heat the oil, add the garlic and chillies and fry for 30 seconds. Add the anchovies, tomatoes and the peppers and cook for a further 1–2 minutes. Drain the pasta and add to the sauce with the capers, toss together, then check the seasoning and add lemon juice to taste. Lay the anchovy fillets on top to garnish and serve immediately.

SPAGHETTI WITH CHILLI AND GARLIC

This simple, classic recipe is known throughout Italy as *aglio olio*. It makes a substantial lunch or supper, and needs only to be followed by a fresh green salad.

● SERVES 4 ● PREPARATION TIME: 10 MINUTES
● COOKING TIME: 15 MINUTES ● 410 CALS PER
SERVING ● 12.6G FAT, OF WHICH 1.6G SATURATED
FAT

350g (12oz) spaghetti
60ml (4 tbsp) olive oil
6 garlic cloves, sliced
1–2 large red chillies, deseeded and sliced
salt and ground black pepper
To garnish:
flatleaf parsley
black olives

NOTES

● *The authentic way to serve pasta is to toss the pasta with the sauce before serving, rather than just spooning it on top.*
● *To remove the smell of garlic from your hands, rub half a cut lemon over them and rinse under warm running water.*

1 Bring a large pan of salted water to the boil, add the pasta and cook according to packet instructions until *al dente*; drain and set aside.

2 Meanwhile, heat the oil in a pan, add the garlic and chillies and cook for 2 minutes or until the garlic is golden and the chillies have softened. Pour over the pasta, toss and season. Garnish with the parsley and olives, then serve immediately.

MEE GORENG

This is a traditional Malaysian dish – Mee meaning 'noodles' and Goreng meaning 'fried' – combining seafood, steak and spices. For a less elaborate dish you can simply omit the squid and replace the raw prawns with cooked peeled prawns – increasing the weight to 225g (8oz).

● SERVES 4–6 ● PREPARATION TIME: 30 MINUTES ● COOKING TIME: ABOUT 10 MINUTES ● 465–310 CALS PER SERVING ● 14.6G–10G FAT, OF WHICH 3.4G–2.3G SATURATED FAT

125g (4oz) rump steak
2 garlic cloves, crushed
30ml (2 tbsp) soy sauce
450g (1lb) squid
175g (6oz) large raw prawns
225g (8oz) medium egg noodles
salt
1–2 hot red chillies
2.5cm (1 inch) piece fresh root ginger
2–3 spring onions
15ml (1 tbsp) vegetable oil
15ml (1 tbsp) sesame or peanut oil
30ml (2 tbsp) hoisin sauce
15ml (1 tbsp) lemon juice
30ml (2 tbsp) Thai fish sauce (nam pla)
125g (4oz) beansprouts

To garnish:
shredded lettuce
lemon wedges

1 Cut the steak into wafer-thin slices across the grain. Place in a shallow dish with half of the garlic and half of the soy sauce. Leave to stand.

2 Rinse the squid then, holding the body in one hand, firmly pull the tentacles with the other hand to remove the soft contents of the body. Cut the tentacles just in front of the eyes and discard the body contents. Cut the tentacles into small pieces.

3 Squeeze out the plastic-like quill from the body and discard. Rinse the body under cold running water, making sure that it is clean inside. Rub off the fine dark skin, then cut the body into rings or small rectangular pieces using a sharp knife.

4 Peel the prawns, leaving the tail end attached. Using a small sharp knife, make a shallow slit along the outer curve from the tail to the head end and remove the dark intestinal vein. Rinse under cold running water, drain and pat dry with kitchen paper.

5 Cook the noodles in a large saucepan of generously salted boiling water. Bring to the boil and turn off the heat. Leave to stand and cook in the residual heat according to packet instructions. Cook the seafood.

6 Chop the chillies (wearing rubber gloves to avoid skin irritation), discarding the seeds if a milder flavour is preferred. Peel and finely chop the ginger. Trim and slice the spring onions. Heat the oils in a wok or large frying pan, add the remaining garlic, chillies, ginger and spring onions, and cook for 2 minutes, stirring all the time.

7 Add the beef and cook for 2 minutes. Add the squid and prawns and cook for 2 minutes. Add the hoisin sauce, lemon juice, fish sauce and remaining soy sauce and cook for 2 more minutes.

8 Drain the noodles and add to the pan with the beansprouts. Heat through for 2 minutes, then add the beaten egg. Cook briefly until the egg is on setting point; remove from the heat. Serve garnished with a mound of shredded lettuce and lemon wedges.

BROAD BEAN AND LEMON RISOTTO

The lemon adds a wonderful contrasting piquancy to the creaminess of the risotto and the buttery broad beans. The broad beans also, in common with other beans and pulses, are a good source of dietary fibre, particularly soluble fibre, which can help reduce high blood cholesterol levels. They also provide useful amounts of vitamin B1 and iron.

- SERVES 4 ● PREPARATION TIME: 25 MINUTES
- COOKING TIME: 35 MINUTES ● 380 CALS PER SERVING 12 ● 12G FAT PER SERVING, OF WHICH 7G SATURATED FAT

350g (12oz) frozen broad beans
salt and ground pepper
25g (1oz) butter
1 medium onion, finely chopped
200g (7oz) arborio (risotto) rice
1 litre (1¾ pints) hot vegetable stock
grated rind and juice of 1 lemon
75g (3oz) freshly grated Parmesan
To garnish:
grated Parmesan
lemon rind

1 Cook the broad beans in a large pan of boiling salted water for 3–5 minutes or until just tender. Plunge into ice-cold water to cool. Drain, peel off the outer skin, if wished, and set aside.

2 Melt the butter in large saucepan, add the onion and cook over a medium heat for 5 minutes or until beginning to soften. Add the rice and continue to cook, stirring, for 1–2 minutes.

3 Pour in a ladleful of the hot stock and simmer gently, stirring frequently until the rice has absorbed most of it. Keep adding the stock in this way until the rice is tender but still has bite to it; this will take about 15–20 minutes. The risotto should look creamy and soft when cooked.

4 Add the broad beans, lemon rind and juice and warm through. Stir in the Parmesan and season to taste.

5 Serve the risotto immediately, garnished with grated Parmesan and lemon rind.

PRAWN AND LEMON RISOTTO

The great thing about risotto is that it is filling without being fattening. This risotto looks as superb as it tastes – dotted with the fresh green of the peas and chives against the creamy yellow of the rice and flecked with gold from the saffron.

● SERVES 4 ● PREPARATION TIME: 15 MINUTES
● COOKING TIME: 40 MINUTES ● 370 CALS PER
SERVING ● 7G FAT, OF WHICH 0.9G SATURATED FAT

225g (8oz) sugar-snap peas, sliced diagonally
175g (6oz) baby courgettes, sliced diagonally
salt and ground black pepper
30ml (2 tbsp) olive oil
1 onion, finely chopped
1.25ml (¼ tsp) saffron strands (optional)
225g (8oz) arborio (risotto) rice
1 garlic clove, crushed
225g (8oz) brown-cap mushrooms, quartered
grated rind and juice of 1 lemon
750ml (1¼ pints) hot fish, chicken or vegetable stock
300g (11oz) cooked prawns
45ml (3 tbsp) finely chopped fresh chives
To garnish:
spring onion curls (see Note)
grated lemon rind

1 Place the sugar-snap peas and courgettes in a large saucepan of boiling salted water, then bring to the boil. Cook for 1–2 minutes, then drain and plunge into ice-cold water.

2 Heat the olive oil in a medium, non-stick saucepan, then add the onion and saffron strands, if using. Cook over a medium heat for 10 minutes or until soft. Add the rice, garlic and mushrooms and cook, stirring for 1–2 minutes; season.

3 Add the grated lemon rind and about one-third of the stock (see Note). Simmer gently, stirring frequently, until most of the liquid has been absorbed. Add another one-third of the stock, then repeat the process.

4 Add the remaining stock. Cover, stirring, for 10 minutes or until the rice is tender and most of the stock has been absorbed.

5 Meanwhile, using a sharp knife, peel away the shells of the cooked prawns. Add the prawns, drained vegetables, 15–30ml (1–2 tbsp) lemon juice and the chives to the pan, then heat for 3–4 minutes. Garnish with spring onion curls and grated lemon rind to serve.

NOTES

● To make spring onion curls, thinly slice the onions lengthways, soak in ice-cold water for 30 minutes, then drain.
● Always use arborio or risotto rice – the grains are thick, short and starchy, giving the risotto its wonderful creamy texture.
● The stock should always be hot when added to the pan to maintain the risotto's temperature.
● Adding the stock gradually gives the risotto its creamy texture.
● Keep the mixture gently simmering and keep testing the rice – it should be soft on the outside but still have a little bite in the centre.

GARLIC AND PARMESAN RISOTTO

Next to pasta, risotto is one of the simplest and most satisfying suppers and just as versatile. It just falls outside the 'quick' category, but it's one of the most delicious one-pot recipes. If you've never tried making a risotto, this is a good one to start with.

● SERVES 4 ● PREPARATION TIME: 5 MINUTES
● COOKING TIME: 35 MINUTES ● 290 CALS PER
SERVING ● 11.5G FAT, OF WHICH 7G SATURATED FAT

750–900ml (1¼ –1½ pints) light vegetable stock
with a splash of white wine (optional)
50g (2oz) butter
175g (6oz) onion, finely chopped
3 garlic cloves, crushed
225g (8oz) arborio (risotto) rice
50g (2oz) grated Parmesan, plus extra, to serve
salt and ground black pepper
60–75ml (4–5 tbsp) chopped fresh parsley

1 Heat the stock and keep it hot over a low heat. Meanwhile, melt half the butter in a large heavy-based saucepan and stir in the onion. Cook for 8–10 minutes until very soft but not coloured, then stir in the garlic and rice. Stir thoroughly over the heat to fry the rice lightly in the butter for 2–3 minutes.

2 Pour in a ladleful of the hot stock and let it simmer gently, stirring frequently until most of the stock has been absorbed. Keep adding the stock in this way until the rice is tender but still has a little bite to it; this will take 20–25 minutes and the end result should look creamy and soft.

3 Stir in the remaining butter, along with the Parmesan, seasoning and parsley. Serve with grated Parmesan.

VARIATIONS

● Fry 125g (4oz) chopped smoked back bacon until browned, add 125g (4oz) sliced mushrooms, cook for 2–3 minutes, then add the rice and cook for 2–3 minutes. Continue as for the Garlic and Parmesan Risotto but omit the Parmesan and serve with one softly poached egg per person. (Remember that the young, the elderly, pregnant women and those suffering from immune-deficiency diseases should avoid raw or lightly cooked eggs, which may contain salmonella.)
● Stir 125g (4oz) diced mozzarella cheese into the risotto just before serving.

NOTE

● When adding the stock, stir continuously to ensure the risotto has a creamy texture.

AUBERGINE AND CHICKPEA PILAF

A simple, yet elegant and fragrant dish, this pilaf uses long-grain rice, which is cooked with chickpeas and delicately spiced with cumin seeds.

● SERVES 6 ● PREPARATION TIME: 10 MINUTES ● COOKING TIME: 20 MINUTES, PLUS 5 MINUTES STANDING ● 290 CALS PER SERVING ● 13G FAT, OF WHICH 4G SATURATED FAT

60–90ml (4–6 tbsp) olive oil
275g (10oz) aubergine, roughly chopped
225g (8oz) onions, finely chopped
25g (1oz) butter
2.5ml (½ tsp) cumin seeds
175g (6oz) long-grain rice
600ml (1 pint) vegetable or chicken stock (see Note)
salt and ground black pepper
400g (15oz) can chickpeas, drained and rinsed
225g (8oz) baby spinach

NOTE

● Use homemade stock for best results, or use a 'fresh', ready-made stock available from chill cabinets in larger supermarkets.

1 Heat half the olive oil in a large pan or flameproof casserole. Fry the aubergine for 4–5 minutes in batches until deep golden brown. Remove from the pan with a slotted spoon and set aside. Add the remaining oil to the pan and cook the onions for 5 minutes or until golden and soft.

2 Add the butter, then stir in the cumin seeds and rice. Fry for 1–2 minutes, pour the stock over, season and bring to the boil. Reduce the heat, then simmer, uncovered, for 10–12 minutes or until most of the liquid has evaporated and the rice is tender.

3 Remove the pan from the heat. Stir in the chickpeas, spinach and reserved aubergine. Cover with a tight-fitting lid and leave to stand for 5 minutes until the spinach is wilted and the chickpeas are heated through. Adjust the seasoning to taste. Fork through the rice grains to separate so they are fluffy. Serve immediately.

RICE AND DAL PILAF

Chana dal is a mustard yellow coloured dal that is sold hulled and split by Indian and Pakistani grocers. Alternatively you can substitute yellow split peas. Here it is cooked with rice, nuts and sesame seeds to make a delicious and nutritious accompaniment. As it is packed with protein, this dish also makes a good basis for a vegetarian meal.

● SERVES 4–6 ● PREPARATION TIME: ABOUT 15 MINUTES, PLUS SOAKING ● COOKING TIME: 30 MINUTES, PLUS STANDING ● 580–355 CALS PER SERVING ● 18.8–12.5G FAT, OF WHICH 2–1.4G SATURATED FAT

50g (2oz) chana dal
350g (12oz) basmati rice
1 medium onion
1–2 garlic cloves (optional)
1 hot green chilli, or 2 dried red chillies
60ml (4 tbsp) vegetable oil
40g (1½oz) cashew nuts
10ml (2 tsp) cumin seeds
4 pieces cassia bark, or 1 cinnamon stick
1 bay leaf
600ml (1 pint) vegetable stock
5ml (1 tsp) salt, or to taste
15ml (1 tbsp) toasted sesame seeds
large pinch of garam masala, to serve

1 Pick over the dal, removing any small stones or green coloured pieces. Wash thoroughly under cold running water, then put in a bowl with plenty of cold water to cover and leave to soak for 3 hours.

2 Wash the rice in a sieve under cold running water, then put in a bowl and add plenty of cold water to cover. Leave to soak for 1 hour.

3 Peel and halve the onion, then cut into thin semi-circular slices. Peel and thinly slice the garlic, if using. Slice the fresh green chilli (wearing rubber gloves to prevent skin irritation), discarding the seeds for a milder flavour. If using dried chillies, leave whole.

4 Heat the oil in a large heavy-based saucepan or flameproof casserole. Add the cashew nuts and fry over a high heat until golden brown. Remove from the pan with a slotted spoon and drain the excess oil on kitchen paper; set aside.

5 Add the onion and garlic to the pan and cook, stirring, until the onion is just tinged with brown. Add the chilli and spices and cook for 1 minute, stirring all the time. Lower the heat slightly. Thoroughly drain the dal and add to the pan. Add the stock and salt.

6 Quickly bring to the boil, stir with a fork, then cover with a tight-fitting lid. Lower the heat and simmer for 10 minutes. Drain the rice and add to the pan; cover again and cook for a further 10 minutes. Shake the pan occasionally as it cooks but resist the temptation to lift the lid or precious steam will escape and the rice is more likely to stick and burn on the base of the pan.

7 Switch off the heat and leave the pan undisturbed for 10 minutes. Turn the rice and dal onto a serving dish and fluff up the grains with a fork. Check the seasoning, adding a little extra salt if necessary. Sprinkle with the cashews, sesame seeds and garam masala before serving.

RICE WITH ASPARAGUS, CRAB AND PINEAPPLE

In this exotic dish, cooked rice is tossed with stir-fried vegetables and spices, and heated through. The combination of flavours is exciting and delicious and that typical sweet and sour taste so inherent of Thai dishes is provided by the fresh pineapple.

- SERVES 4 ● PREPARATION TIME: 30 MINUTES
- COOKING TIME: 15 MINUTES, PLUS THE RICE
- 250 CALS PER SERVING ● 12G FAT, OF WHICH 2G SATURATED FAT

2 fresh small green chillies, seeded
2 garlic cloves, peeled
4 spring onions, trimmed
225g (8oz) thin asparagus spears, trimmed
125g (4oz) fresh pineapple slices
30ml (2 tbsp) sunflower oil
5ml (1 tsp) paprika
2.5ml (½ tsp) ground coriander
1.25ml (¼ tsp) cayenne pepper
225g (8oz) cooked Thai fragrant rice (see below)
150g (5oz) white crab meat, fresh or frozen and thawed
2 eggs, beaten
15ml (1 tbsp) Thai fish sauce (nam pla)
15ml (1 tbsp) lime juice
salt and ground black pepper
lime wedges, to serve

1 Finely chop the chillies, garlic and spring onions; cut the asparagus spears into short lengths. Remove the core from the pineapple slices and cut into chunks.

3 Add the eggs to the pan and stir over a high heat for 2–3 minutes until just set. Add the pineapple chunks, fish sauce and lime juice. Cover and heat through for 5 minutes. Season with salt and pepper to taste. Serve at once, with the lime wedges.

NOTE

● When possible buy fresh crab meat from your fishmonger or supermarket fresh fish counter; alternatively buy freshly frozen meat. Both of these are superior to canned crab meat which should only be used as a last resort.

2 Heat the oil in a wok, add the chillies, garlic, spring onions and spices and fry over a low heat for 5 minutes. Increase the heat and add the asparagus. Stir-fry for 2 minutes, then add the rice and crab meat and stir-fry for a further 2–3 minutes.

THAI FRAGRANT RICE

Thai fragrant rice is available from some supermarkets. To cook perfect Thai rice, wash 225g (8oz) Thai fragrant rice under cold running water for several minutes, until the water runs clear. Put the rice in a heavy-based saucepan and add 300ml (½ pint) cold water. Cover and bring quickly to the boil. As soon as the water boils, remove the lid and stir over a medium heat until all the water has evaporated. Replace the lid (making sure it fits tightly) and set over a low heat for 20 minutes allowing the rice to steam. The resulting rice should be light, soft and fluffy.

VEGETABLES AND SALADS

An amazing selection of vegetables can be bought these day – and, if you grow your own produce, you will know how good really fresh vegetables taste. Spring and summer months offer a wonderful variety including tender asparagus, broad beans, the sweetest peas, a huge selection of salad leaves, tender young beans and fennel and a vast array of herbs like parsley, basil, chervil and mint. And of course there are also the earthy root vegetables that winter brings, plus Chinese greens and the more unusual vegetables from overseas that are readily available – although often at a price.

Low in fat, high in fibre and full of vitamins and minerals, vegetables are nutritionally excellent. Choose the freshest produce and preferably vegetables that are in season to ensure they contain the maximum amount of goodness.

In this chapter you will find suggestions for salad and vegetable dishes, hot and cold, light or filling that can be served as starters, side dishes, light meals or as part of a buffet. They range from the simple, yet visually stunning Three Tomato Salad to the more substantial Wild Rice and Thyme Salad. Chinese Braised Vegetables can be served as a side dish or with rice as a main course, while the Sweet Potato Purée makes an ideal accompaniment to many spicy dishes. Okra Tagine, Winter Vegetable Roast and Stir-fried Summer Vegetables on the other hand are meals in themselves. Not all the recipes are vegetable only – chicken, sausages and seafood are also included in this varied selection.

MUSTARD-SEEDED OKRA

Okra, known as lady's fingers, is available from most major supermarkets. It has a juicy texture and needs to be seasoned generously to taste. If it's unavailable, you could use green beans or broccoli as an alternative.

● SERVES 8 ● PREPARATION TIME: 10 MINUTES
● COOKING TIME: 5 MINUTES ● 40 CALS PER SERVING ● 2G FAT, OF WHICH 0.5G SATURATED FAT

700g (1½lb) okra (see Note)
salt and ground black pepper
15ml (1 tbsp) oil
30ml (2 tbsp) mustard seeds
1 garlic clove

1 Trim the okra, then cook it in a large pan of boiling, salted water for 3–4 minutes or until tender; drain.

2 Place the oil, mustard seeds and crushed garlic in a large, dry saucepan and cook until the mustard seeds change colour and become golden brown and pop – take care, they may splutter! Toss the okra through the flavourings, season well and serve.

GRILLED PEPPERS WITH PINENUTS

Look for the sweetest, juiciest peppers for this dish. The soured cream and pinenuts are the perfect complements for the sweet peppers.

● SERVES 2 ● PREPARATION TIME: 5 MINUTES
● COOKING TIME: 5–10 MINUTES ● 185 CALS
PER SERVING ● 13.5G FAT, OF WHICH 1.4G
SATURATED FAT

2 ramiro sweet pointed, yellow peppers
olive oil, for brushing
5ml (1 tsp) crushed coriander seeds
30ml (2 tbsp) mixed pinenuts and flaked almonds
soured cream, to serve
fresh chopped oregano, to garnish

Brush the yellow peppers with a little olive oil and sprinkle with 5ml (1 tsp) crushed coriander seeds. Grill the peppers for 5–10 minutes until charred and tender. Sprinkle over the mixed pinenuts and flaked almonds for the last 2 minutes of the cooking time. Season and serve with soured cream and garnish with the oregano.

NOTE

● Look out for ramiro sweet pointed peppers – long thin peppers with a delicious sweet flavour, or Italian-style extra sweet peppers for the best results. These are available from some major supermarkets.

GLAZED SHALLOTS WITH BALSAMIC VINEGAR

Here the shallots are caramelised, giving them a wonderful sweetness. The balsamic vinegar adds the final concentration of flavour to these golden, tender onions.

● SERVES 8–10 ● PREPARATION TIME: 20 MINUTES ● COOKING TIME: 15–20 MINUTES ● 69–55 CALS PER SERVING ● 4.3–3.5G FAT, OF WHICH 2.7–2.2G SATURATED FAT

1kg (2¼lb) medium shallots, peeled, roots left intact
40g (1½oz) butter
15ml (1 tbsp) caster sugar
salt and ground black pepper
30ml (2 tbsp) balsamic vinegar

NOTES

● *If the shallots aren't cooked but are starting to overbrown, add a little cold water to the saucepan. This will bring the temperature down so you can continue to cook them without burning.*
● *Suitable for freezing.*

1 Place the shallots in a large saucepan of cold water; bring to the boil and cook for 5 minutes or until just soft; drain.

2 Heat the butter in a wide, heavy-based saucepan. Add the shallots, caster sugar and seasoning. Cook over a moderate heat, stirring occasionally, for 15–20 minutes or until the shallots are brown, shiny and cooked through to the centre. Add the vinegar; bring to the boil and bubble until the liquid has evaporated. Serve immediately.

WINTER VEGETABLE ROAST

Any seasonal root vegetables can be used in this recipe, but make sure you use a good mix of pale and colourful vegetables.

● SERVES 6 ● PREPARATION TIME: 20 MINUTES
● COOKING TIME: 50 MINUTES ● 260 CALS PER
SERVING ● 19G FAT, OF WHICH 1.2G SATURATED FAT

1.4kg (3lb) mixed root vegetables, such as carrots,
sweet potato, parsnips, celeriac, turnips, squash or
salsify, and pumpkin
150g (5oz) shallots, skin removed and root
left intact
60ml (4 tbsp) olive oil
salt and ground black pepper
150g (5oz) spicy sausages, such as merguez, twisted
in half and cut in two
125g (4oz) vacuum-packed chestnuts

2 Place all the vegetables in a roasting tin, drizzle with olive oil and season.

3 Cook on the top shelf of the oven at 200°C (400°F) Mark 6 for 25 minutes, add the sausages and return to the oven for 15 minutes, stirring occasionally. Finally, add the chestnuts and cook for 15 minutes or until the vegetables are golden brown.

1 Peel and cut the vegetables into rough chunks keeping the sweet potato and pumpkin in larger pieces. Cut the shallots in half lengthways if large.

BROAD BEANS WITH ARTICHOKES AND CUMIN

A slightly unusual, but delicious combination of flavours are blended together for a tasty dish that can be served in its own right or as a starter with warmed flatbread or French bread.

- SERVES 6 ● PREPARATION TIME: 10 MINUTES
- COOKING TIME: 20 MINUTES ● 115 CALS PER
SERVING ● 5G FAT, OF WHICH 0.8G SATURATED FAT

450g (1lb) shelled, small broad beans
salt and ground black pepper
1 onion, peeled
400g (14oz) can artichoke hearts, drained
75g (3oz) sliced raw cured ham, such as jamón
serrano, or prosciutto
30ml (2 tbsp) olive oil
2 garlic cloves, crushed
5ml (1 tsp) ground cumin
2 bay leaves
pinch of powdered saffron
60ml (4 tbsp) dry white wine
45ml (3 tbsp) chopped fresh parsley

1 Cook the broad beans in boiling salted water until just tender, refresh in cold water, then drain.

2 Meanwhile, chop the onion, halve the artichoke hearts and slice the ham into small pieces.

3 Heat the oil in a large sauté pan. Add the onion and garlic and fry until just beginning to brown. Stir in the cumin and cook for 1 minute more.

4 Mix in the artichokes, broad beans, bay leaves, saffron and seasoning. Pour in the wine with 100ml (4fl oz) water. Cover and allow to simmer for 5 minutes.

5 Stir in the ham and chopped parsley, then simmer for 2–3 minutes. Check the seasoning and serve immediately.

FRENCH BEANS WITH TOMATOES AND HERBS

A simple, but great way to utilise the wonderful produce of summer: tender French beans are cooked with tomatoes that are reduced to a sweet sauce, then served with fresh herbs.

● SERVES 6 ● PREPARATION TIME: 15 MINUTES
● COOKING TIME: ABOUT 20 MINUTES ● 81 CALS
PER SERVING ● 4.5G FAT, OF WHICH 0.7G
SATURATED FAT

400g (1lb) tomatoes
1 large onion
700g (1½ lb) French beans
salt and ground black pepper
30ml (2 tbsp) olive oil
1 garlic clove
15ml (1 tbsp) chopped fresh parsley
fresh basil leaves

3 Heat the oil in a saucepan. Add the onion and fry until beginning to colour. Stir in the tomatoes with the garlic. Cook covered, for about 5 minutes

4 Mix in the beans, cover and cook gently for a further 10 minutes, or until the beans are tender and the sauce is reduced. Stir in the herbs and season with salt and pepper to taste.

1 To peel the tomatoes, make four slits through the skin at the core with a sharp knife. Immerse the tomatoes in boiling water for 30 seconds, cool, then peel away the skin. Roughly chop the tomatoes. Peel and chop the onion.

2 Halve the French beans and cook in boiling salted water for 2 minutes only; drain.

CHINESE BRAISED VEGETABLES

This authentic tasting Chinese vegetable dish is quick and easy to prepare and the ingredients are all readily available.

● SERVES 8 ● PREPARATION TIME: 20 MINUTES, PLUS SOAKING ● COOKING TIME: 5–6 MINUTES ●
110 CALS PER SERVING ● 5G FAT, OF WHICH 0.5G SATURATED FAT

10 dried Chinese mushrooms
1 Chinese cabbage
2 onions, peeled
2 carrots, peeled
16 baby corn
225g (8oz) broccoli
2.5cm (1 inch) piece fresh root ginger
45ml (3 tbsp) oil
1 garlic clove, crushed
175ml (6fl oz) chicken stock
15ml (1 tbsp) cornflour
30ml (2 tbsp) light soy sauce
5ml (1 tsp) caster sugar

1 Soak the mushrooms in hot water for 20 minutes. Squeeze out as much water as possible from the mushrooms, then discard the stalks and thinly slice the caps.

2 Cut the cabbage into 2.5cm (1 inch) strips. Cut the onions into eighths and separate into layers; thinly slice the carrots. Halve the corn. Divide the broccoli into small florets. Peel and grate the ginger.

3 Heat the oil in a wok or large frying pan. Add the garlic, cabbage, onions, carrots, baby corn, broccoli, sliced mushrooms and ginger and stir-fry for 2 minutes. Stir in the stock, cover and cook for 2–3 minutes. Blend the cornflour with the soy sauce until you have a smooth paste.

4 Remove the vegetables from the wok or pan, using a slotted spoon, and keep on one side. Stir the cornflour mixture into the wok and bring to the boil, stirring all the time. Boil for 1 minute. Add the sugar. Return the vegetables to the pan and toss lightly to heat through. Serve at once.

CORIANDER ROSTI

Here the potatoes are grated and mixed with onions and plenty of fresh coriander and then roasted to create a delicious accompaniment to any dish with which you would serve potatoes.

- SERVES 6–8 ● PREPARATION TIME: 15 MINUTES
- COOKING TIME: 1 HOUR 15 MINUTES
- 100 CALS PER ROSTI ● 2.3G FAT, OF WHICH 1.4G SATURATED FAT

1.4kg (3lb) baking potatoes
2 onions
40g (1½oz) butter
15ml (1 tbsp) chopped fresh coriander
salt and ground black pepper
fresh coriander sprigs, to garnish

1 Prick the potatoes with a fork and bake them at 200°C (400°F) Mark 6 for 40 minutes until slightly softened but not cooked right through.

2 Peel and finely chop the onions. Heat the butter in a large pan and sauté the onions, without browning, for 5–7 minutes until soft.

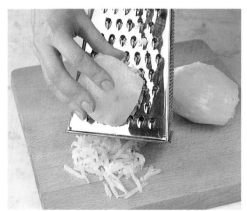

3 Leave the potatoes in their skins until cool enough to handle, then peel and grate coarsely. Gently stir the potatoes into the onion with the coriander. Season well.

4 Spoon the potatoes into 16 mounds onto a greased baking sheet. Bake at 200°C (400°F) Mark 6 for 40 minutes or until golden and crisp. Garnish with coriander.

RATATOUILLE

This truly French dish is one of those all-time favourites that can be served as a dish in its own right or as an accompaniment.

● SERVES 6 ● PREPARATION TIME: 20 MINUTES
● COOKING TIME: ABOUT 40 MINUTES ● 140 CALS
PER SERVING ● 7.3G FAT, OF WHICH 1.1G
SATURATED FAT

2 onions, peeled
350g (12oz) aubergine
450g (1lb) small courgettes
450g (1lb) tomatoes
1 green pepper, halved, cored and deseeded
1 red pepper, halved, cored and deseeded
50ml (2fl oz) olive oil
1 large garlic clove, crushed
15ml (1 tbsp) chopped fresh basil
10ml (2 tsp) chopped fresh thyme
30ml (2 tbsp) chopped fresh parsley
30ml (2 tbsp) tomato purée
salt and ground black pepper

1 Thinly slice the onions. Quarter the aubergine lengthways, then slice. Slice the courgettes. Immerse the tomatoes in boiling water for 30 seconds, cool, then peel away the skins. Deseed and roughly chop the tomatoes. Roughly chop the peppers.

2 Heat the oil in a large saucepan or flameproof casserole. Add the onions and garlic and fry for about 5 minutes or until soft, but not brown.

3 Add the aubergine, courgettes, tomatoes, peppers, herbs, tomato purée and seasoning. Fry, stirring, for 2–3 minutes, then cover tightly and simmer for 30–40 minutes or until all the vegetables are tender. If necessary boil, uncovered, to reduce the liquid. Check seasoning. Serve hot or cold.

NOTE

● Suitable for freezing.

CHICKPEAS WITH SPINACH

This accompaniment goes well with most meat curries. It is also excellent with fish. For a quick supper dish as a meal in itself, use canned rather than fresh chickpeas.

● SERVES 4–6 ● PREPARATION TIME: 10 MINUTES, PLUS SOAKING FOR DRIED CHICKPEAS ● COOKING TIME: 2¼–3¼ HOURS, OR 15 MINUTES IF USING CANNED CHICKPEAS ● 272–181 CALS PER SERVING ● 10–6.5G FAT, OF WHICH 1.1–0.8G SATURATED FAT

225g (8oz) dried chickpeas, or 2 x 425 g (15oz)
cans chickpeas
5ml (1 tsp) salt, or to taste
4 tomatoes
450g (1lb) spinach leaves
30ml (2 tbsp) ghee or vegetable oil
2.5cm (1 inch) piece fresh root ginger, peeled and
finely chopped
3 garlic cloves, peeled and crushed
10ml (2 tsp) ground coriander
5ml (1 tsp) ground cumin
10ml (2 tsp) paprika
handful of fresh coriander, roughly torn
ground black pepper
fresh coriander sprigs, to garnish

NOTES

● *The cooking time for dried chickpeas will depend on their 'freshness'. If they have been stored for a long time and look shrivelled, they may take even longer than 3 hours to cook.*
● *Suitable for freezing.*

VARIATION

● *Use another pulse in place of the chickpeas. Black-eyed beans are particularly good; cook as above.*

1 Pick over the dried chickpeas if using, discarding any small stones or shrivelled peas. Rinse thoroughly in plenty of cold running water, then put the chickpeas into a bowl and add plenty of cold water to cover. Leave to soak overnight.

2 Drain the dried chickpeas, put them in a large saucepan with plenty of water and bring to the boil. Lower the heat and simmer gently for 2–3 hours or until tender, adding salt towards the end of the cooking time. Drain well. If using canned chickpeas, simply drain and rinse under cold running water.

3 Immerse the tomatoes in boiling water for 30 seconds, cool, then peel away the skins. Finely chop the tomato flesh. Trim and chop the spinach.

4 Heat the ghee or oil in a heavy-based saucepan. Add the ginger, garlic and spices and cook for 2 minutes, stirring all the time. Add the chickpeas and stir to coat in the spice mixture.

5 Add the tomatoes, coriander and spinach. Cook for 2 minutes, then cover and simmer gently for 10 minutes. Season with salt and pepper before serving. Garnish with coriander sprigs.

OKRA TAGINE

Tagine is named after the domed terracotta dish in which it is traditionally cooked. Preserved lemons, if available, can also be added to the dish. Serve with bread, rice or couscous to soak up the juices.

● SERVES 4–6 ● PREPARATION TIME: 15 MINUTES ● COOKING TIME: ABOUT 40 MINUTES ● 140–93 CALS PER SERVING ● 7–4.7G FAT, OF WHICH 1.1–0.7G SATURATED FAT

2 onions
2.5ml (½ tsp) saffron strands
30ml (2 tbsp) olive oil
3 garlic cloves, crushed
5ml (1 tsp) ground ginger
5ml (1 tsp) turmeric
5ml (1 tsp) caraway seeds
2.5ml (½ tsp) ground cloves
10ml (2 tsp) paprika
finely grated rind and juice of 1 lemon
300ml (½ pint) vegetable stock
1 large head (or 2 small heads) of fennel
handful of fresh coriander or parsley
3 fresh oregano sprigs
425g (15oz) can plum tomatoes
350g (12oz) okra
8 baby courgettes, about 225g (8oz)
salt and ground black pepper
handful of black olives
harissa, to serve (see Note)

NOTE

● *Harissa is a hot red chilli paste sold in delicatessens and specialist food stores. It is a traditional accompaniment to many North African dishes.*

1 Peel and roughly chop the onions. Put the saffron in a small bowl, pour on 150ml (¼ pint) warm water and leave to soak.

2 Meanwhile heat the oil in a large casserole dish, add the onions and garlic and sauté until softened. Add all the spices and cook, stirring constantly, for 2 minutes. Stir in the lemon rind and juice, the saffron with its soaking liquid, and the stock. Slowly bring to the boil.

3 Meanwhile, trim the fennel and cut into 6 wedges. Roughly chop half of the herbs. Add the fennel and chopped herbs to the casserole and season liberally with salt and pepper. Lower the heat, cover and simmer gently for about 15 minutes or until the fennel is softened.

4 Meanwhile drain the tomatoes, being careful not to break them up. Trim the stalk ends of the okra if necessary, without cutting right through into the pods. Halve the baby courgettes lengthways.

5 Add the tomatoes, okra and baby courgettes to the casserole. Simmer gently for 10–15 minutes until the okra and courgettes are cooked. Check the seasoning and adjust, if necessary.

6 Add the remaining herbs and the olives. Serve immediately, with harissa to accompany.

VARIATIONS

● *Add 175g (6oz) cooked or rinsed canned pulses, such as chickpeas, with the fennel.*
● *Add 150ml (¼ pint) thick low-fat yogurt with the tomatoes and okra, for a milder flavour.*

CHICKPEAS WITH GINGER AND TOMATOES

This accompaniment is excellent served with baked potatoes or grilled sausages, or as part of an Indian meal. The flavour is improved if the dish is made the day before required and reheated. If you don't have the time for soaking and cooking dried chickpeas, used canned ones instead – they work equally well (see Variation).

● SERVES 6 ● PREPARATION TIME: 5 MINUTES, PLUS SOAKING TIME ● COOKING TIME: 1 3/4–2 1/4 HOURS ● 165 CALS PER SERVING ● 4G FAT, OF WHICH 0.6G SATURATED FAT

225g (8oz) dried chickpeas
salt and ground black pepper
5cm (2 inch) piece fresh root ginger
1–2 garlic cloves
15ml (1 tbsp) olive or vegetable oil
10ml (2 tsp) garam masala
425g (15oz) can chopped tomatoes
2 spring onions
150ml (¼ pint) thick low-fat yogurt
5ml (1 tsp) mild curry paste
30ml (2 tbsp) chopped fresh mint
30ml (2 tbsp) chopped fresh coriander (optional)
To garnish:
fresh coriander sprigs
fresh mint sprigs

1 Put the chickpeas in a large bowl and pour on cold water to cover. Soak overnight.

2 The next day, drain the chickpeas and put them in a large saucepan with enough fresh cold water to cover. Bring to the boil and boil steadily for 10 minutes, then lower the heat and simmer for about 1½ –2 hours or until the chickpeas are really tender, adding salt towards the end of the cooking time. Drain.

3 Peel and finely chop the ginger and garlic. Heat the oil in the saucepan and add the ginger, garlic and garam masala. Sauté for 2 minutes, then add the tomatoes and chickpeas and bring to the boil. Reduce the heat and simmer gently for 15 minutes.

4 Meanwhile, trim and finely chop the spring onions. Place in a bowl with the yogurt, curry paste, mint, and coriander, if using. Mix thoroughly and season liberally with salt and pepper.

5 Turn the chickpeas into a serving bowl and swirl in the yogurt mixture. Serve immediately, garnished with coriander and mint sprigs.

VARIATION

● Replace the dried chickpeas with 2 x 425g (15oz) cans of chick peas. Drain and rinse thoroughly under cold running water. Add to the tomato mixture, in step 3.

GRILLED VEGETABLE SALAD

Highly colourful, this Mediterranean salad contains all the best of summer fare: asparagus, courgettes, sweet peppers and cherry tomatoes. Choose the freshest full-flavoured ingredients.

● SERVES 4–6 ● PREPARATION TIME: 20 MINUTES
● COOKING TIME: ABOUT 20 MINUTES
● 216–144 CALS PER SERVING ● 16.6–11.1G FAT, OF WHICH 2.4–1.6G SATURATED FAT

1 red pepper
1 green pepper
350g (12oz) baby courgettes
about 6 garlic cloves
1 bunch asparagus
olive oil, for brushing
few cherry tomatoes

Dressing:
10ml (2 tsp) balsamic or garlic vinegar
5ml (1 tsp) runny honey
5ml (1 tsp) Dijon mustard
75ml (5 tbsp) olive oil
salt and ground black pepper
chopped fresh herbs, such as basil, marjoram, parsley and chives, to garnish

1 Halve the peppers and remove the seeds and cores. Cut each half into four pieces. Halve the courgettes lengthways. Remove the loose, papery outer skins from the garlic cloves, but leave the inner skins attached.

2 Pour enough water into a saucepan to come to a depth of about 5cm (2 inches) and bring to the boil. Add the peppers and garlic, bring back to the boil and boil for 1 minute. Remove the peppers with a slotted spoon (leaving the garlic in the water), refresh the peppers under cold running water and leave to drain. Repeat with the courgettes, using the same water. Drain the garlic.

3 Steam the asparagus: tie in a bundle, tips upwards, and stand in a saucepan containing about 5cm (2 inches) simmering water. Cover the tips with a tent of foil and cook for 5–8 minutes depending on their thickness, until just tender. Drain, arrange on a serving plate and leave to cool.

4 Brush the blanched peppers, courgettes and garlic with a little olive oil and cook under a hot grill until they are flecked with brown. Turn the vegetables over, brush with more olive oil and cook the other side. Leave to cool, then arrange the grilled vegetables on the serving plate with the asparagus. Halve the cherry tomatoes and scatter over the vegetables.

5 To make the dressing, whisk the vinegar, honey and mustard together in a small bowl, then gradually whisk in the olive oil to make a very thick dressing. Season with salt and pepper. Drizzle over the vegetables and sprinkle with herbs to serve.

ROASTED PEPPER SALAD

This roasted pepper salad is served with a sauce of ginger, soy sauce and chilli for a spicier dish. Use a good combination of different coloured peppers for the best result.

● SERVES 4 ● PREPARATION TIME: 10 MINUTES
● COOKING TIME: 10–15 MINUTES ● 70 CALS
PER SERVING ● 0.8G FAT, OF WHICH 0.2G
SATURATED FAT

2 red peppers
1 yellow pepper
1 orange pepper

Dressing:
½ small red chilli
½ small green chilli
15g (½oz) fresh root ginger
1 small bunch spring onions
60ml (4 tbsp) soy sauce
60ml (4 tbsp) lemon juice
15ml (1 tbsp) white wine vinegar
30ml (2 tbsp) runny honey

1 Halve the peppers and place them cut-side down, on the rack in the grill pan. Place under a hot grill for about 10–15 minutes until the skin is blackened and charred. Cover the peppers with a clean damp tea towel and allow to cool.

2 For the dressing: halve, deseed and finely chop the chillies (wearing rubber gloves to avoid skin irritation).

3 Peel and finely chop the ginger; thinly slice the spring onions.

4 Whisk together all the ingredients for the dressing, except the chillies, until thoroughly combined. Lastly, add the chopped chillies.

5 Remove the skins, cores and seeds from the peppers and cut the flesh into thick slices. Spoon the salad dressing over the peppers to serve.

GRILLED AUBERGINES

Baby aubergines are ideal for this recipe. If you are lucky enough find these, allow one per person, otherwise half an aubergine each should be ample as an accompaniment. If you're really short of time you could omit the degorging, but it does draw out any bitter juices and reduces the amount of oil the aubergines absorb during cooking. Serve with grilled meat or fish.

● SERVES 4 ● PREPARATION TIME: 25 MINUTES
● COOKING TIME: 15–20 MINUTES ● 80 CALS PER SERVING ● 6.3G FAT, OF WHICH 1G SATURATED FAT

2 medium aubergines
salt and ground black pepper
2 garlic cloves
1 green chilli
15ml (1 tbsp) chopped fresh rosemary
finely grated rind and juice of 1 lemon
45ml (3 tbsp) chopped fresh parsley
olive oil, for basting

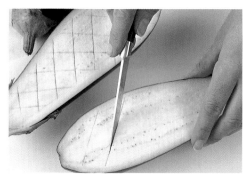

1 Trim the aubergines and cut in half lengthways. Deeply score the flesh in a criss-cross pattern, cutting almost, but not right through to the skin. Place in a colander, sprinkle generously with salt and leave to degorge for 20 minutes.

2 Meanwhile, peel and finely chop the garlic. Chop the chilli (wearing rubber gloves to avoid skin irritation), discarding the seeds if a milder flavour is preferred. Mix the chilli with the garlic, rosemary, lemon rind and parsley.

3 Drain the aubergines and rinse with cold water. Squeeze dry. Brush the scored sides with olive oil and place, cut-side uppermost, on the grill rack. Grill – not too close to the heat – for 10 minutes. Spread with the herb mixture and drizzle with a little more olive oil. Position the grill pan closer to the heat source and grill for a further 5–10 minutes or until the aubergines are tender, brushing with more oil occasionally.

4 Arrange on a serving platter and sprinkle with a little lemon juice and olive oil. Serve immediately.

VARIATIONS

● Replace the chilli and herb topping with a coriander pesto. Place a handful of coriander leaves in the food processor with 1 green chilli, 2 peeled garlic cloves and 60ml (4 tbsp) oil. Work to a paste and season with salt and ground black pepper to taste. Spread on the aubergines and grill as above.
● For a more substantial dish, to serve as a light lunch or supper, top with slices of feta cheese and accompany with a tomato salad.

NOTE

● If the aubergines are quite plump, increase the initial cooking time to 15–20 minutes.

AUBERGINES STUDDED WITH GARLIC AND ROSEMARY

Roasting aubergines in this manner gives them a wonderful aroma and makes them deliciously soft inside. They are equally good served hot or cold, as an accompaniment to grilled or roast meats. Use long, thin aubergines, if possible, rather than plump ones.

● SERVES 6–8 ● PREPARATION TIME: 20 MINUTES ● COOKING TIME: 45 MINUTES–1 HOUR ● 70–53 CALS PER SERVING ● 4.7G–3.5G FAT, OF WHICH 0.8G–0.6G SATURATED FAT

4 medium aubergines
12 fat garlic cloves
handful of fresh rosemary sprigs
salt and ground black pepper
olive oil, for basting

1 Preheat the oven to 180°C (350°F) Mark 4. Peel the garlic cloves and cut into chunky slivers.

NOTE

● You may prefer to remove the rosemary before serving as it is a little indigestible.

2 Using a small sharp knife, make deep incisions all over each aubergine. Push a sliver of garlic into each one. Insert a small sprig of rosemary into each slit, too.

3 Lay the aubergines in a baking dish and drizzle with olive oil. Sprinkle with salt and pepper to taste. Bake in the oven for 45 minutes–1 hour, or until tender.

VARIATION

● Use courgettes instead of aubergines, but make a line of slits along the top of the courgettes rather than all over. Insert lardons of bacon into the slits with the garlic.

STIR-FRIED SUMMER VEGETABLES

A simple stir-fry is an ideal way to feast on the abundance of summer vegetables. Choose small, tender young vegetables – baby carrots, finger-thick courgettes, slender green beans, mangetout, sugar-snap peas, or baby corn. Serve the sauce separately in a small jug, to allow guests to help themselves.

● SERVES 4–6 ● PREPARATION TIME: 15 MINUTES
● COOKING TIME: 5 MINUTES ● 144–96 CALS PER
SERVING ● 7–4.8G FAT, OF WHICH 1–0.7G
SATURATED FAT

175g (6oz) baby courgettes (with flowers if possible)
175g (6oz) baby carrots
125g (4oz) baby French beans
125g (4oz) mangetout or sugar-snap peas
125g (4oz) baby corn
3–4 spring onions
175g (6oz) beansprouts
2.5cm (1 inch) piece fresh root ginger (optional)
1 garlic clove
30ml (2 tbsp) sunflower oil
30ml (2 tbsp) light soy sauce
salt and ground black pepper
5–10ml (1–2 tsp) sesame oil
Sauce:
45ml (3 tbsp) sherry
45ml (3 tbsp) light soy sauce
5ml (1 tsp) runny honey
fresh coriander sprigs, to garnish

NOTE

● *Vary the vegetables according to whatever is readily available. Broccoli florets, fine asparagus spears and finely sliced water chestnuts are suitable choices.*

1 First prepare the vegetables. Halve the courgettes lengthways. Scrub the carrots and trim, leaving a tuft of stalk on each one. Top and tail the French beans and peas. Halve the baby corn diagonally. Trim the spring onions and shred finely. Rinse the beansprouts and drain thoroughly.

2 To prepare the sauce, simply mix the sherry, soy sauce and honey together in a small jug; set aside.

3 Peel and finely chop the ginger, if using, and garlic. Heat the oil in a wok or large frying pan and add the ginger and garlic to flavour the oil. When the oil is very hot, add the carrots and French beans and fry, turning constantly, for 2–3 minutes.

4 Add the courgettes, mangetout or sugar-snap peas, corn cobs, spring onions and beansprouts, together with the soy sauce. Stir-fry for 2 minutes. Taste and season with salt and pepper if necessary. Sprinkle with the sesame oil. Serve immediately, garnished with coriander sprigs. Serve the sauce separately.

VARIATION

● *To serve the stir-fry as a main course, including rice noodles or egg noodles will make the dish more substantial. Cook the noodles according to the packet instructions until almost tender. Drain, then add to the stir-fry and cook, turning constantly, for 1 minute. Serve immediately.*

SWEDE AND CARROTS WITH MUSTARD SEEDS AND GINGER

Swede has often been a much maligned vegetable, yet it has a distinctive flavour which is enhanced by herbs, spices and aromatic ingredients. Swede and carrots go well together, and the addition of mustard seeds and ginger make the combination just a little bit different.

● SERVES 4 ● PREPARATION TIME: 20 MINUTES
● COOKING TIME: 15 MINUTES ● 105 CALS PER SERVING ● 6G FAT, OF WHICH 3.5G SATURATED FAT

450g (1lb) swede
450g (1lb) carrots
2 pieces preserved stem ginger in syrup, drained
25g (1oz) butter
5ml (1 tsp) black mustard seeds
coarse sea salt and ground black pepper
fresh parsley or chervil sprigs, to garnish

1 Peel the swede and cut into small dice. Peel the carrots and slice thinly. Cook the vegetables separately in boiling salted water until tender.

2 Meanwhile, finely chop the stem ginger. Melt the butter in a small heavy-based saucepan. Add the mustard seeds and heat gently until the seeds begin to pop. Add the chopped ginger and cook for 1 minute over a low heat.

NOTE

● *Use a heavy-duty potato masher or a vegetable mill for mashing. Do not use a food processor as this results in an unpleasant glutinous texture.*

3 Drain the cooked swede and carrots thoroughly, then mash together thoroughly, ensuring there are no lumps. Season liberally with freshly ground black pepper and stir in half of the mustard and ginger mixture.

4 Transfer the mashed swede and carrots to a warmed serving dish and drizzle the remaining mustard and ginger mixture over the top. Garnish with parsley or chervil and serve at once.

VARIATION

● *Make a mustard and ginger cauliflower cheese for those not watching their fat intake by tossing cooked cauliflower florets in half of the mustard mixture. Transfer to a gratin dish and spoon on the cheese sauce. Top with the remaining mustard mixture and grated cheese, then brown under the grill.*

SUGAR-SNAP PEAS IN A MINTED-LEMON DRESSING

Sugar-snap peas are available all year round and make an excellent accompaniment. Here they are served in a light crème fraîche dressing, flavoured with fresh mint and lemon. Fresh peas are equally good served this way – it's well worth seeking them out during their short season or, better still, grow some yourself… the taste of freshly picked home-grown peas is incomparable.

● SERVES 4 ● PREPARATION TIME: 10 MINUTES
● COOKING TIME: 5–10 MINUTES ● 73 CALS PER SERVING ● 3.3G FAT, OF WHICH 2G SATURATED FAT

400–450g (14oz–1lb) sugar-snap peas
Dressing:
60ml (4 tbsp) reduced-fat crème fraîche
15ml (1 tbsp) finely shredded or chopped fresh mint
finely pared or grated rind and juice of ½ lemon
90ml (3fl oz) low-fat yogurt
coarse sea salt and ground black pepper
fresh mint sprigs, to garnish

1 Top and tail the sugar-snap peas, then steam or cook them in boiling water until just tender (see Note).

2 Meanwhile, gently heat the crème fraîche in a small saucepan, then add the finely chopped mint, lemon rind and juice, stirring gently. When the dressing is warmed through, add the yogurt; do not overheat at this stage otherwise the dressing may curdle. Season with salt and pepper to taste.

3 Drain the sugar-snap peas and transfer to a warmed serving dish. Pour over the minted-lemon dressing. Garnish with mint sprigs and serve at once.

NOTE

● Steam the sugar-snap peas for the shortest possible time to retain their flavour and bite.

VARIATIONS

● Instead of sugar-snap peas, use mangetout or fresh peas. You will need 675g (1½lb) fresh peas in pods to give the correct shelled weight. Steam or cook in boiling water for 5–10 minutes until tender; continue as above.
● Young broad beans are also delicious steamed and served with this sauce.

ASPARAGUS OR SAMPHIRE SALAD

This salad is delicious with vegetarian dishes, fish and chicken. Samphire, a tender seaweed, is in season between May and September – you may be able to buy it at a fishmonger's.

● SERVES 6 ● PREPARATION TIME: 10 MINUTES
● COOKING TIME: 20 MINUTES, PLUS 5 MINUTES
STANDING ● 45 CALS PER SERVING ● 3.8G FAT, OF
WHICH 2.3G SATURATED FAT

25g (1oz) butter
350g (12oz) fine asparagus, trimmed, or 350g
(12oz) samphire, well washed and drained
salt and ground black pepper
grated rind and juice of 1 lemon
To garnish:
finely grated lemon rind
fresh herbs (optional)

Melt the butter in a frying pan or wok. Add the asparagus or samphire and stir-fry for 5–10 minutes or until tender. Season; add the lemon rind and juice. Garnish and serve.

MESCLUN WITH TOASTED SEEDS

The French term mesclun refers to an assortment of wild salad greens that typically would have been picked fresh from the fields for this simple, yet lovely leafy salad. Toasted seeds and nuts are added to enhance the dish. Use your own favourite selection of salad leaves and herbs and include a few edible flowers, if available.

● SERVES 4 ● PREPARATION TIME: 5 MINUTES
● COOKING TIME: 2–3 MINUTES ● 177 CALS PER SERVING ● 20G FAT, OF WHICH 2.7G SATURATED FAT

25g (1oz) sunflower seeds
25g (1oz) pumpkin seeds
30ml (2 tbsp) poppy seeds
175g (6oz) assorted salad leaves, such as rocket, lamb's lettuce (mâche), watercress, oakleaf, lollo rosso, chicory
25g (1oz) assorted fresh herb leaves, such as parsley, chives, basil, chervil, tarragon
Dressing:
60ml (4 tbsp) extra-virgin olive oil
10ml (2 tsp) champagne or sherry vinegar
a pinch of sugar
salt and ground black pepper
edible flowers, to garnish (optional)

NOTE

● *For convenience, use one of the ready-prepared packets of mixed salad leaves which are available from most supermarkets.*

VARIATION

● *For a more substantial salad suitable to serve as a light lunch, add 125g (4oz) crumbled feta or diced gruyère cheese to the salad dressing along with some croûtons and seedless grapes.*

1 Heat a heavy-based frying pan over a medium heat. Add the sunflower, pumpkin and poppy seeds and stir-fry for 2–3 minutes until they are golden and begin to release their aroma. Immediately transfer the seeds to a plate and allow to cool.

2 Wash the salad leaves if necessary and shake well to remove all the excess water, pat dry. Place the leaves in a large bowl with the herbs.

3 Blend all the dressing ingredients together until evenly combined.

4 Pour the dressing over the leaves and herbs, and toss gently until coated. Scatter over the toasted seeds and edible flowers, if using. Serve at once.

TOMATO AND PEACH SALAD WITH AVOCADO SALSA

This is a really attractive plate for a summer buffet, especially if served alfresco. Alternatively it can be served as a starter salad with a meat or fish main course to follow. Add a few chive flowers or other edible flowers, if available.

● SERVES 4 ● PREPARATION TIME: 15 MINUTES
● COOKING TIME: 3 MINUTES ● 120 CALS PER
SERVING ● 9G FAT, OF WHICH 1.5G SATURATED FAT

1 large ripe beef tomato
2 large firm, but ripe peaches
Avocado Salsa:
½ small ripe avocado
1–2 spring onions, trimmed
1 small red chilli
1 garlic clove, crushed
7.5ml (1½ tsp) lime juice
7.5ml (1½ tsp) chopped fresh coriander or chives
7.5ml (1½ tsp) extra virgin olive oil
salt and ground black pepper
Dressing:
15ml (1 tbsp) caster sugar
5ml (1 tsp) lemon juice
2.5ml (½ tsp) Dijon mustard
30ml (2 tbsp) extra-virgin olive oil
To garnish:
snipped fresh chives
fresh coriander sprigs
lime wedges

1 First prepare the avocado salsa. Peel and dice the avocado; finely chop the spring onions; halve, deseed and finely chop the chilli (wearing rubber gloves to avoid skin irritation). Mix these ingredients together in a bowl and gently stir in the garlic, lime juice, coriander or chives and olive oil. Season to taste and set aside until required.

NOTE

● *Allow the salsa to stand while preparing the rest of the salad, but leave it no longer or the avocado will discolour and spoil the appearance of the dish.*

2 To prepare the dressing, dissolve the sugar in 50ml (2fl oz) water in a small pan, over a low heat. Bring to the boil and simmer for 3 minutes. Remove from the heat, allow to cool, then stir in the lemon juice and mustard. Gradually whisk in the oil until amalgamated and season to taste.

3 Thinly slice the tomato. Halve, stone and slice the peaches. Arrange the tomato and peach slices in overlapping circles on a large serving plate.

4 Spoon the avocado salsa into the centre of the plate and drizzle over the dressing. Sprinkle with the snipped chives and garnish with coriander sprigs and lime wedges. Serve immediately.

VARIATION

● *Omit the salsa and, instead, fan out a thinly sliced large avocado in between the tomato and peach slices.*

THREE TOMATO SALAD

Anyone who believes that all tomato salads taste the same should sample this one. Here the individual flavours and textures of the different types of tomato are very apparent. It is, however, essential to use ripe, flavourful tomatoes. Look out for vine-ripened tomatoes, or those labelled 'grown for flavour' or, better still, use home-grown tomatoes.

● SERVES 4–6 ● PREPARATION TIME: 10 MINUTES, PLUS STANDING TIME ● 215–110 CALS PER SERVING ● 17–11.3G FAT, OF WHICH 4–2.8G SATURATED FAT

30ml (2 tbsp) small French capers, washed (see Note)
2 large ripe beef tomatoes
3 ripe plum tomatoes
125g (4oz) red or yellow cherry tomatoes
40g (1½oz) small Niçoise olives

Dressing:
60ml (4 tbsp) extra virgin olive oil
30ml (2 tbsp) lemon juice
5ml (1 tsp) Dijon mustard
1.75ml (¼ tsp) runny honey
salt and ground black pepper

To serve:
15g (½oz) fresh basil leaves
50g (2oz) Pecorino cheese or Parmesan

1 Soak the capers in cold water for 30 minutes, then drain and pat dry.

2 Remove any stalks still attached to the tomatoes. Thinly slice the beef tomatoes and arrange in overlapping slices on a large serving platter.

NOTE

● *Small French capers come either packed in salt or in balsamic vinegar and are available from delicatessens. They have a firm, slightly crunchy texture, whereas the larger capers packed in brine can be soggy and taste strongly of brine. You can use ordinary capers for this recipe, but wash and dry them well before using.*

3 Slice the plum tomatoes lengthways and arrange over the beef tomatoes. Halve the cherry tomatoes and place in the centre of the plate.

4 Stone the olives, if preferred, and scatter them and the capers over the tomatoes.

5 To prepare the dressing, place all the ingredients in a screw-topped jar and shake well until amalgamated.

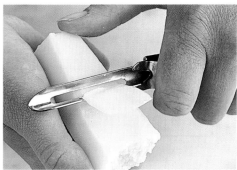

6 Drizzle a generous amount of dressing over the tomatoes. Cover and leave to stand for 30 minutes to infuse. Scatter the basil leaves over the salad, then top with Pecorino cheese or Parmesan shavings. Serve at once.

CARROT SALAD

This pretty salad is a good accompaniment to spicy meat and fish dishes. You could replace the orange slices with mango or papaya, or use blood oranges when they are in season. A few black olives scattered on top of the salad just before serving provide a striking contrast to the vivid shades of orange.

- SERVES 4–6 ● PREPARATION TIME: 20 MINUTES
- COOKING TIME: ABOUT 5 MINUTES ● 160–104 CALS PER SERVING ● 11.6–7.7G FAT, OF WHICH 1.4–1G SATURATED FAT

450g (1 lb) carrots
2 small thin-skinned oranges
few fresh chives, snipped
few small fresh mint leaves
Dressing:
1–2 garlic cloves
1 green chilli
1 red chilli
60ml (4 tbsp) vegetable oil
5ml (1 tsp) black mustard seeds
5ml (1 tsp) cumin seeds
15ml (1 tbsp) orange juice
15ml (1 tbsp) lemon juice
salt and ground black pepper
few drops of orange flower water (optional, see Note)

NOTE

- *If using orange flower water, apply sparingly as the flavour can be overpowering.*

VARIATION

- *Soak a handful of sultanas or raisins in a little orange juice until plump. Scatter over the salad before serving. For a more substantial salad, add a handful of cooked chickpeas, too.*

1 Grate the carrots, using the coarse side of a grater. (Do not use a food processor as it tends to make them very wet.) Pat dry with kitchen paper.

2 Peel the oranges, as you would an apple, removing all the bitter white pith. Do this over a bowl to catch the juice (use for the dressing). Cut the oranges into very thin slices. Arrange the orange slices and carrots on a large serving plate and scatter with the chives and mint leaves.

3 To make the dressing, peel and thinly slice the garlic. Slice the chillies (wear rubber gloves to avoid irritation), and remove the seeds for a milder flavour.

4 Heat half the oil in a small frying pan, add the garlic and cook for 1–2 minutes until just golden brown. Add the mustard and cumin seeds and cook over a high heat for 1 minute, stirring all the time. Remove from the heat and add the remaining oil. Leave to cool.

5 Add the orange and lemon juices to the dressing with the chillies and salt and pepper to taste. Pour the dressing over the salad and turn the carrots and orange slices to ensure that they are evenly coated.

6 Leave the salad to stand at room temperature for 30 minutes to infuse the flavours. Sprinkle with a few drops of orange flower water just before serving, if using.

CHILLED MELON AND GINGER SALAD

This simple summer salad features the classic combination of melon and ginger. Here the mellow colours of several different melons blend together beautifully to make a very pretty dish. Serve as a light starter or, if you prefer fruit at the end of the meal, as a refreshing final course.

● SERVES 6 ● PREPARATION TIME: 15 MINUTES, PLUS CHILLING ● COOKING TIME: 10 MINUTES
● 86 CALS PER SERVING ● 0.5G FAT, OF WHICH 0.1G SATURATED FAT

1 small charentais or cantaloupe melon
1 small ogen or galia melon
½ large honeydew melon
350g (12oz) water melon
Dressing:
30ml (2 tbsp) caster sugar
15ml (1 tbsp) chopped preserved stem ginger in syrup (drained)
30ml (2 tbsp) orange juice
10ml (2 tsp) lemon juice

NOTE

● *If you can't find all the different types of melon suggested, make up the quantities using whatever is available.*

1 First make the dressing. Place the sugar and ginger in a small saucepan with 120ml (4fl oz) water. Heat gently to dissolve the sugar, then bring to the boil and simmer for a further 10 minutes.

2 Transfer to a bowl and stir in the orange and lemon juices. Set aside to cool.

3 Peel each melon and discard the seeds. Cut the flesh into thin wedges and mix together in a large bowl.

4 Pour over the cooled dressing, stir well, cover and chill for 1 hour before serving.

ORIENTAL CHICKEN SALAD

The longer you leave the chicken to marinate the more flavour the chicken will retain. Apart from the time it takes to marinate the chicken, this is a quick and easy dish to prepare.

- SERVES 4 ● PREPARATION TIME: 20 MINUTES, PLUS MARINATING ● COOKING TIME: ABOUT 20 MINUTES
- 300 CALS PER SERVING ● 9.9G FAT, OF WHICH 2.2G SATURATED FAT

15ml (1 tbsp) peeled and finely chopped fresh root ginger
1 large garlic clove, crushed
200ml (7fl oz) orange juice
60ml (4 tbsp) lemon juice
60ml (4 tbsp) light soy sauce
60ml (4 tbsp) sherry
15ml (1 tbsp) white wine vinegar
5ml (1 tsp) runny honey
4 chicken breast fillets, skinned, about 450g (1lb) total weight
1 small head Chinese leaves
1 head radicchio
1 bunch spring onions
175g (6oz) baby corn, halved lengthways
125g (4oz) beansprouts
15ml (1 tbsp) sunflower oil
salt and ground black pepper
To garnish:
15ml (1 tbsp) sesame seeds, toasted
25g (1oz) alfalfa sprouts (optional)

2 Shred the Chinese leaves and radicchio. Slice the spring onions. Cook the corn in boiling water for about 5 minutes. Add the beansprouts to the saucepan and cook for a further 30 seconds. Drain and blot dry with absorbent kitchen paper. Cool.

4 Toss all the salad ingredients together and divide between four serving plates. Slice the warm chicken breasts and arrange on top of the salad, using the marinade as a dressing. Garnish with toasted sesame seeds and alfalfa sprouts, if using.

3 Remove the chicken breasts from the marinade with a slotted spoon, reserving the marinade. Heat the oil in a large non-stick frying pan and fry the chicken for 10–12 minutes, turning frequently, until browned and cooked through. Add the reserved marinade and simmer to thicken slightly. Adjust the seasoning, if necessary.

1 Mix together the first eight ingredients and place in a large, shallow non-metallic dish. Make three shallow cuts in the flesh of each chicken breast and place in the marinade. Cover and refrigerate for at least 3–4 hours.

INDONESIAN FRUIT AND PRAWN SALAD WITH CHILLI DRESSING

This Indonesian salad is an unusual combination of exotic fruits and cooked prawns. Adorned with a hot and sour dressing, it is bursting with a whole range of exciting flavours. Serve it as a light summer lunch, or as part of a cold buffet.

- SERVES 4 ● PREPARATION TIME: 15 MINUTES
- COOKING TIME: 2 MINUTES ● 186 CALS PER SERVING ● 6.4G FAT, OF WHICH 1G SATURATED FAT

1 firm ripe papaya
1 pink grapefruit
1 small firm ripe mango
1 large firm ripe banana
12 large cooked Mediterranean prawns, or 4 cooked lobster tails

Dressing:
22.5ml (1½ tbsp) lemon juice
15ml (1 tbsp) rice wine vinegar
15ml (1 tbsp) caster sugar
5ml (1 tsp) dark soy sauce
1.25ml (¼ tsp) crushed red chillies
30ml (2 tbsp) groundnut oil
a pinch of salt
orange rind shreds, to garnish

NOTE

● *The best way to test the papaya and mango for ripeness is by gently squeezing them. There should be a small amount of give, but the fruits should not feel soft. You may prefer to buy them in advance and store in a warm dark place for several days to ripen.*

1 First make the dressing. Place the lemon juice, vinegar, sugar, soy sauce and chillies in a small saucepan and heat gently to dissolve the sugar. Remove from the heat and whisk in the oil and salt. Leave to cool.

2 Prepare the fruits. Peel and halve the papaya, then scoop out the seeds and thinly slice the flesh. Peel the grapefruit, removing all of the white pith, and cut out the segments free from the membranes. Peel the mango, cut the flesh away from the stone, then cut into slices. Peel and slice the banana into rings.

3 Arrange the fruits on a large serving platter and spoon over the dressing. Peel the prawns or lobster tails, leaving on the tail-end shells. Arrange these on top of the salad and garnish with orange rind shreds. Serve immediately.

VEGETARIAN DISHES

The ever-growing number of vegetarians has led to a greater demand for more interesting and varied recipes for meals without meat. It has also meant that vegetarian alternatives to meat are more readily available. Quorn and tofu are just two examples.

This trend towards a meat-free diet has been led mainly because of the belief that it is a healthier way of eating, high in fibre and low in fat. But variety is important in all diets, and it is essential to balance your diet if you are vegetarian and include nuts, seeds, beans and grains as well as dairy products.

The following recipes offer a comprehensive selection of imaginative, sometimes exotic and nutritionally sound dishes, including Curried Tofu Burgers and Quorn Kebabs with Tomato Salsa, that demonstrate what can be done with a few simple ingredients. Stuffed Peppers, Spicy Vegetable Chilli and Baked Black-eyed Bean Casserole show how the creative use of herbs, spices and other condiments can lift the simple vegetable or bean to great culinary heights.

New ideas for vegetarian dishes have come from all over the world. There are recipes from the eastern Mediterranean, Italy, and India for lentils, beans, grains and vegetables; even those who are most sceptical of vegetarianism will find something to tantalise their tastebuds.

LEMON DAL

The lemon rind and juice used in this recipe add a wonderful tang that contrasts well with the creaminess of the lentils. These are cooked down to a smooth, moist, almost purée-like consistency.

● SERVES 4–6 ● PREPARATION TIME: 10 MINUTES
● COOKING TIME: 30 MINUTES ● 291–194 CALS
PER SERVING ● 11.8–7.9G FAT, OF WHICH 1.5–1G
SATURATED FAT

225g (8oz) masoor dal (split red lentils)
1 onion
1 garlic clove (optional)
1 hot red chilli (optional)
60ml (4 tbsp) oil
2.5ml (½ tsp) ground turmeric
salt, to taste
finely grated rind and juice of 1 lemon
5ml (1 tsp) cumin seeds

NOTE

● Masoor dal or red split lentils are readily available. They should be washed thoroughly before use.

1 Rinse the masoor dal (red split lentils) under cold water to remove any grit; then drain them well. Peel and halve the onion, then cut into thin slices. Crush the garlic, if using. Chop the chilli, if using (wearing rubber gloves to avoid skin irritation), discarding the seeds if a milder flavour is preferred.

2 Heat half the oil in a heavy-based saucepan. Add the onion and cook over a high heat for about 5 minutes or until the onions are golden brown. Remove the onions from the saucepan with a slotted spoon and drain on absorbent kitchen paper.

3 Add the turmeric to the oil that is remaining in the saucepan and cook the turmeric, stirring constantly, for 1 minute. Add the masoor dal, salt and lemon rind and juice. Cook, stirring, for 1 minute, then add 300ml (½ pint) water.

4 Bring to the boil, cover the saucepan with a tight-fitting lid, turn the heat to its lowest setting and cook for 25–30 minutes without lifting the lid to prevent steam escaping. When cooked, the dal should be soft and all the water absorbed.

5 When the dal is almost ready, heat the remaining oil in a small saucepan. Add the cumin seeds and the garlic and chilli, if using. Cook, stirring, for 2 minutes.

6 Beat the dal to a smooth, moist consistency. If it's too dry, add a spoonful of hot water; if too moist, cook, stirring over a high heat, to evaporate the moisture. Season with salt, if wished.

7 Turn into a warmed serving dish. Pour the hot oil mixture over and scatter the fried onions on top. Serve immediately.

TUSCAN BEAN STEW

Beans are an excellent source of dietary fibre, which helps reduce high blood cholesterol levels. Their other advantage, particularly if you have a hearty appetite, is that they are incredibly filling. Use a mixture of beans for this recipe.

● SERVES 4 ● PREPARATION TIME: 30 MINUTES
● COOKING TIME: 50 MINUTES ● 255 CALS PER
SERVING (PLUS 40 CALS PER PESTO CROÛTE)
● 7G FAT, OF WHICH 1G SATURATED FAT

30ml (2 tbsp) olive oil
175g (6oz) red onions, finely chopped
4 garlic cloves, crushed
30ml (2 tbsp) sun-dried tomato paste
2.5ml (½ tsp) chilli powder (optional)
125g (4oz) carrots, sliced
75g (3oz) celery sticks, sliced
4 tomatoes, preferably plum, peeled, deseeded and
roughly chopped
2 fresh thyme sprigs or a large pinch of dried thyme
2 bay leaves
salt and ground black pepper
450ml (¾ pint) vegetable stock
2 x 400g (14oz) cans beans, such as butter,
flageolet, kidney or chickpeas, drained and rinsed
50g (2oz) French beans, trimmed and cut into
short lengths
small fresh thyme sprigs, to garnish
pesto croûtes, to serve (see Note)

NOTE

● To make pesto croûtes, toast sliced French bread, drizzle with a little olive oil and spread with ready-made pesto.

1 In a non-stick saucepan, heat the oil, add the onions and cook for 10 minutes or until soft. Add the garlic, tomato paste and chilli powder, if using; cook for 1–2 minutes.

2 Add the next five ingredients and season. Pour in the stock, bring to the boil and simmer; stirring occasionally, for 20–30 minutes or until soft.

3 Add the beans and French beans, then simmer for 5–10 minutes or until the beans are heated through and the French beans are just tender, but still have some bite. Serve hot, garnished with thyme and accompanied with the pesto croûtes.

MIXED LENTIL CASSEROLE

Here the shallots are caramelised, giving them a wonderful sweetness. The balsamic vinegar adds the final concentration of flavour to these golden, tender onions.

● SERVES 6 ● PREPARATION TIME: 20 MINUTES
● COOKING TIME: ABOUT 1 HOUR ● 240 CALS
PER SERVING ● 7.3G FAT, OF WHICH 1.1G
SATURATED FAT

5ml (1 tsp) cumin seeds
15ml (1 tbsp) coriander seeds
5ml (1 tsp) mustard seeds
3 onions, peeled
450g (1lb) carrots, peeled
350g (12oz) leeks
350g (12oz) mooli (white radish), peeled
450g (1lb) button mushrooms
45ml (3 tbsp) olive oil
2 garlic cloves, crushed
25g (1oz) fresh root ginger, peeled and grated
1.25ml (¼ tsp) turmeric
175g (6oz) split red lentils
50g (2oz) brown or green lentils
750ml (1¼ pints) boiling water
salt and ground black pepper
60ml (4 tbsp) chopped fresh coriander

2 Slice the onions, carrots and leeks. Roughly chop the mooli; halve the mushrooms if large.

1 Crush the cumin, coriander and mustard seeds using a mortar and pestle (or in a strong bowl using the end of a rolling pin).

3 Heat the oil in a very large flameproof casserole. Add the onions, carrots, leeks and mooli, and fry for 2–3 minutes, stirring constantly. Add the mushrooms, garlic, ginger, turmeric and crushed spices, and fry for a further 2–3 minutes, stirring.

4 Stir in the lentils with the boiling water. Season with salt and pepper and return to the boil. Preheat the oven to 180°C (350°F) Mark 4. Transfer the dish to the oven, cover and cook for about 45 minutes or until the vegetables and lentils are tender. Stir in the chopped coriander just before serving.

VEGETABLE CHILLI

Using canned kidney beans makes this dish easy to prepare. You can adjust the amount of chilli powder depending on how hot you like it. Serve with plain boiled rice.

● SERVES 8 ● PREPARATION TIME: 20 MINUTES ● COOKING TIME: ABOUT 1 HOUR ● 225 CALS PER SERVING ● 4.7G FAT, OF WHICH 0.7G SATURATED FAT

30ml (2 tbsp) oil
2 onions, peeled and chopped
2 large garlic cloves, crushed
1–2 green chillies, deseeded and chopped
1 bay leaf
1 cinnamon stick
4 cloves
15ml (1 tbsp) paprika
10ml (2 tsp) ground cumin
2.5ml (½ tsp) chilli powder, to taste
5ml (1 tsp) dried marjoram
30ml (2 tbsp) tomato purée
225g (8oz) button mushrooms, sliced
1 large green pepper, cored, deseeded and chopped
900g (2lb) mixed vegetables, including carrots, aubergines, parsnips, potatoes and celery, prepared and cut into chunks
2 x 400g (14oz) cans chopped tomatoes
2 x 425g (15oz) cans red kidney beans, drained and rinsed
pinch of sugar
5ml (1 tsp) vinegar
45ml (3 tbsp) chopped fresh coriander
salt and ground black pepper

NOTES

● *This is delicious served with grated cheese and topped with soured cream or low-fat yogurt. If preferred, use cooked dried kidney beans; you will need 225g (8oz) dried weight.*
● *Suitable for freezing.*

1 Heat the oil in a large heavy-based saucepan. Add the onions, garlic and chillies and fry, stirring, for 3–4 minutes. Add the bay leaf, all the spices, the marjoram and tomato purée, and cook for a further 2 minutes, stirring.

2 Add all the fresh vegetables and cook, stirring for 1–2 minutes. Add the tomatoes. Bring to the boil, stirring occasionally. Add enough water just to cover the vegetables, half cover the pan and simmer for 35–45 minutes.

3 Add the kidney beans with the sugar, vinegar and half the coriander. Add extra chilli powder, if you like it spicier, and season with salt and pepper. Bring to the boil, lower the heat and simmer for 10 minutes, stirring occasionally. If there is too much liquid, leave the lid off during this time to evaporate the liquid. If dry, add a little water and cover.

4 Remove from the heat. Stir in the remaining coriander, then leave to stand for 5 minutes. Taste and adjust the seasoning, if necessary.

CURRIED TOFU BURGERS

Tofu is the perfect basis for vegetarian burgers. It holds together well and absorbs flavours easily. Here it is flavoured with subtle curry spices. Try serving these with a fruity chutney.

● SERVES 4 ● PREPARATION TIME: 20 MINUTES
● COOKING TIME: 6–8 MINUTES ● 215 CALS PER SERVING ● 15G FAT, OF WHICH 1.7G SATURATED FAT

I large carrot, peeled
I large onion, peeled
15ml (1 tbsp) oil
10ml (2 tsp) coriander seeds, finely crushed
(optional)
I garlic clove, crushed
5ml (1 tsp) curry paste
5ml (1 tsp) tomato purée
225g (8oz) packet tofu
25g (1oz) fresh wholemeal breadcrumbs
25g (1oz) mixed nuts, finely chopped
salt and ground black pepper
plain flour, for coating
oil, for grilling

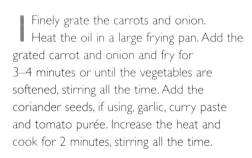

1 Finely grate the carrots and onion. Heat the oil in a large frying pan. Add the grated carrot and onion and fry for 3–4 minutes or until the vegetables are softened, stirring all the time. Add the coriander seeds, if using, garlic, curry paste and tomato purée. Increase the heat and cook for 2 minutes, stirring all the time.

2 Mash the tofu using a potato masher, then stir the mashed tofu into the vegetables with the breadcrumbs and nuts until well combined. Season with salt and pepper, then beat thoroughly until the mixture starts to stick together. With lightly floured hands, shape the mixture into eight burgers.

3 Brush the burgers lightly with oil on both sides and cook under a hot grill for about 3 minutes on each side or until they are golden brown all over. Drain on absorbent kitchen paper and serve hot.

QUORN KEBABS WITH TOMATO SALSA

These Quorn kebabs are unusual and delicious. The Quorn is marinated in a lightly spiced ginger and orange sauce and grilled with pieces of corn cob. They also work well as a vegetarian barbecue dish. Serve with natural low-fat yogurt, if wished.

● SERVES 4 ● PREPARATION TIME: 20 MINUTES
● COOKING TIME: 6 MINUTES ● 227 CALS
PER SERVING ● 12.6G FAT, OF WHICH 1.9G
SATURATED FAT

350g (12oz) Quorn, cubed
2 corn cobs, each weighing about 200g (7oz)
Marinade:
15ml (1 tbsp) Cajun seasoning
5ml (1 tsp) mild chilli seasoning
30ml (2 tbsp) bottled ginger and orange sauce
finely grated rind and juice of 2 limes
30ml (2 tbsp) olive oil
Tomato Salsa:
1 large tomato
1 small red pepper
1 very small red chilli
3 spring onions
¼ small cucumber
30ml (2 tbsp) chopped fresh parsley
15ml (1 tbsp) olive oil
salt and ground black pepper

1 In a non-metallic bowl, mix together the ingredients for the marinade. Stir in the Quorn cubes and leave to marinate for at least 15 minutes.

2 Meanwhile, make the tomato salsa. Finely dice the tomato and red pepper, discarding the core and seeds. Finely chop the chilli (wearing rubber gloves to avoid skin irritation). Slice the spring onions; finely dice the cucumber. Mix these prepared ingredients with the parsley, oil and seasoning.

3 Remove the Quorn from the marinade with a slotted spoon. Cut the corn cobs into thin slices and thread onto fine skewers with the Quorn cubes, taking care that the Quorn does not break up.

4 Brush the kebabs with the remaining marinade and grill for about 6 minutes, turning them and basting occasionally, until the Quorn is heated through and the corn is evenly browned. Serve with the tomato salsa.

STUFFED PEPPERS

Glorious to look at and more so to taste, these stuffed peppers are filled with rice, mushrooms and pinenuts and flavoured with a hint of ginger and soy sauce. Serve with crusty bread.

● SERVES 6 ● PREPARATION TIME: 30 MINUTES
● COOKING TIME: 30 MINUTES ● 265 CALS
PER SERVING ● 13.8G FAT, OF WHICH 3.3G
SATURATED FAT

6 red peppers
1 onion, peeled
2.5cm (1 inch) piece fresh root ginger, peeled
25g (1oz) butter or margarine
1 garlic clove, crushed
125g (4oz) long-grain rice
450ml (¾ pint) vegetable stock
15ml (1 tbsp) tomato purée
125g (4oz) mushrooms, sliced
50g (2oz) pine nuts or flaked almonds, toasted
10ml (2 tsp) soy sauce
salt and ground black pepper
30ml (2 tbsp) oil

1 Cut a 2.5cm (1 inch) lid from the stem end of each pepper. Scoop out the core and seeds. Blanch the shells and lids in boiling water for about 2 minutes; drain and cool.

2 Finely chop the onion and ginger. Melt the butter in a saucepan and gently fry the onion, ginger and garlic until softened. Stir in the rice and cook for 1–2 minutes.

3 Add the stock, tomato purée and mushrooms. Bring to the boil and simmer for 13–15 minutes or until the rice is tender and all the stock has been absorbed.

4 Stir in the nuts and soy sauce. Check the seasoning. Use this mixture to fill the pepper cavities.

5 Replace the lids, then stand the peppers in a deep ovenproof dish and pour over the oil. Cover with foil or a lid and bake at 190°C (375°F) Mark 5 for 30 minutes or until the peppers are tender.

JACKET POTATOES WITH CHILLI

Providing a hearty meal, these jacket potatoes are filled with a nutritious chilli bean stew that is quick and easy to prepare for a family lunch or supper. Serve with a mixed salad.

● SERVES 4 ● PREPARATION TIME: 10 MINUTES
● COOKING TIME: ABOUT 1 HOUR 30 MINUTES
● 250 CALS PER SERVING ● 1.1G FAT, OF WHICH 0.1G SATURATED FAT

4 large potatoes, each weighing about 175g (6oz)
oil for coating (optional)
salt and ground black pepper
Hot Chilli Bean Filling:
400g (14oz) can chopped tomatoes
10ml (2 tsp) tomato purée
2 garlic cloves, crushed
2.5ml (½ tsp) chilli powder
2.5ml (½ tsp) dried oregano
400g (14oz) can red kidney beans, drained and rinsed
30ml (2 tbsp) chopped fresh coriander or fresh parsley
fresh coriander sprigs, to garnish

1 Scrub the potatoes and prick all over with a fork. If you prefer baked potatoes with softish skins, put the potatoes into the oven while still wet. For crunchy skins, rub them all over with a little oil and sprinkle with salt.

2 Bake the potatoes at 200°C (400°F) Mark 6 for about 1½ hours or until the potatoes feel soft when gently squeezed, turning them over once during cooking.

3 Meanwhile make the filling. Put all the ingredients in a saucepan, season with salt and pepper, and bring to the boil. Cook vigorously for 15–20 minutes or until reduced and thickened.

4 When the potatoes are cooked, cut them in half and mash the flesh lightly with a fork. Pile the filling on top. Serve garnished with coriander.

VARIATION

● *Omit the chilli bean filling and serve the potatoes topped with a mixture of grated carrot and low-fat cheese.*

BAKED BLACK-EYED BEAN CASSEROLE

This casserole is based on the American recipe for Boston Baked Beans. The beans are cooked long and slow in a rich sauce of cider, tomatoes, treacle and mustard. Serve with garlic bread or jacket potatoes, and accompanied by a crisp, colourful salad.

● SERVES 4 ● PREPARATION TIME: 10 MINUTES, PLUS SOAKING ● COOKING TIME: 2–2½ HOURS ● 335 CALS PER SERVING ● 6.6G FAT, OF WHICH 1.1G SATURATED FAT

225g (8oz) black-eyed beans
1 large garlic clove
1 large onion
30ml (2 tbsp) olive oil
600ml (1 pint) dry cider
150ml (¼ pint) passata
30ml (2 tbsp) tomato purée
15ml (1 tbsp) black treacle
15ml (1 tbsp) demerara sugar
5ml (1 tsp) French mustard
coarse sea salt and ground black pepper
fresh parsley sprigs, to garnish

1 Soak the black-eyed beans overnight in plenty of cold water.

2 Drain the beans, rinse thoroughly and place in a large saucepan. Cover with plenty of fresh cold water, bring to the boil and boil steadily for 10 minutes. Remove any scum with a slotted spoon. Lower the heat, cover and simmer for a further 20 minutes. Do not add seasoning at this stage as it toughens the beans. Drain the beans.

3 Preheat the oven to 170°C (325°F) Mark 3. Peel and finely chop the garlic. Peel and chop the onion.

4 Heat the oil in a saucepan, add the onion and garlic and fry gently until tender. Add the cider, passata, tomato purée, black treacle, sugar and mustard. Bring to the boil.

5 Transfer the black-eyed beans to a casserole and add the prepared sauce. Stir well until evenly mixed, then cover and cook in the oven for 1½–2 hours or until the beans are tender. Check and stir the beans occasionally during cooking and add a little extra cider or water if necessary to prevent them drying out; the finished sauce should be thick and syrupy. Season with salt and pepper to taste.

6 Serve in warmed bowls and garnish with the parsley sprigs to serve.

VARIATION

● Instead of black-eyed beans, use haricot beans or another pulse variety, adjusting the cooking time accordingly.

NOTE

● The cooking time for pulses varies considerably. The longer the beans have been stored, the longer they will take to cook.

SPICY VEGETABLE COUSCOUS WITH HARISSA

This is a spicy version of vegetable couscous, not for the faint-hearted. Harissa, the traditional accompaniment to couscous, is a fiery hot red chilli paste, flavoured with garlic, coriander, cumin and mint. It is used widely in North African cookery and is available from ethnic shops in tubes or small cans. If you can't find it, make your own substitute (see Note).

● SERVES 4–6 ● PREPARATION TIME: 30 MINUTES ● COOKING TIME: ABOUT 20 MINUTES ● 460–308 CALS PER SERVING ● 10.8–7G FAT, OF WHICH 5.7–3.8G SATURATED FAT

2 small onions
1 bunch of baby fennel, or 1 large fennel bulb
225g (8oz) pumpkin
225g (8oz) small whole baby carrots
450g (1lb) quick-cook couscous
40g (1½oz) butter
2 garlic cloves, crushed
good pinch of saffron strands
2 cinnamon sticks
30ml (2 tbsp) coriander seeds, crushed
5ml (1 tsp) paprika
1 red chilli
225g (8oz) tomatoes
225g (8oz) courgettes
175g (6oz) shelled fresh or frozen broad beans (optional)
50g (2oz) raisins
450ml (¾ pint) vegetable stock
salt and ground black pepper
15ml (1 tbsp) harissa, plus extra to serve (see Note)
chopped fresh coriander, to garnish

HARISSA

● If harissa is unobtainable, flavour 30ml (2 tbsp) tomato purée with a little crushed garlic and paprika and cayenne pepper, to taste.

1 Peel and quarter the onions. Trim the baby fennel or quarter, core and chop the large fennel, if using. Peel and chop the pumpkin. Trim and scrub the carrots.

2 Put the couscous in a bowl and moisten with some water, according to packet instructions. Drain well and place in a steamer or colander lined with muslin. Steam over boiling water for about 20 minutes, forking it through occasionally, until tender and fluffed up.

3 Meanwhile, cook the vegetables: melt the butter in a large saucepan and add the onions, garlic, fennel, pumpkin and carrots. Cook, stirring, for 3 minutes. Crumble in the saffron and stir in the cinnamon, coriander, paprika and chilli. Lower the heat, cover and cook for 5 minutes.

4 Meanwhile, finely slice the chilli; skin and chop the tomatoes; thickly slice the courgettes; skin the broad beans, if using. Add these vegetables to the saucepan with the raisins and stock. Season with salt and pepper to taste. Cook, uncovered, over a medium heat for 10–12 minutes, stirring frequently, until the vegetables are tender and the stock has reduced a little.

5 Just before serving, pour about 200ml (7fl oz) of the cooking liquor into a small bowl and stir in the harissa paste.

6 Pile the couscous onto a warmed platter or individual plates and top with the vegetables. Sprinkle with coriander and serve with more harissa paste.

VEGETABLE COUSCOUS

Couscous is a staple food in Algeria, Morocco and Tunisia, and is produced from semolina grains. It is often served with chicken or lamb or – as it is here – couscous grains are steamed over a nourishing vegetable stew. Use quick-cook couscous – which needs to be moistened before cooking but doesn't require lengthy soaking. Vary the vegetables as you like.

● SERVES 4 ● PREPARATION TIME: 15 MINUTES
● COOKING TIME: 15 MINUTES ● 260 CALS
PER SERVING ● 5.4G FAT, OF WHICH 0.6G
SATURATED FAT

225g (8oz) quick-cook couscous
225g (8oz) aubergine
175g (6oz) courgettes
175g (6oz) carrots, peeled
1 large onion, peeled
15ml (1 tbsp) oil
2 garlic cloves, crushed
10ml (2 tsp) ground cumin
2.5ml (½ tsp) mild chilli seasoning
2.5ml (½ tsp) ground ginger
60ml (4 tbsp) tomato purée
1 bay leaf
175g (6oz) canned chickpeas, drained, or frozen broad beans
750ml (1¼ pints) vegetable stock
salt and ground black pepper

To garnish:
chopped fresh parsley
paprika (optional)

1 Moisten the couscous according to the packet instructions. Cut the aubergine and courgettes into chunks. Chop the carrots. Finely chop the onion. Heat the oil in a saucepan (over which a steamer, metal sieve or colander will fit). Add the onion, carrots, garlic and spices and cook gently, stirring occasionally, for 1 minute.

2 Add the tomato purée, bay leaf, aubergine, courgettes and chickpeas or broad beans. Stir in the stock. Cover and bring to the boil, then uncover and boil rapidly for 8 minutes.

3 Meanwhile, fork the couscous through to break up any lumps and spread in a steamer, metal sieve, or colander lined with a double thickness of muslin.

4 Place the couscous container over the cooking vegetables. Cover and cook for 5 minutes or until the vegetables are tender, the sauce is well reduced and the couscous is piping hot. Check the seasoning.

5 Spoon the couscous onto a warmed serving dish and fork through. Pile the vegetables and juices on top. Garnish with plenty of chopped parsley and sprinkle with paprika to serve, if desired.

VARIATIONS

● Use another pulse in place of the chickpeas. Black-eyed beans are particularly good; cook as above.
● Replace the tomato purée with 350g (12oz) fresh tomatoes, skinned and quartered.
● Include other vegetables, such as cauliflower florets, sliced leeks and diced red pepper.

DESSERTS

Desserts need not be fattening – think of all the wonderful fruits available through the year, from the soft summer fruits and berries to the many varieties of apples, pears and exotic fruits which have become so readily available. A fruit salad makes an excellent end to a meal while compotes of poached fruits in winter are comforting and warming. Spices, citrus juices and natural fruit juices can be added to flavour and sweeten desserts instead of piling on the sugar; fruit can be macerated in juices or alcohol to add an extra dimension; and low-fat yogurt or crème fraîche can be used as accompaniments or ingredients instead of cream. Dried fruits, too, give flavour and texture to puddings.

You can create good hearty desserts without too many calories. Try the delicious but light Apricot and Cardamom Crumble, Raspberry Cheesecakes, and Chocolate Pancakes. They are all indulgent, but not too high in fat. For a lighter end to the meal there are airy souffés made with mango or prunes and Armagnac.

Refreshing sorbets that cleanse the palate are ideal low-fat desserts: choose from lemon sorbet, raspberry and cocoa sorbets and three classics – melon, orange and strawberry.

Remember that presentation plays a major role and can quickly transform a simple dessert into a spectacular one. A fine dusting of icing sugar, a fresh sprig of mint or a slice of fruit can add welcome colour and interest to a dessert.

SPICED PEACHES

This highly attractive dessert oozes with flavour. Serve the peaches in a glass bowl with the syrup and leave the spices in as they make a pretty garnish.

- SERVES 8 ● PREPARATION TIME: 30 MINUTES
- COOKING TIME: 1 HOUR 20 MINUTES, PLUS COOLING AND STANDING ● 100 CALS PER SERVING
- 0.2G FAT; NO SATURATED FAT

125g (4oz) caster sugar
2.5ml (½ tsp) black peppercorns
4 bay leaves
finely grated rind and juice of 1 lemon
8 large ripe peaches

1 Place the caster sugar in a large saucepan with 450ml (¾ pint) water, the peppercorns, bay leaves and the grated rind and juice of the lemon. Bring the mixture slowly to the boil, then simmer for 5 minutes.

2 Stone and quarter the peaches, then add to the saucepan Return the mixture to the boil, then cover and bubble gently for 10 minutes or until the peaches are just soft. Lift the peaches out of the liquor and set aside to cool.

3 Bring the liquor to the boil again and bubble until it has a light syrupy consistency (this will take about 15–20 minutes). Reserve the peppercorns and bay leaves as these will add flavour to the peaches later when the peaches are soaked in the syrup.

4 When the peaches are cool enough to handle, carefully peel off the skins, if wished, as this will help the fruit to absorb the flavours from the syrup. Pour the hot syrup over the peaches, then cover and leave in a cool place for 12 hours before serving.

GINGER-GLAZED PINEAPPLE

Ginger is used in the glaze to enhance the hot, caramelised pineapple, giving it a subtle, fresh dimension.

● SERVES 8 ● PREPARATION TIME: 30 MINUTES
● COOKING TIME: 10 MINUTES ● 65 CALS PER
SERVING ● 0.3G FAT; NO SATURATED FAT

2 medium ripe pineapples
30ml (2 tbsp) light soft brown (muscovado) sugar
10ml (2 tsp) ground ginger
low-fat yogurt, to serve
5ml (1 tsp) runny honey (optional)
ground ginger, for dusting

1 Cut both pineapples into four lengthways, keeping the stalk on. Remove the fibrous core and, to give a neat appearance to the finished dish, use a large, serrated knife to cut the flesh away from the skin – this will keep the shape of the pineapple. Reserve the skin 'shells'. Cut the flesh into pieces and return to the pineapple 'shell'. Wrap the green leaves of the stalk in foil so that they don't burn while grilling. Mix the brown sugar and ground ginger together.

2 Sprinkle each pineapple quarter with the sugar mixture. Place on foil-lined baking sheets and cook under a preheated grill for 10 minutes or until golden and caramelised.

3 Mix the yogurt with the runny honey, if using. Serve the pineapple with the yogurt and dust with ground ginger.

BAKED PEARS WITH APRICOTS AND ALMONDS

The more luscious and ripe the pears for this dish, the better. The yogurt and honey really enhance the finished dish.

- SERVES 4 ● PREPARATION TIME: 15 MINUTES
- COOKING TIME: 25–30 MINUTES ● 240 CALS PER SERVING ● 7G FAT, OF WHICH 0.5G SATURATED FAT

50g (2oz) ready-to-eat dried apricots
50g (2oz) ground almonds
50g (2oz) raisins
50g (2oz) caster sugar
1 large egg white
2 large ripe pears
Greek yogurt and a little warm honey, for drizzling (optional)

1 Roughly chop the dried apricots and place them in a small bowl with the almonds, raisins and sugar. Add the egg white and mix well.

2 Halve the pears lengthways then, using a teaspoon, remove the core. Pile the almond mixture into the centre of the pears.

3 Place the pears in an ovenproof dish and bake at 180°C (350°F) Mark 4 for 25–30 minutes or until soft. Serve immediately with a spoonful of Greek yogurt drizzled with honey, if wished.

POACHED PEARS WITH FUDGE SAUCE

Poached pears are low in calories, so you can afford to serve them with a more indulgent sauce, like this delicious fudge one.

● SERVES 4 ● PREPARATION TIME: 15 MINUTES
● COOKING TIME: 25 MINUTES, PLUS COOLING
● 225 CALS PER SERVING ● 8G FAT, OF WHICH 7G SATURATED FAT

225g (8oz) granulated sugar
2 cinnamon sticks
4 medium firm pears, peeled, stalk intact
50g (2oz) butter
75g (3oz) light brown sugar
30ml (2 tbsp) golden syrup
50ml (2fl oz) double cream
tuile or brandysnap baskets (optional, see below)
maple syrup (low-fat option, to serve)

NOTE

● Use a saucepan large enough for the pears to stand upright, to poach evenly. The cooking time depends on the pears' ripeness – when cooked they will be transparent.
● If you can only find cigar-shaped brandysnaps, to make baskets place on a baking sheet and warm through at 180°C (350°F) Mark 4 for 1 minute. Remove from the oven and unroll them so they flatten, then return to the oven for a further 1 minute. Remove from the oven. Place over an upturned tumbler to shape into a basket.

TUILE BASKETS

● MAKES 24 ● 55 CALS PER SERVING ● 2.5G FAT, OF WHICH 2G SATURATED FAT

Line baking sheets with greaseproof paper. Whisk 3 large egg whites with 100g (3½oz) each sifted icing sugar and plain flour. Stir in 75g (3oz) melted unsalted butter. Cover and chill for 30 minutes. Place teaspoonfuls of the mixture well apart on the baking sheets, spread out into 9cm (3½ inch) circles. Bake at 200°C (400°F) Mark 6 for 12 minutes or until just brown at the edges. Over an upturned tumbler, mould quickly into baskets while still warm. These will keep in an airtight tin for up to a week.

1 Place the granulated sugar and the cinnamon sticks in a saucepan (see Note), add 500ml (1 pint) water and heat gently, stirring occasionally, until the sugar dissolves. Bring to the boil and bubble for 2 minutes. Meanwhile, carefully remove the core from the pears using the tip of a vegetable peeler or the sharp edge of a teaspoon.

2 Place the pears immediately in the sugar syrup and cover the saucepan with a circle of greaseproof paper, followed by a lid. Bring the pears to the boil, reduce the heat and cook gently for 20–25 minutes or until tender (see Note). Set aside.

3 Place the butter, brown sugar, syrup and cream in a saucepan. Heat gently until melted, then bring to the boil and bubble for 1 minute.

4 Lift the pears out of the syrup, sit in a tuile or brandysnap basket (see Note), then spoon the warm fudge sauce over. Alternatively, to make the fat content negligible, substitute the fudge sauce with a liittle maple syrup. Serve immediately.

PEAR GALETTES WITH CHOCOLATE SAUCE

These little galettes are easy to make using ready-to-bake dough – and they're delicious, too.

● MAKES 6 ● PREPARATION TIME: 15 MINUTES
● COOKING TIME: 10 MINUTES ● 220 CALS PER
SERVING ● 9G FAT, OF WHICH 3G SATURATED FAT

1 tube ready-to-bake pain au chocolat dough with
chocolate pieces (see Note)
flour, to dust
2 firm, but ripe pears, cored and cut into thick slices
ground cinnamon
30ml (6 tsp) soft dark brown sugar
150ml (¼ pint) semi-skimmed milk
cinnamon and icing sugar, to dust

NOTE

● *If you can't find ready-to-bake pain au*
chocolat dough, use 350g (12oz) puff pastry
and 40g (1½oz) plain chocolate, broken into
small pieces. Roll out the pastry and complete
the recipe, cooking at the same temperature for
20 minutes.

1 Place a baking sheet in the oven at 200°C (400°F) Mark 6 to heat. Unroll the dough onto a lightly floured work surface; set aside the chocolate pieces. Using a cup or saucer, cut six circles, about 10cm (4 inches) in diameter, and place on a second baking sheet.

2 Quarter the pears and core them with a sharp knife. Cut the flesh into thick slices and arrange these on top of the dough. Sprinkle each one with a little cinnamon and 5ml (1 tsp) sugar.

3 Place the second baking sheet in the oven on top of the hot baking sheet and cook for 6–8 minutes or until the galettes are golden brown.

4 Meanwhile, to make the chocolate sauce, bring the milk to the boil, then whisk in the reserved chocolate pieces. Bubble for about 3 minutes or until the sauce is syrupy.

5 Dust the galettes with a little cinnamon and icing sugar. Serve with the warm chocolate sauce.

PEARS IN MALMSEY MADEIRA

Malmsey Madeira is the sweetest, darkest and richest type of Madeira. Here it is made into a thick syrup in which the pears are poached.

● SERVES 6 ● PREPARATION TIME: 15 MINUTES
● COOKING TIME: 30 MINUTES–1 HOUR, PLUS COOLING ● 270 CALS PER SERVING ● NO FAT

300ml (½ pint) Malmsey Madeira or a dark cream sherry
225g (8oz) caster sugar
grated rind of 2 lemons
1 vanilla pod, split
6 firm under-ripe pears (see Note)

NOTES

● *Suitable for freezing: complete the recipe, then pack and freeze.*
● *Slightly under-ripe pears will keep their shape better when poaching.*
● *If you don't have a canelle knife, you can use a vegetable peeler to peel away thin strips of skin from the pears.*
● *If wished, carefully remove the core of the pears by using the tip of a vegetable peeler, working from the base of the fruit.*

1 Pour the Malmsey Madeira and 150ml (¼ pint) water into a pan and add the caster sugar, lemon rind and vanilla pod. Heat gently until the sugar is dissolved and boil for 3 minutes. Set aside.

2 Decorate the pears by using a canelle knife to etch spirals or stripes into the skin of the fruit, working from the stem end, retaining the stalks.

3 Stand the pears in the smallest saucepan that will take them. Pour the syrup over the top and tuck the lemon rind and vanilla pods among them. Cover tightly, bring to the boil and simmer gently until tender, anything from 30 minutes–1 hour, depending on the ripeness of the pears,

4 Lift the pears out of the syrup; set aside. Boil the syrup until reduced by half. Strain over the pears. Serve at room temperature.

FRUIT KEBABS WITH SPICED PEAR DIP

This delicious, fruity, energy-boosting pudding with just 125 calories can be rustled up in hardly any time. You could use a mixture of oranges, apricots, peaches and plums if you prefer.

● MAKES 6 KEBABS ● PREPARATION TIME: 20 MINUTES, PLUS SOAKING ● COOKING TIME: 8 MINUTES ● 125 CALS PER KEBAB, INCLUDING DIP ● 3G FAT, OF WHICH 0.3G SATURATED FAT

Spiced Pear Dip:

150g (5oz) ready-to-eat dried pears, soaked in hot water for about 30 minutes
juice of 1 orange
5ml (1 tsp) finely chopped fresh root ginger
2.5ml (½ tsp) vanilla extract
50ml (2fl oz) very low-fat plain yogurt
2.5ml (½ tsp) ground cinnamon, plus extra, to dust
5ml (1 tsp) dark runny honey
25g (1oz) hazelnuts, toasted and roughly chopped

Fruit Kebabs:

3 large fresh figs, cut into quarters
1 large ripe mango, skinned and stoned, flesh cut into large cubes
1 baby pineapple or 2 thick slices, skin removed and flesh cut into large cubes
15ml (1 tbsp) dark runny honey

1 To make the dip, drain the pears and place in a food processor or blender with the orange juice, ginger, vanilla extract, yogurt, cinnamon and 50ml (2fl oz) water and process until smooth. Spoon the dip into a bowl. Drizzle with the runny honey, sprinkle with the toasted hazelnuts and dust with a little ground cinnamon. Cover and set aside in a cool place until ready to serve.

2 Preheat the grill to its highest setting. To make the kebabs, thread alternate pieces of fruit on to six 20.5cm (8 inch) wooden kebab skewers, using at least two pieces of each type of fruit per skewer. Place the skewers on a foil-covered tray and cover the ends of the skewers with strips of foil to prevent them burning. Drizzle with honey and grill for about 4 minutes on each side, close to the heat, until lightly charred. Serve warm or at room temperature with the dip.

RHUBARB AND RASPBERRY MERINGUES

Forced rhubarb arrives in the shops in late January or early February. It has a delicate flavour which marries well with ginger, but you could use a pinch of cinnamon as an alternative.

● SERVES 4 ● PREPARATION TIME: 15 MINUTES
● COOKING TIME: 10–15 MINUTES ● 90 CALS PER
SERVING ● 0.2G FAT; NO SATURATED FAT

450g (1lb) rhubarb
2.5cm (1 inch) piece stem ginger (optional)
1 orange
75g (3oz) caster sugar
75g (3oz) frozen raspberries
1 large egg white

1 Clean and cut the rhubarb into 2.5cm (1 inch) pieces. Finely chop the stem ginger, if using.

2 Thinly grate the orange rind with a zester. Squeeze the juice out of the orange and set aside. You will need to add a little to prevent the rhubarb becoming too dry.

3 Place the rhubarb in a large saucepan with 25g (1oz) caster sugar, the chopped stem ginger, if using, and the orange rind. Cover and cook gently for 2–3 minutes, adding a little orange juice as necessary. Add the raspberries. Spoon the mixture into four 150ml (5fl oz) ramekins or ovenproof cups.

4 Whisk the egg white and remaining sugar together until foamy. Place the bowl over a saucepan of simmering water and continue to whisk for 5 minutes or until stiff and shiny.

5 Place a spoonful of meringue mixture on top of each ramekin and bake at 180°C (350°F) Mark 4 for 5–10 minutes or until lightly golden.

WARM TROPICAL FRUITS WITH SABAYON SAUCE

You can use any fruits for this pudding. The sabayon is easy but requires patience when whisking. To save time, you can omit the sauce, sprinkle the fruit with icing sugar and brown under the grill, reducing the calories to 135 cals per serving.

● SERVES 4 ● PREPARATION TIME: 25 MINUTES
● COOKING TIME: 15 MINUTES ● 250 CALS PER SERVING ● 0.5FAT; NO SATURATED FAT

4 passion fruit
125g (4oz) fresh lychees or 425g (15oz) can
1 large mango, peeled and sliced
1 medium ripe pineapple, peeled and sliced
2 bananas, peeled and thickly sliced
1 large egg, plus 2 large egg yolks
50g (2oz) caster sugar
90ml (6 tbsp) sweet white wine or orange-flavoured liqueur

NOTE

● *The mixture may curdle if it becomes too hot. If possible, use a ceramic bowl which will heat more quickly than Pyrex, giving a thicker mixture. The sauce is ready when it's thick enough to leave a ribbon trail.*

1 Remove the flesh from the passion fruit. Peel and remove the stones from the lychees (if using canned, drain). Place all the fruit in four shallow 12.5cm (5 inch) diameter ovenproof dishes. Cover with foil; bake at 200°C (400°F) Mark 6 for 15 minutes.

2 Meanwhile, place the egg and yolks, sugar and sweet white wine or orange-flavoured liqueur in a bowl, then whisk until beginning to thicken. Place over a saucepan of simmering water, with the bowl just touching the water, and whisk for 10–15 minutes until fluffy (see Note).

3 Preheat the grill. Remove the fruit from the oven and spoon the sauce over. Grill until golden. Serve immediately.

HOT MANGO SOUFFLÉS WITH PAPAYA SAUCE

These little fruit-flavoured soufflés are turned out while hot onto a pool of slightly sharp, scented papaya sauce – and the crunchy almond layer in the base becomes a nutty, golden topping. The thought of tipping a hot soufflé out of its dish to serve may worry even the most confident cook, but this recipe works like a dream.

● SERVES 6 ● PREPARATION TIME: 55 MINUTES ● COOKING TIME: 6–8 MINUTES ● 310 CALS PER SERVING ● 9.4G FAT, OF WHICH 4.8G SATURATED FAT

50g (2oz) butter, melted
150g (5oz) caster sugar
25g (1oz) blanched almonds
2 ripe mangoes, each weighing about 350g (12oz)
20ml (4 tsp) cornflour
30ml (2 tbsp) orange juice
5ml (1 tsp) finely grated orange rind
6 egg whites
Papaya Sauce:
2–3 papayas
30–45ml (2–3 tbsp) caster sugar
10–15ml (2–3 tsp) lemon juice

1 Brush six deep ramekins evenly and generously with the butter, then dust with 40g (1½oz) of the sugar, tapping out any excess sugar. Chop the almonds coarsely and divide equally between the ramekins.

2 Peel the mangoes and cut the flesh away from the stones. Purée the mango flesh in a food processor or blender until smooth.

3 Pour the mango purée into a small, heavy-based saucepan and cook over a low heat for 20 minutes, stirring frequently, until reduced to a thick paste.

4 Put the remaining sugar in a small heavy-based pan, with 45ml (3 tbsp) water and dissolve over a low heat, stirring occasionally. Boil rapidly for 2 minutes, then stir the syrup into the mango purée.

5 In a small bowl, blend the cornflour with the orange juice to a smooth paste, then stir into the mango purée, with the orange rind. Place in a saucepan and cook, stirring, over a medium heat until boiling and thickened. Remove from the heat and cover the surface with dampened greaseproof paper; set aside to cool.

6 Meanwhile, make the papaya sauce. Halve the papayas, scoop out the seeds and discard, then peel away the skin. Purée the flesh in a food processor or blender until smooth. Add sugar and lemon juice to taste; set aside.

7 Preheat the oven to 220°C (425°F) Mark 7 and preheat a baking sheet. Whisk the egg whites in a large bowl until holding soft peaks, then whisk one-third of the egg whites into the mango mixture. Carefully fold in the remaining egg whites.

8 Spoon the mixture into the ramekins until they are full. Place on the preheated baking sheet and bake just above the centre of the oven for 6–8 minutes until well risen and golden.

9 Meanwhile, spoon the papaya sauce onto individual plates. When the soufflés are ready, gently unmould them, using a palette knife, place them onto the sauce and serve at once.

PLUMS WITH CARAMELISED FRUIT BREAD

This simple-to-make dish is also perfect for a special breakfast or brunch. Make sure you choose ripe fruit as it will be sweeter and have a better flavour, which means you can cut down on sugar.

● SERVES 4 ● PREPARATION TIME: 10 MINUTES
● COOKING TIME: 16 MINUTES ● 250 CALS PER SERVING ● 9G FAT, OF WHICH 4G SATURATED FAT

700g (1½lb) dessert plums, stoned and cut into quarters
60ml (4 tbsp) caster sugar
8 slices fruit or cinnamon bread, about 5mm (¼ inch) thick
1 large egg
45ml (3 tbsp) milk
25g (1oz) unsalted butter
Greek yogurt, to serve

NOTE

● You can buy the fruit a few days in advance and keep in a dark, warm place to ripen further. A ripe banana gives off ethylene gas which helps other fruit ripen, so try adding one to the fruit bowl.

1 Place the plums in a heavy-based saucepan, sprinkle over 30ml (2 tbsp) caster sugar and cook over a gentle heat, stirring occasionally, for 8–10 minutes or until the plums just begin to soften.

2 Meanwhile, using a large plain cutter or upturned tumbler as a guide, cut each slice of the fruit or cinnamon bread into a circle. Beat together the egg and the milk.

3 Heat the butter in a non-stick frying pan. Dip the bread into the egg mixture, making sure it's well coated. Once the butter is hot, add the bread and sprinkle with 15ml (1 tbsp) of the caster sugar. Fry over a medium heat for about 3 minutes, turn over and sprinkle with the remaining sugar; fry for a further 3 minutes or until golden.

4 Place the cooked fruit bread on a plate, then top with the warm plums and a spoonful of Greek yogurt.

APRICOT AND CARDAMOM CRUMBLE

A good fruit crumble is delicious but can be high in calories and fat. This version is nice and light, but it won't disappoint.

● SERVES 6 ● PREPARATION TIME: 15 MINUTES
● COOKING TIME: 25 MINUTES ● 230 CALS PER
SERVING ● 10.5G FAT, OF WHICH 5G SATURATED FAT

700g (1½lb) fresh apricots, stoned and cut into
quarters
30–45ml (2–3 tbsp) caster sugar
3–4 green cardamom pods, split, seeds reserved and
crushed (see Note)
50g (2oz) plain flour
50g (2oz) jumbo rolled oats
50g (2oz) light brown sugar
50g (2oz) butter, cut into cubes
25g (1oz) hazelnuts, browned and roughly chopped
Greek yogurt, to serve (optional)

NOTES

● *If you don't have a pestle and mortar to*
crush the cardamom seeds, wrap them in a
small piece of clingfilm, place on a chopping
board and crush with the base of a heavy pan.
● *Choose apricots with the warmest colour – a*
slight pink blush means they're ripe.

1 Mix the apricots with the caster sugar and place in a 1.3 litre (2¼ pint) capacity ovenproof dish or divide between six individual ovenproof dishes.

2 Place the crushed cardamom seeds, flour, oats and light brown sugar in a large bowl, then rub in the butter until the mixture resembles rough breadcrumbs. Mix in the chopped hazelnuts.

3 Spoon the crumble mixture over the fruit. Bake at 190°C (375°F) Mark 5 for 25–30 minutes or until golden brown. Serve warm with a little Greek yogurt, if wished.

SUMMER PUDDING

What would summer be without summer pudding? Oozing with red fruits and moist with their juices that saturate the bread, it epitomises summer. Serve with low-fat cream or fat-free yogurt.

● SERVES 8 ● PREPARATION TIME: 20 MINUTES, PLUS CHILLING ● COOKING TIME: 10 MINUTES ● 250 CALS PER SERVING ● 1G FAT, OF WHICH 0.2G SATURATED FAT

175g (6oz) redcurrants, stalks removed
350g (12oz) blackcurrants, stalks removed
225–275g (8–10oz) granulated sugar
finely grated rind of 1 large orange
225g (8oz) raspberries, hulled
225g (8oz) loganberries, hulled
12 thick slices white bread, about 2 days old, crusts removed

NOTE

● Suitable for freezing.

1 Place the redcurrants, blackcurrants, sugar and orange rind in a large saucepan. Cover and cook gently until the juices flow and the sugar has dissolved. Add the raspberries and loganberries, and continue cooking for about 5 minutes until they are softened. Remove from the heat and leave to cool.

2 Cut a round from one of the slices of bread, large enough to fit in the base of a 1.7 litre (3 pint) pudding basin. Place the round in the basin, then line the sides of the basin with slightly overlapping slices of bread; reserve the rest for the centre and top.

3 Remove the orange rind from the fruit. Spoon half of the fruit and juice into the bread-lined basin, then place a layer of bread on top. Add the remaining fruit and juice, then cover completely with the remaining bread, trimmed to fit if necessary.

4 Cover the pudding with a plate or saucer which just fits inside the basin. Place heavy weights on top and chill overnight. To serve, remove the weights and saucer, gently loosen the pudding from the basin with a palette knife, and turn it out onto a serving plate.

VARIATION

● Autumn Pudding: Replace the summer fruits with 900g (2lb) mixed autumn fruits such as apples, blackberries and plums. Put the fruit, 90ml (6 tbsp) water and 50g (2oz) sugar in a saucepan. Cover and cook as above.

SPICED WINTER FRUIT COMPOTE

Dried fruits are poached in apple and wine syrup – double-scented with star anise and cinnamon – then served whole with a dollop of 0% fat Greek yogurt or crème fraîche. Include other dried fruits if you wish – healthfood shops and many larger supermarkets now stock a good variety, especially around Christmas.

● SERVES 6 ● PREPARATION TIME: 10 MINUTES, PLUS COOLING ● COOKING TIME: 50 MINUTES
● 155 CALS PER SERVING ● 0.4G FAT; NO SATURATED FAT

75g (3oz) ready-to-eat dried pears
75g (3oz) ready-to-eat dried figs
75g (3oz) ready-to-eat dried apricots
75g (3oz) ready-to-eat dried prunes
300ml (½ pint) apple juice (approximately, see Note)
300ml (½ pint) dry white wine
1 star anise
½ cinnamon stick
light muscovado sugar, to taste
To serve:
150ml (¼ pint) 0% fat Greek yogurt
pinch of ground cinnamon

NOTES

● *Ready-to-eat dried fruits are already slightly rehydrated. However, different varieties soak up more or less liquid during cooking, so it is important to keep a watch and add a little more apple juice, if necessary.*
● *Suitable for freezing.*

1 Put the dried fruits in a saucepan with the apple juice, the wine, star anise and cinnamon stick. Place over a low heat and bring slowly to the boil.

2 Reduce the heat, cover the pan and simmer for 45 minutes until the fruits are plump and tender. Check the liquid during cooking to ensure there is sufficient; add a little more apple juice if necessary.

3 Turn the compote into a bowl. Taste the cooking liquid for sweetness, adding a little sugar if necessary. Allow to cool to room temperature.

4 To serve, divide the compote between individual glass dishes. Accompany with crème fraîche or Greek yogurt, topped with a light sprinkling of cinnamon.

VARIATION

● *Replace the figs with apple rings and the pears with raisins.*

BLACK FOREST ROULADE

Chocolate and cherries are a classic combination. This pudding is made lighter by mixing whipping cream with 0% fat Greek yogurt which complements the richness of the sponge.

● SERVES 10 ● PREPARATION TIME: 35 MINUTES, PLUS COOLING AND CHILLING ● COOKING TIME: 20 MINUTES ● 230 CALS PER SERVING ● 11.7G FAT, OF WHICH 6.3G SATURATED FAT

2 x 425g (15oz) cans morello cherries, drained, stoned and halved
30ml (2 tbsp) Amaretto (optional)
125g (4oz) plain chocolate, chopped into small pieces
4 large eggs, separated
125g (4oz) caster sugar, plus 5ml (1 tsp) for filling
142ml carton whipping cream
75ml (3fl oz) 0% fat Greek yogurt
cocoa powder and icing sugar, to dust

1 Line a 23 x 33cm (9 x 13 inches) Swiss roll tin with non-stick baking parchment. Place the cherries in a bowl, reserving a few to decorate, and pour the Amaretto over, if using. Place the chocolate in a heatproof bowl over a pan of just simmering water and stir until melted. Cool. Place the egg yolks and 125g (4oz) sugar in a separate large bowl and whisk until thick and creamy. Whisk in the melted chocolate.

2 In a clean bowl, using an electric hand whisk, whisk the egg whites until stiff and shiny. Lightly fold into the chocolate mixture.

3 Pour the mixture into the prepared Swiss roll tin and level the surface. Bake at 180°C (350°F) Mark 4 for 20 minutes or until firm to the touch.

4 Turn the roulade out on to a large sheet of greaseproof paper and carefully peel off the baking parchment. Cover with a damp cloth. Leave to cool for 30 minutes.

5 Lightly whip the cream, add 5ml (1 tsp) sugar and stir in the Greek yogurt. Spread the cream mixture over the cold roulade and scatter the cherries on top. Roll up from one of the narrow ends, using the paper to help. Chill for 30 minutes.

6 Slice the roulade into ten pieces and arrange each slice on a plate. Dust with cocoa powder and icing sugar and decorate with the reserved cherries to serve.

NOTE

● Suitable for freezing: complete the recipe to the end of step 4. Wrap carefully in greaseproof paper, then freeze.

CHOCOLATE PANCAKES

Y ou can use any fruit instead of the banana filling, or serve the pancakes with chocolate sauce and vanilla ice cream or frozen yogurt.

● MAKES 12 PANCAKES; SERVES 6 ● PREPARATION TIME: 15 MINUTES, PLUS CHILLING ● COOKING TIME: 30–40 MINUTES ● 140 CALS PER PANCAKE ● 4.5G FAT, OF WHICH 2.4G SATURATED FAT

150g (5oz) plain chocolate
100g (3½oz) plain flour
1 large egg
pinch of salt
300ml (½ pint) skimmed milk
25g (1oz) butter
15ml (1 tbsp) light brown sugar
4 medium bananas, thickly sliced
120ml (8 tbsp) brandy
vegetable oil, for brushing
icing sugar, to dust
Greek yogurt or quark, to serve
chocolate shavings, to decorate

NOTE

● *Suitable for freezing: make and wrap the pancakes as for step 3, then freeze for up to one month. Thaw at a cool temperature for 3 hours. Complete as for step 4.*

1 Place 50g (2oz) of chocolate in a food processor and chop. Add the flour, egg, salt and milk and process until smooth. Cover and chill for 30 minutes.

2 Melt the butter and sugar in a frying pan. Add the bananas and stir-fry over a medium heat for 3 minutes. Add the brandy (take care when doing this as it may ignite in the warm pan) and continue to simmer until the bananas soften and the liquid is syrupy (about 2 minutes). Set aside.

3 Lightly brush an 18cm (7 inch) non-stick crêpe or small frying pan with oil and heat. Stir the batter and coat the base of the pan thinly, with about 60ml (4 tbsp). Cook for 2 minutes or until golden brown, then turn over. Cook for a further 1 minute. Transfer to a plate, cover and keep warm. Cook the remaining batter in the same way.

4 Chop the remaining chocolate. Place 2 dessertspoonfuls of banana filling over one half of each pancake; sprinkle with some of the chocolate. Fold in half, then in half again. Keep warm while filling the remaining pancakes. Dust with icing sugar, decorate and serve warm with Greek yogurt or quark.

RASPBERRIES WITH CHOCOLATE MALLOW

If you want a chocolate fix without many calories this is the dessert for you. It's deceptively chocolatey and rich, yet it's low in calories and contains very little fat.

● SERVES 6 ● PREPARATION TIME: 15 MINUTES
● COOKING TIME: 25 MINUTES ● 110 CALS PER
SERVING ● 2G FAT, OF WHICH 0.5G SATURATED FAT

225g (8oz) raspberries
grated rind of ½ orange
15ml (1 tbsp), plus 125g (4oz) caster sugar
3 large egg whites
15ml (1 tbsp) cocoa powder
15g (½oz) hazelnuts, toasted and roughly chopped

WATCHPOINT

● *The young, the elderly, pregnant women or anyone with immune-deficiency diseases should avoid raw or lightly cooked eggs, which may contain salmonella.*

1 Divide the raspberries, grated orange rind and 15ml (1 tbsp) caster sugar between six (150ml) ¼ pint ovenproof ramekins.

2 Place the egg whites in a bowl with 125g (4oz) caster sugar over a saucepan of gently simmering water. Using an electric hand whisk, whisk the egg whites and sugar until very stiff and shiny. Remove the bowl from the heat and whisk for 4–5 minutes or until the bowl is cool. At the last moment, fold in the cocoa powder.

3 Spoon the meringue over the fruit and sprinkle the chopped hazelnuts on top.

4 Bake at 150°C (300°F) Mark 2 for 20–25 minutes or until the meringue is lightly coloured, crisp on the outside and soft in the middle. Serve immediately.

PRUNE AND ARMAGNAC SOUFFLÉ WITH CARAMELISED WALNUTS

Prunes and Armagnac are a classic combination. Here the prunes are soaked overnight in the Armagnac so they ooze with the flavour of the alcohol.

● SERVES 6 ● PREPARATION TIME: 30 MINUTES, PLUS SOAKING ● COOKING TIME: 35 MINUTES
● 185 CALS PER SERVING ● 8.4G FAT, OF WHICH 3.3G SATURATED FAT

125g (4oz) ready-to-eat dried prunes, stoned and chopped
45ml (3 tbsp) Armagnac or brandy
25g (1oz) butter, plus extra for greasing
15ml (1 tbsp) chopped toasted hazelnuts
15ml (1 tbsp) brioche crumbs (optional)
25g (1oz) plain white flour
200ml (7fl oz) milk
3 large eggs, separated
50g (2oz) caster sugar
vanilla essence
icing sugar, to dust
Caramelised Walnuts (see below) and vanilla ice cream or frozen yogurt, to serve

CARAMELISED WALNUTS

Place 100g (3½oz) shelled walnuts and 125g (4oz) caster sugar in a saucepan with one thick slice of lemon, the finely grated rind of ½ orange and ½ split vanilla pod. Add 200ml (7fl oz) water, bring to the boil and simmer gently for 30 minutes. Drain the walnuts, discard the lemon wedges and orange rind and reserve the syrup. Spread the walnuts on a greased non-stick baking tray. Cook at 190°C (375°F) Mark 5 for 7–10 minutes or until golden; cool.

1 Soak the prunes overnight in the Armagnac or brandy. Grease six 150ml (¼ pint) ramekins. Mix the hazelnuts with the brioche crumbs, if using, and use this mixture to dust the ramekins.

2 Melt the butter in a saucepan, add the flour and mix to a smooth paste. Pour in the milk, stirring continuously, and bring to the boil. Cool the mixture a little, beat in the egg yolks, then stir in the prunes and Armagnac. Whisk the egg whites to a soft peak, add the caster sugar and whisk until stiff. Fold the egg whites into the mixture with a few drops of vanilla essence.

3 Fill the ramekins with the prune mixture and place the ramekins in a roasting tin. Add enough hot water to the roasting tin to come halfway up the sides of the moulds.

4 Cook at 190°C (375°F) Mark 5 or 20–25 minutes or until firm to the touch in the centre. Dust with icing sugar and serve with Caramelised Walnuts and vanilla ice cream or frozen yogurt.

CARROT AND CARDAMOM PUDDINGS

Deliciously moist and delicately flavoured with the cardomoms, these individual carrot puddings make an unusual and tasty end to a meal.

● SERVES 6 ● PREPARATION TIME: 20 MINUTES, PLUS INFUSING AND COOLING ● COOKING TIME: 45 MINUTES ● 100 CALS PER SERVING ● 3G FAT, OF WHICH 1.9G SATURATED FAT

150ml (¼ pint) skimmed milk
30ml (2 tbsp) caster sugar, plus extra, for dusting
3 cardamom pods, crushed
2.5ml (½ tsp) vanilla essence
20g (¾oz) unsalted butter, plus melted butter, for greasing
20g (¾ oz) plain flour
2 large egg yolks
40g (1½oz) sultanas
175g (6oz) carrots, peeled and finely grated
grated rind of 1 orange
4 large egg whites
To decorate:
Caramel Flowers (see right)
vanilla pods
orange zest
shredded cinnamon stick
Cinnamon Crème Anglaise, to serve (see below)

WATCHPOINT

● The young, elderly, pregnant women and those with immune-deficiency diseases should avoid raw or lightly cooked eggs, which may contain salmonella.

CARAMEL FLOWERS

● SERVES 6 ● 80 CALS PER FLOWER ● NO FAT

Line a baking sheet with oiled greaseproof paper. Place 120ml (8 tbsp) caster sugar in a small heavy-based saucepan with 30ml (2 tbsp) water and the crushed seeds from two cardamom pods.

Slowly dissolve the sugar, then increase heat and cook until the sugar is a medium caramel colour. Dip the base of the saucepan quickly in cold water, then immediately drizzle the caramel onto the lined baking sheet, using a fork to make abstract flower shapes about 4cm (1½ inch) in diameter. Allow to cool, peel the greaseproof paper away from the caramel and use to decorate the Carrot and Cardamom Puddings.

CINNAMON CRÈME ANGLAISE

● MAKES ABOUT 450ML (¾ PINT) ● 83 CALS PER SERVING ● 4G FAT, OF WHICH 1G SATURATED FAT

Place 450ml (¾ pint) skimmed milk, 5ml (1 tsp) ground cinnamon, a crumbled cinnamon stick and a split vanilla pod in a saucepan. Bring to the boil and set aside for 20 minutes to infuse. In a bowl, beat together 25g (1oz) caster sugar and 3 large egg yolks. Strain the infused milk into the egg mixture and stir until evenly combined. Return the mixture to the clean saucepan and cook gently, stirring until thickened (don't boil). Strain and serve warm with the Carrot and Cardamom Puddings.

1 Place the milk, sugar and cardamom pods in a saucepan and bring to the boil. Remove from the heat and set aside for 15 minutes to infuse. Strain, then add the vanilla essence.

2 Brush six 200ml (7fl oz) dariole moulds or ramekins with a little melted butter and dust with caster sugar. Melt the butter in a saucepan, stir in the flour and cook for 30 seconds. Add the milk, bring to the boil, stirring. Leave to cool a little, then beat in the egg yolks. Add the sultanas, carrots and orange rind.

3 Whisk the egg whites to medium peaks and fold in. Divide the mixture between the moulds. Place in a roasting tin. Add enough hot water to come halfway up the sides of the dishes.

4 Cook at 180°C (350°F) Mark 4 for 10 minutes. Decorate with Caramel Flowers, vanilla pods, orange zest and cinnamon. Serve with Cinnamon Crème Anglaise.

RED FRUIT TERRINE

Choose the best quality summer fruits for this highly attractive, fruit-filled dessert. Serve with low-fat single cream or fat-free yogurt.

● SERVES 6 ● PREPARATION TIME: 50 MINUTES, PLUS CHILLING ● COOKING TIME: 3 MINUTES ● 100 CALS PER SERVING ● 0.2G FAT; NO SATURATED FAT

65g (2½oz) caster sugar
250ml (9fl oz) medium-dry white wine
45ml (3 tbsp) lemon juice
20ml (4 tsp) powdered gelatine
225g (8oz) redcurrants
225g (8oz) medium ripe strawberries, hulled
225g (8oz) raspberries
6 mint leaves
redcurrant sprigs, to decorate

2 Sprinkle gelatine over 60ml (4 tbsp) water in a small bowl and leave to soak for 2–3 minutes. Stand the bowl over a pan of gently simmering water for 2–3 minutes until the gelatine is dissolved. Add to the syrup and leave to cool.

4 Place a 1.1 litre (2 pint) non-stick loaf tin in a roasting tin containing ice cubes and cold water to come halfway up the sides of the tin. Place a layer of redcurrants in the loaf tin; spoon over the liquid jelly to cover. Leave to set.

1 Put the sugar and 250ml (9 fl oz) water in a heavy-based saucepan. Dissolve over a low heat, then bring to the boil and let bubble for 1 minute. Pour into a bowl, cool, then add the wine and lemon juice.

3 Strip the redcurrants off the stalks and slice the strawberries.

5 Layer the remaining fruit in the tin, with the mint leaves. Carefully spoon over the jelly to fill. Leave the mould in the roasting tin until the jelly is just set. Transfer to the refrigerator and leave until set completely – at least 3 hours or preferably overnight.

6 Fill a large bowl with hot water. Dip the loaf tin in the water for 3–4 seconds. Immediately invert onto a flat platter, gently shaking the tin to release the jelly. Lift off the tin. Decorate the fruit terrine with tiny sprigs

FRUIT TERRINE WITH STRAWBERRY SAUCE

This splendid terrine has alternate layers of vivid orange and ruby red jelly set with raspberries and orange segments. A peppery strawberry sauce – flavoured with balsamic vinegar – is the ideal complement.

● SERVES 6 ● PREPARATION TIME: 25 MINUTES, PLUS SETTING ● 150 CALS PER SERVING ● 0.2G FAT; NO SATURATED FAT

300ml (½ pint) orange juice
300ml (½ pint) ruby red orange juice
1½ x 11g (0.4oz) sachets powdered gelatine
15ml (1 tbsp) Grand Marnier or other orange-flavoured liqueur
50g (2oz) caster sugar
225g (8oz) raspberries
3 oranges
Sauce:
225g (8oz) strawberries, hulled
50g (2oz) caster sugar
10ml (2 tsp) balsamic vinegar (optional)
5–10ml (1–2 tsp) ground black pepper

NOTE

● *Make sure that each layer of jelly is only just set, before you add the next one: the surface should be slightly sticky. If it is set too firmly, the layers may not hold together once the terrine is turned out. Keep the jelly for subsequent layers at room temperature – place the jugs of jelly in a pan of lukewarm water if they begin to set.*

1 Line a 1.2 litre (2 pint) loaf tin with clingfilm. Pour 45ml (3 tbsp) of each orange juice into separate small heatproof bowls. Sprinkle on the gelatine, dividing it equally between them. Leave to soften for a few minutes, then stand the bowls in a pan of hot water until the gelatine has dissolved. Add each gelatine liquid to the appropriate remaining fruit juice.

2 Stir the orange liqueur and half of the sugar into the orange-coloured jelly, then pour half of this into the prepared mould. Scatter over half of the raspberries. Chill until just set (see Note).

3 Meanwhile, cut the peel and white pith from the oranges, then cut out the segments. Cut each segment into two or three pieces; drain in a sieve.

4 When the first layer of orange jelly has just set, arrange the orange segments on top. Stir the remaining sugar into the ruby red orange jelly, pour gently over the orange jelly and chill again until just set.

5 Pour the remaining orange-coloured jelly on top and scatter over the remaining raspberries. Return to the refrigerator and leave to set firmly.

6 To make the strawberry sauce, put the strawberries in a food processor or blender with the sugar, vinegar and pepper, and purée until smooth. Chill.

7 To serve, turn out the terrine onto a board and carefully peel off the clingfilm. Cut into slices, using a large serrated knife that has been dipped into hot water. Pour the strawberry sauce onto individual plates and arrange a slice or two of the fruit terrine on top of each serving.

ORANGES IN CARAMEL

The oranges are gently poached in a caramel syrup and served with crunchy pieces of caramel, for a sweet, yet refreshing dessert. Serve well chilled.

● SERVES 6 ● PREPARATION TIME: 25 MINUTES, PLUS CHILLING ● COOKING TIME: 25–30 MINUTES ● 285 CALS PER SERVING ● 0.2G FAT; NO SATURATED FAT

225g (8oz) granulated sugar
6 large oranges
30–45ml (2–3 tbsp) Grand Marnier or other orange-flavoured liqueur
Caramel Chips:
75g (3oz) granulated sugar

1 Put the sugar and 50ml (2fl oz) water in a saucepan and heat gently until dissolved, brushing down the sides of the pan with hot water. Bring to the boil, then boil until the syrup turns a golden caramel.

2 Immediately plunge the base of the pan into cold water to prevent further cooking. Carefully pour 300ml (½ pint) boiling water into the pan. Reheat gently until the caramel has completely dissolved.

3 Meanwhile, thinly pare the rind from two of the oranges, taking care not to remove the white pith. Cut the rind into very fine shreds and set aside. Using a very sharp knife, remove the skin and white pith from all the oranges.

4 Add the oranges and shredded rind to the caramel, cover and cook very gently for 25–30 minutes, turning frequently until the oranges are tender; do not overcook – they must retain a good shape. Transfer the oranges and syrup to a large serving dish. Pour in the liqueur and leave to cool. Cover and chill in the refrigerator.

5 To make the caramel chips, dissolve the sugar in 75ml (3fl oz) water in a saucepan over low heat. Increase the heat and boil rapidly, without stirring, to a rich brown caramel. Pour into a greased shallow tin; leave until set. Transfer to a chopping board and crush with a rolling pin. Sprinkle the chips over the oranges just before serving.

APPLE AND BLACKBERRY SNOW

This delightfully light dessert welcomes in the start of autumn by incorporating the best of the season's fruits – juicy blackberries and sweet apples.

● SERVES 6 ● PREPARATION TIME: 15 MINUTES, PLUS CHILLING ● COOKING TIME: 12 MINUTES ● 125 CALS PER SERVING ● 0.2G FAT; NO SATURATED FAT

900g (2lb) cooking apples, peeled and sliced
60ml (4 tbsp) fruit juice
grated rind of 1 lemon
225g (8oz) blackberries
90ml (6 tbsp) caster sugar
1 large egg white
fresh mint leaves, to decorate

WATCHPOINT

● *The young, the elderly, pregnant women and those suffering from immune-deficiency diseases should not eat raw or lightly cooked eggs, which may contain salmonella.*

1 Place the apples and fruit juice in a saucepan over a low heat and cook, uncovered, for 10 minutes or until soft. Transfer the apples to a food processor and blend until smooth. Stir in the lemon rind, cover and chill for 1 hour.

2 Place the blackberries and 30ml (2 tbsp) of caster sugar in a saucepan and heat gently for 2–3 minutes or until the blackberries begin to soften and their juices start to run.

3 Whisk the egg white until stiff, adding the remaining sugar gradually until the mixture forms stiff peaks. Fold the egg white into the apple purée. Divide the blackberries and the juice among six serving glasses, spoon the apple mixture on top, decorate with the mint leaves and serve.

RASPBERRY CHEESECAKES

With a base of rich Madeira cake and topping of fresh raspberries and ricotta cheese, these individual cheesecakes will serve a special occasion well.

● SERVES 6 ● PREPARATION TIME: 25 MINUTES, PLUS SOAKING ● COOKING TIME: 3 MINUTES, PLUS CHILLING ● 210 CALS PER SERVING ● 10G FAT, OF WHICH 5.5G SATURATED FAT

250g (9oz) Madeira cake
180ml (6½fl oz) fresh orange juice
350g (12oz) raspberries
250g (9oz) ricotta cheese
caster sugar, to taste
10ml (2 tsp) powdered gelatine
fresh raspberries or strawberries, to decorate

NOTE

● *To make the foil collars, take strips of foil 20 x 30cm (7½ x 11½ inches); fold twice lengthways into bands 5cm (2 inches) wide. Curl round in circles and secure the collars with a metal paper clip.*

1 Cut the cake lengthways into six slices. Using a round cutter stamp out six 7cm (2¾ inch) circles of cake.

2 Make six foil collars (see Note). Slip one around each cake circle and transfer to a baking sheet. Spoon 15ml (1 tbsp) of the orange juice over each cake circle.

3 Whizz 225g (8oz) of the raspberries in a food processor, then sieve. Mix together the purée and ricotta cheese, and add the caster sugar to taste.

4 Put 30ml (2 tbsp) of the orange juice in a small heatproof bowl, then sprinkle the gelatine over the top and leave to soak for 5 minutes. Place the bowl over a saucepan of simmering water, stir until melted, allow to cool a little, then stir into the raspberry purée. Spoon the mixture over the cake circles and chill in the refrigerator for 2 hours or until set.

5 Whizz the remaining raspberries in a food processor with the remaining orange juice, then sieve and sweeten to taste with sugar.

6 Remove the foil collars. Decorate each cheesecake with a few strawberries or raspberries. Serve with the raspberry purée.

MELON WITH SUMMER FRUITS

Cubes of scented, pale green and orange melon are tossed with red summer fruits in a melon sauce to make a delightful fruit salad. Charentais melon, with its pinky orange flesh, provides colour contrast as well as superb flavour, although a yellow-fleshed melon could be used instead. Serve on its own or with vanilla ice cream or 0% fat Greek yogurt, if wished.

● SERVES 4 ● PREPARATION TIME: 20 MINUTES, PLUS STANDING ● 132 CALS PER SERVING ● 0.5G FAT, OF WHICH 0.1G SATURATED FAT

½ galia or ogen melon
1 charentais melon
150ml (¼ pint) freshly squeezed orange juice
30ml (2 tbsp) melon liqueur or Grand Marnier
(optional)
125g (4oz) strawberries
225g (8oz) raspberries
lemon balm sprigs, to decorate (optional)

NOTE

● *Choose melons that are very ripe. A ripe melon should give slightly to pressure at the stem end. However, if lots of people have already tested the melons on a fruit stall, the melon may be soft through bruising rather than ripeness. So check the smell too – a ripe melon will be heavily scented.*

VARIATION

● *Omit the raspberries and strawberries from the salad and replace with 2 mangoes. Peel, then cut into 3 wedges around the stone. Cut the mango flesh into cubes, adding any rough shaped pieces to the portion of melon which is to be puréed. Serve with scoops of orange sorbet instead of ice cream.*

1 Cut the melons into thick wedges, then scoop out the seeds using a tablespoon and remove the skin, using a sharp knife. Cut the galia or ogen melon and half of the charentais melon into cubes and place in a serving bowl.

2 Roughly chop the remaining charentais melon and place in a food processor or blender with the orange juice. Process until smooth. Stir in the liqueur, if using, then pour over the melon cubes.

3 Halve or quarter the strawberries, depending on their size, and add to the melon with the raspberries. Leave at room temperature for at least half an hour to allow the flavours to mingle before serving.

4 Decorate with lemon balm sprigs if available, then serve.

FRAGRANT FRUIT SALAD

The spiciness of the stem ginger and ginger wine used in this recipe contrasts beautifully with sweet exotic fruits, including lychees, mangoes, pineapple and kiwi fruit.

● SERVES 8 ● PREPARATION TIME: 35 MINUTES, PLUS CHILLING ● COOKING TIME: 5 MINUTES ● 160 CALS PER SERVING ● 0.5G FAT, OF WHICH 0.1G SATURATED FAT

2 pieces preserved stem ginger in syrup
50g (2oz) caster sugar
grated rind and juice of 1 lemon
60ml (4 tbsp) ginger wine
700g (1½lb) lychees
3 ripe mangoes
450g (1lb) fresh pineapple or 425g (15oz) can in natural juice
4 ripe kiwi fruit, peeled
50g (2oz) Cape gooseberries, to decorate (optional)

1 Finely chop the ginger. Put the sugar in a saucepan with 150ml (¼ pint) water and the lemon rind and juice. Heat gently to dissolve the sugar, bring to the boil and simmer for 1 minute. Remove from the heat, stir in the ginger and ginger wine. Pour into a bowl; cool.

2 Peel the lychees, cut in half and remove the shiny stones. Peel the mangoes and cut the flesh away from the stones. Cut the flesh into cubes.

3 If using fresh pineapple, peel, slice and remove the core. Cut into cubes. Slice the kiwi fruit. Add the fruit to the syrup and stir gently. Cover and chill for several hours.

4 If using Cape gooseberries, peel back each calyx (papery husk) to form a 'flower'. Clean the orange berries by wiping with a damp cloth. Arrange on top of the fruit salad to serve.

FRUIT SALAD

The best way to end a spicy meal is with fruit. If you're looking for something a little more sophisticated, try this tempting fruit salad – enhanced with a cardamom and mint-scented syrup. Choose ripe fruit in optimum condition; under-ripe mangoes and pineapples are simply not worth eating. Pineapples should have a rich golden brown skin and a sweet aroma. Mangoes should give slightly when pressed. Include other fruits, such as guavas, watermelon, lychees and rambutans, when available and as the mood takes you.

● SERVES 6 ● PREPARATION TIME: 20 MINUTES, PLUS INFUSING AND CHILLING ● COOKING TIME: 5 MINUTES ● 125 CALS PER SERVING ● 0.3G FAT; NO SATURATED FAT

50g (2oz) caster sugar
4 green cardamom pods
6 large fresh mint sprigs
finely grated rind and juice of 1 lime
1 ripe pineapple
1 large ripe mango
3 small juicy oranges
1 papaya

1 Put the sugar in a small heavy-based saucepan with 200ml (7fl oz) water. Crush the cardamoms with a rolling pin to split the pods slightly. Crush 4 mint sprigs in the same way. Add the crushed mint and cardamoms to the saucepan.

2 Heat the mixture gently until the sugar dissolves, then bring to the boil and boil for 1 minute. Allow to cool and infuse for at least 1 hour or until completely cold. Discard the mint sprigs and cardamom pods.

3 Strip the leaves from the remaining mint sprigs and add them to the sugar syrup with the lime rind and juice. Pour into a bowl and chill while preparing the fruit.

4 Peel the pineapple, using a sharp knife, then remove any brown 'eyes' with the tip of the knife. Halve and discard the tough central core. Cut the flesh into large chunks. Cut the mango across either side of the stone, then cut the flesh into large slices and peel off the skin. Chop the flesh surrounding the stone.

5 Peel the oranges, then cut each one into wedges. Cut the papaya in half and scoop out the seeds with a teaspoon. Cut the flesh into slices and remove the skin.

6 Arrange the fruit in a shallow serving dish and pour over the syrup. Cover the bowl and chill in the refrigerator for 30 minutes before serving.

NOTE

● *Don't cut the fruit up too small; keep the pieces chunky and attractive. Include a wedge of watermelon and/or papaya if you like.*

WARM SALAD OF SUMMER FRUITS WITH PORT

This is lovely way to use up any leftover summer fruits after making a summer pudding perhaps, or at the end of the berry season. The fruits are warmed through in a red wine and port syrup – just long enough to soften them slightly. A spoonful of low-fat crème fraîche is the perfect accompaniment.

● SERVES 4 ● PREPARATION TIME: 10 MINUTES
● COOKING TIME: 5–6 MINUTES ● 170 CALS PER SERVING ● 0.4G FAT; NO SATURATED FAT

250g (8oz) strawberries
250g (8oz) cherries
2 firm, but ripe nectarines or peaches
175g (6oz) raspberries
175g (6oz) blueberries
125g (4oz) blackberries
50g (2oz) granulated sugar
75ml (3fl oz) fruity red wine
30ml (2 tbsp) ruby port or brandy
15ml (1 tbsp) balsamic vinegar
juice of 1 orange
a pinch of ground mixed spice
strawberry leaves or herb sprigs, to decorate

1 Prepare the fruits. Hull the strawberries and halve, if large. Stone the cherries if wished. Halve and stone the nectarines or peaches, then cut into thin wedges. Combine all of the fruits together in a bowl.

VARIATION

● For a winter version, put 675g (1½lb) of mixed dried fruits in a bowl, pour on boiling tea to cover and leave to soak overnight. Drain and reserve 75ml (3fl oz) of the tea. Continue from step 2, replacing the wine and port with the reserved tea and 30ml (2 tbsp) brandy.

2 Place the sugar in a heavy-based pan over a low heat until melted, then increase the heat and cook without stirring, to a golden caramel; do not let it burn.

3 Meanwhile, in a jug mix together the wine, port, vinegar and orange juice. Stir in the mixed spice. Protecting your hand with an oven glove, pour this mixture into the pan, taking care as the caramel will immediately spit and splatter. Stir over a low heat for 1–2 minutes until the syrup is smooth and thickened slightly.

4 Add all the fruits to the pan. Toss in the hot syrup for 1 minute until they start to soften, then remove from the heat and leave to cool slightly. Pour into a serving bowl and scatter with strawberry leaves or herb sprigs, to decorate.

EXOTIC FRESH FRUIT SALAD

Exotic fruits are just what's required to round off a Thai meal, which is likely to have been spicy and hot. Feel free to choose your favourite fruits but, if you are serving a complete Thai dinner, try to be as authentic as possible.

● SERVES 4 ● PREPARATION TIME: 20 MINUTES, PLUS INFUSING ● COOKING TIME: 5–6 MINUTES
● 136 CALS PER SERVING● 0.5G FAT, OF WHICH 0.1G SATURATED FAT

225g (8oz) wedge watermelon
225g (8oz) wedge galia or ogen melon
1 small papaya
1 small mango
125g (4oz) fresh pineapple
2 small bananas
Jasmine Syrup:
1 jasmine tea bag
2 strips lime peel
30ml (2 tbsp) lime juice
25g (1oz) sugar
finely shredded lime rind, to decorate (optional)

VARIATION

● *Other teas, including fruit-flavoured infusions, can be substituted for the jasmine tea – simply choose your favourite.*

1 First make the syrup. Put the tea bag in a small bowl, pour on 150ml (¼ pint) boiling water and leave to stand for 10 minutes. Discard the tea bag and pour the tea into a small pan. Add the lime peel, lime juice and sugar and heat gently, stirring until the sugar is dissolved. Simmer gently for 5 minutes, remove from the heat and leave to go cold.

2 Prepare the fruit. Scoop out the seeds from both melon wedges and carefully cut the flesh away from the skin. Slice the flesh and place in a large bowl.

3 Halve the papaya, scoop out and discard the seeds, then slice the flesh.

4 Peel the mango and cut down either side of the central stone; cube the flesh.

5 Peel and core the pineapple, cut into slices and then quarter each slice. Peel and slice the bananas. Combine all the fruits together in a bowl.

6 Pour over the cold tea syrup and leave to marinate for 10 minutes before serving. Decorate with shredded lime rind, if using.

PEACHES WITH A HOT ZABAGLIONE SAUCE

The ripe golden fruits of high summer are at their headiest served with a frothy sweet wine sauce. You can use either peaches or nectarines for this dessert, but make sure they are perfectly ripe to ensure the optimum flavour.

● SERVES 4 ● PREPARATION TIME: 5 MINUTES
● COOKING TIME: 7–8 MINUTES ● 130 CALS
PER SERVING ● 4.8G FAT, OF WHICH 1.3G
SATURATED FAT

4 ripe peaches or nectarines
60ml (4 tbsp) Marsala wine
25g (1oz) caster sugar
2 eggs, plus 1 extra yolk

1 Put the peaches or nectarines into a heatproof bowl (see Note) and pour on sufficient boiling water to cover. Leave for 1 minute, then drain and peel away the skins. Halve and stone the peaches, and arrange rounded-side up on individual plates.

2 Immediately before serving, mix the wine and sugar together in a heatproof bowl. Set the bowl over a pan of boiling water and stir gently until the sugar dissolves completely.

3 In a separate bowl, beat the eggs and extra yolk lightly together, then whisk into the hot wine mixture. Continue whisking over boiling water until the zabaglione has increased in volume and forms a thick, billowy froth, thick enough to leave a trail on the surface when the whisk is lifted.

4 Pour the hot zabaglione sauce over the peaches and serve immediately.

NOTE

● *A thin metal bowl is best for making zabaglione, but a heatproof glass one will do – and has the added advantage that you can lift it to see when all the liquid has been absorbed into the mounting froth.*

VARIATION

● *When peaches and nectarines are not in season, you could use canned peach halves in natural juice.*

THREE CLASSIC SORBETS

These are three of the most refreshing sorbets imaginable! The orange sorbet is delicately flavoured with exotic orange flower water and orange juice; the strawberry sorbet has a hint of rich balsamic vinegar which is imperceptible but brings out the flavour of the strawberries; and the melon sorbet is a real taste of sunshine!

● EACH SORBET SERVES 4–6 ● PREPARATION TIME: 20 MINUTES PER SORBET, PLUS FREEZING ● 165–280 CALS PER SERVING ● 0.1–0.2G FAT; NO SATURATED FAT

Melon Sorbet:
about 900g (2lb) very ripe cantaloupe or other orange-fleshed melon (see Note)
225g (8oz) caster sugar
juice of 1 lemon or 2 limes
1 egg white

Orange Sorbet:
200g (7oz) caster sugar
10 juicy oranges
30ml (2 tbsp) orange flower water
1 egg white

Strawberry Sorbet:
450g (1lb) fresh sweet strawberries
250g (9oz) caster sugar
15ml (1 tbsp) balsamic vinegar
1 egg white

NOTE

● *The melon must be as ripe as possible to ensure the intense sweet flavour.*
● *When making sorbets and ice creams chill all the ingredients before freezing – this speeds up the freezing process. Transfer the sorbets to the refrigerator about 30 minutes before serving to soften slightly.*

WATCHPOINT

● *The young, elderly, pregnant women and those with immune-deficiency diseases should avoid raw or lightly cooked eggs, which may contain salmonella.*

1 To make the melon sorbet, halve and deseed the melon, cutting out any bad parts. Scoop out the melon flesh into a blender or food processor. Process until smooth, then press through a sieve into a bowl. Cover and chill for 2–3 hours.

2 Pour 300ml (½ pint) water into a saucepan, add the sugar and heat gently to dissolve. Boil for 1 minute. Cool, then chill.

3 Stir the syrup into the chilled melon, then add lemon or lime juice to taste. Beat the egg white until just frothy and whisk into the melon mixture. Pour into a shallow freezer tray and freeze until the sorbet is almost frozen. Mash well with a fork and refreeze until solid. Alternatively, freeze in an ice cream maker according to the manufacturer's instructions, for optimum results.

4 To make the orange sorbet, pour 200ml (7fl oz) water into a saucepan and add the sugar. Proceed as for step 2, but add the finely grated rind of the oranges and their juice. Leave to cool, stir in the orange flower water, then chill. Strain, whisk in the egg white and freeze as in step 3.

5 To make the strawberry sorbet, pour 250ml (9fl oz) water into a saucepan and add the sugar. Proceed as in step 2. Meanwhile, wash and hull the strawberries. Place in a blender or food processor and process until smooth. Pass through a sieve, if preferred. Chill.

6 Stir the syrup and balsamic vinegar into the strawberry purée and beat in the egg white as in step 3. Freeze as in step 3.

LEMON SORBET

A light refreshing sorbet that can be served as a palate cleanser between courses, if wished, or as a light dessert.

- SERVES 3–4 ● PREPARATION TIME: 10 MINUTES, PLUS FREEZING ● 170–130 CALS PER SERVING
- NO FAT

350ml (12fl oz) sugar syrup (see below)
finely grated rind and juice of 3 lemons
1 egg white

SUGAR SYRUP

Put 125g (4oz) granulated sugar in a heavy-based saucepan. Add 300ml (½ pint) water and heat gently until the sugar dissolves. Do not stir, but occasionally loosen the sugar from the base of the pan to help it dissolve. Bring to the boil and boil for 2 minutes. Leave to cool and use as required.

1 Prepare the sugar syrup as far as dissolving the sugar. Add the pared lemon rinds and simmer gently for about 10 minutes. Leave to cool completely.

3 Using an electric whisk, whip the egg white until forming stiff peaks. Turn the sorbet into a bowl and beat gently to break down the ice crystals.

2 Stir in the lemon juice and strain into a shallow non-metal, freezer tray. Cover and freeze for about 3 hours until mushy. Alternatively, freeze in an ice cream machine following the manufacturer's instructions.

4 Fold in the egg white. Return the sorbet to the freezer tray, cover and freeze for 4 hours or until firm. Place the sorbet in the refrigerator for about 30 minutes to soften slightly before serving.

WATCHPOINT

- *The young, elderly, pregnant women and those with immune-deficiency diseases should avoid raw or lightly cooked eggs, which may contain salmonella.*

NOTE

- *When making sorbets and ice creams it is best to have all the ingredients chilled before freezing – this speeds up the freezing process.*

VARIATIONS

- *For orange or lime sorbet, make as above, using the grated rind and juice of 2 oranges or 5 limes instead of the lemons.*

RASPBERRY AND COCOA SORBETS

This duo of sorbets tastes as exciting as it looks. Dark chocolate makes a surprisingly good sorbet – cocoa is used here to give a wonderfully intense flavour. The refreshing raspberry sorbet provides a lovely colour and flavour contrast. Crisp dessert biscuits are a perfect accompaniment.

● SERVES 6 ● PREPARATION TIME: 40 MINUTES, PLUS FREEZING ● COOKING TIME: 5 MINUTES ● 230 CALS PER SERVING ● 1.7G FAT, OF WHICH 0.9G SATURATED FAT

Chocolate Sorbet:

40g (1½oz) cocoa powder
100g (3½oz) granulated sugar
5ml (1 tsp) vanilla essence
1 egg white

Raspberry Sorbet:

175g (6oz) caster sugar
450g (1lb) raspberries
juice of 2 lemons
1 egg white
125g (4oz) raspberries, to serve
lemon balm or mint leaves, to decorate
icing sugar, for dusting

1 To make the chocolate sorbet, place the cocoa powder, sugar and 450ml (¾ pint) water in a heavy-based saucepan. Dissolve over a low heat, stirring occasionally, then bring to the boil and boil for 2 minutes, without stirring. Remove from the heat, stir in the vanilla essence and leave to cool.

2 Pour the cocoa mixture into a freezer tray and freeze for 2–3 hours until slushy. Whisk the egg white until holding soft peaks. Whizz the sorbet in a food processor, or tip into a bowl and beat well, then fold in the egg white. Return to the freezer container, cover and freeze for 3–4 hours until firm.

3 To make the raspberry sorbet, place the sugar in a saucepan with 150ml (¼ pint) water and dissolve over a low heat, stirring occasionally, then bring to the boil and boil for 2 minutes, without stirring.

4 Whizz the raspberries in a food processor or blender, add the syrup and process again, then sieve to remove the pips. Add the lemon juice and leave to cool. Pour into a freezer tray, then freeze for 2–3 hours until slushy. Whisk the egg white until holding soft peaks. Briefly process or beat the sorbet, then fold in the egg white. Return to the container, cover and freeze for 3–4 hours until firm.

5 To serve, transfer the sorbets to the refrigerator for 20 minutes to soften, then arrange quenelles of alternate flavours onto individual serving plates. Scatter with raspberries and lemon balm or mint leaves. Dust with icing sugar and serve at once.

VARIATION

● *Use 10 passion fruit in place of the raspberries. Scoop out the pulp and place in a saucepan with 30ml (2 tbsp) water. Cook over a low heat for 5 minutes, then push through a fine sieve. Substitute oranges for the lemons and continue from step 4.*

MANGO, GINGER AND CITRUS SORBET

Mangoes are ideal for making sorbets as their creamy texture lends itself perfectly to the freezing process. As the flesh starts to freeze very few ice crystals form – ensuring a smooth-textured result. The sweetness of the ginger and mango is balanced by the lime juice to produce a tangy, refreshing dessert.

● SERVES 4–6 ● PREPARATION TIME: 25 MINUTES, PLUS FREEZING ● COOKING TIME: 3–4 MINUTES ● 163–109 CALS PER SERVING ● 0.4–0.3G FAT, OF WHICH 0.2G–0.1G SATURATED FAT

2 large mangoes, each weighing about 400g (14oz)
25g (1oz) preserved stem ginger in syrup
50ml (2fl oz) syrup from the stem ginger jar
50g (2oz) caster sugar
finely grated rind and juice of 3 limes

I Peel the mangoes, using a potato peeler, then cut down either side of the central stone; cut away as much of the remaining flesh as possible. Chop the mango flesh and purée in a blender or food processor until very smooth. Transfer to a bowl and set aside. Finely chop the stem ginger and stir into the purée.

2 Place the ginger syrup in a small pan with the sugar, lime rind and juice, and add 90ml (3fl oz) water. Heat gently, stirring until the sugar is dissolved. Bring to the boil and simmer for 3 minutes. Remove from the heat and leave to cool.

3 Strain the cooled syrup through a fine sieve into the puréed mango mixture and stir well. Transfer to a freezer tray and freeze for 2 hours.

4 Remove from the freezer and beat well to break down any ice crystals that may have formed. Return to the freezer for a further 1 hour, then beat again. Repeat the process once more. Freeze for several hours until firm, or until required.

5 Transfer the sorbet to the refrigerator about 20 minutes before serving to soften slightly. Scoop into individual glass dishes to serve.

GLOSSARY

A brief guide to cooking methods, terms and ingredients.

Acidulated water Water to which lemon juice or vinegar has been added in which fruit or vegetables, such as pears or Jerusalem artichokes, are immersed to prevent discoloration.

Al dente Italian term used to describe food, especially pasta and vegetables, which are cooked until tender but still firm to the bite.

Antipasto Italian selection of cold meats, fish, salads and so on served as a starter.

Arrowroot Fine, white powder used as a thickening agent for sauces. Unlike cornflour, arrowroot gives a sauce a clear gloss.

Au gratin Describes a dish which has been coated with sauce, sprinkled with breadcrumbs or cheese and browned under the grill or in the oven. Low-sided gratin dishes are used.

Bain-marie Literally, a water bath, used to keep foods, such as delicate custards and sauces, at a constant low temperature during cooking. On the hob a double saucepan or heatproof bowl placed over a pan of simmering water is used; for oven cooking, the baking dish(es) is placed in a roasting tin containing enough hot water to come halfway up the sides.

Balsamic vinegar Italian oak-aged vinegar, dark brown in colour with a superior sweet, mellow flavour.

Baste To spoon the juices and melted fat over meat, poultry, game or vegetables during roasting to keep them moist. The term is also used to describe spooning over a marinade.

Beat Method of incorporating air into an ingredient or mixture by agitating it vigorously with a spoon, fork, whisk or electric mixer. The technique is also used to soften ingredients.

Beurre manié Equal parts of flour and butter kneaded together to form a paste. Used for thickening soups, stews and casseroles. It is whisked into the hot liquid a little at a time at the end of cooking.

Bind To mix beaten egg or other liquid into a dry mixture to hold it together.

Blanch To immerse food briefly in fast-boiling water to loosen skins, such as peaches or tomatoes, or to remove bitterness, or to destroy enzymes and preserve the colour, flavour and texture of vegetables (especially prior to freezing).

Bouquet garni Small bunch of herbs – usually a mixture of parsley stems, thyme and a bay leaf – tied in muslin and used to flavour stocks, soups and stews.

Braise To cook meat, poultry, game or vegetables slowly in a small amount of liquid in a pan or casserole with a tight-fitting lid. The food is usually first browned in oil or fat.

Brochette Food cooked on a skewer or spit.

Brûlée A French term, literally meaning 'burnt' used to refer to a dish with a crisp coating of caramelised sugar.

Bulghar wheat Partially processed cracked wheat which readily absorbs moisture and therefore cooks quickly. It is used extensively in Middle Eastern cooking, as an alternative to rice. Also known as pourgouri, bulghul and cracked wheat.

Calorie Strictly a kilocalorie, this is used in dietetics to measure the energy value of foods.

Caper Small bud of a flowering Mediterranean shrub, usually packed in brine. Small French capers in balsamic vinegar are the best variety.

Caramelise To heat sugar or sugar syrup slowly until it is brown in colour; i.e. forms a caramel.

Casserole Strictly speaking, a dish with a tight-fitting lid used for slow-cooking meat, poultry and vegetables. Now applied to the food cooked in this way.

Chill To cool food in the refrigerator.

Chine To sever the rib bones from the backbone, close to the spine. This is done to meat joints, such as loin of pork or lamb, to make them easier to carve into chops after cooking.

Clarify To remove sediment or impurities from a liquid. Butter which is clarified will withstand a higher frying temperature. To clarify butter, heat until melted and all bubbling stops. Remove from the heat and let stand until the sediment has sunk to the bottom, then gently pour off the fat, straining it through muslin.

Compote Mixture of fresh or dried fruit stewed in sugar syrup. Served hot or cold.

Concassé Diced ingredient; the term is most often applied to skinned, seeded tomatoes.

Coulis A smooth fruit or vegetable purée, thinned if necessary to a pouring consistency.

Court bouillon Aromatic cooking liquid containing wine, vinegar or lemon juice, used for poaching delicate fish, poultry or vegetables.

Couscous Processed semolina grains; a staple food in North African countries.

Croûtons Small pieces of fried or toasted bread, served with soups and salads.

Crudités Raw vegetables, usually cut into slices or sticks, typically served with a dipping sauce as an appetiser.

Curdle To cause sauces or creamed mixtures to separate once the egg is added, usually by overheating or over-beating.

Cure To preserve fish, meat or poultry by smoking, drying or salting.

Daube Braising meat and vegetables with stock, often with wine and herbs added.

Deglaze To heat stock, wine or other liquid with the cooking juices left in the pan after roasting or sautéeing, stirring to dissolve the sediment on the base of the pan.

Degorge To draw out moisture from a food, e.g. salting aubergines to remove bitter juices.

Dice To cut food into small cubes.

Draw To remove the entrails from poultry or game.

Dredge To sprinkle food generously with flour, sugar, icing sugar etc.

Dust To sprinkle lightly with flour, cornflour, caster sugar, icing sugar etc.

E numbers Used on food packaging to denote the additives in the product.

Emulsion A mixture of two liquids which do not dissolve into one another, e.g. oil and vinegar. Vigorous shaking or heating will emulsify them, as for a vinaigrette.

Extract Concentrated flavouring which is used in small quantities, e.g. yeast extract, vanilla extract.

Fermentation Term used to denote chemical changes deliberately or accidentally brought about by fermenting agents, such as yeast or bacteria. The process is utilised for making bread, yogurt and wine.

Fines herbes Classic French mixture of chopped herbs, i.e. parsley, tarragon, chives and chervil.

Fry To cook food in hot fat or oil. There are various methods: shallow-frying in a little fat in a shallow pan; deep-frying where the food is totally immersed in oil; dry-frying in which fatty foods are cooked in a non-stick pan without extra fat; see also Stir-frying.

Garnish A decoration, usually edible, such as parsley or lemon, which is added to a savoury dish to enhance its appearance.

Ghee Clarified butter widely used in Indian cookery.

Glaze A glossy coating given to sweet and savoury dishes to improve their appearance and sometimes flavour. Ingredients for glazes include beaten egg, egg white, milk and syrup.

Gluten A protein constituent of grains, such as wheat and rye, which develops when the flour is mixed with water giving the dough elasticity.

Griddle A flat, heavy, metal plate used on the hob for cooking scones or for searing savoury ingredients.

Grind To reduce foods such as nuts and spices to small particles in a food mill, pestle and mortar, electric grinder or food processor.

Hull To remove the stalk and calyx from soft fruits, such as strawberries.

Infuse To impart flavour to a liquid by immersing flavourings, such as aromatic vegetables, herbs and spices, usually bringing to the boil, then leaving to stand for a while.

Julienne Fine 'matchstick' strips of vegetables or citrus zest, sometimes used as a garnish.

Macerate To soften and flavour raw or dried foods by soaking in a liquid, e.g. soaking fruit in alcohol.

Mandolin(e) A flat wooden or metal frame with adjustable blades for cutting vegetables.

Marinate To soak raw meat or vegetables – usually in a mixture of oil, wine, vinegar and flavourings – to soften and impart flavour. The mixture, which is known as a marinade, may also be used to baste the food during cooking.

Monosodium Glutamate Common food additive of vegetable origin – used as a flavour enhancer.

Parboil To boil a vegetable or other food for part of its cooking time before finishing it by another method.

Passata A purée of plum tomatoes, used in many Italian dishes. Available ready-made from supermarkets.

Pâté A savoury mixture of finely chopped or minced meat, pulses and/or vegetables, usually served as a starter with bread or toast and crudités.

Pectin A naturally occurring substance found in most fruit and some vegetables which is necessary for setting jams and jellies.

Pestle and mortar Heavy marble or porcelain bowl with a heavy grinding tool for grinding herbs, spices etc.

Pesto A paste-like sauce made from puréed herbs and oil, used to add flavour to pasta and vegetables. A classic pesto is made from basil, pine nuts, garlic and olive oil.

Pith The bitter white skin under the thin zest of citrus fruit.

Poach To cook food gently in liquid at or just below simmering point, so that the surface of the liquid is just trembling.

Purée Fruit or vegetable pounded, sieved or liquidised to a smooth pulp. Purées often form the basis for soups and sauces.

Reduce To fast-boil stock or other liquid in an uncovered pan to evaporate water and concentrate the flavour.

Refresh To cool hot vegetables very quickly and stop the cooking process – by plunging into ice-cold water or holding under running water.

Salsa Piquant sauce made from chopped fresh vegetables and sometimes fruit.

Sauté To cook food in a small quantity of fat over a high heat, shaking the pan constantly – usually in a sauté pan (a frying pan with straight sides and a wide base).

Scald To pour boiling water over food to clean it, or loosen skin, eg tomatoes. Also used to describe heating milk to just below boiling point.

Score To cut parallel lines in the surface of food to improve its appearance or help it cook more quickly.

Sear To brown meat or vegetables quickly in a little hot fat before grilling or roasting.

Seasoned flour Flour mixed with a little salt and pepper, used for dusting meat and vegetables etc before frying.

Shred To grate cheese or slice vegetables into very fine pieces or strips.

Sieve To press food through a perforated sieve to obtain a smooth texture.

Sift To shake dry ingredients through a sieve to remove lumps.

Simmer To keep a liquid just below boiling point.

Skim To remove froth, scum or fat from the surface of stock, stews, jam etc. Use either a skimmer, a spoon or a sheet of absorbent kitchen paper.

Steam To cook food in the steam of rapidly boiling water.

Sterilise To destroy bacteria in foods by heating.

Stew To cook food such as meat or vegetables slowly in flavoured liquid which is kept at simmering point.

Stir-fry To cook small even-sized pieces of food rapidly in a little fat, tossing constantly over a high heat, usually in a wok.

Sweat To cook chopped or sliced vegetables in a little fat without liquid in a covered pan over a low heat.

Tepid The term used to describe temperature at approximately blood heat, i.e. 37°C (98.7°F).

Whipping (whisking) Beating air rapidly into a mixture either with a manual or electric whisk.

Worcestershire sauce A pungent flavouring sauce. Most brands contain anchovies.

Wok Large Chinese pan with a rounded base and sloping sides, used mainly for stir-frying but can also be used with a steamer.

Zest The thin coloured outer layer of citrus fruit (oranges, lemons, limes etc) which contains essential oil.

Zester Small bevelled tool with five holes drawn across citrus fruit to remove the zest in fine strips.

INDEX